MATTHEW BRZEZINSKI

A TOUCHSTONE BOOK
PUBLISHED BY SIMON & SCHUSTER
New York   London   Toronto   Sydney   Singapore

CASINO MOSCOW

A Tale of
Greed and Adventure
on Capitalism's
Wildest Frontier

TOUCHSTONE
Rockefeller Center
1230 Avenue of the Americas
New York, NY 10020

First Touchstone Edition 2002

TOUCHSTONE and colophon are registered trademarks
of Simon & Schuster, Inc.

For information about special discounts for bulk purchases,
please contact Simon & Schuster Special Sales:
1-800-456-6798 or business@simonandschuster.com

Designed by Brooke Koven
Manufactured in the United States of America

3   5   7   9   10   8   6   4   2

The Library of Congress has cataloged the Touchstone edition as follows:

Brzezinski, Matthew
Casino Moscow : a tale of greed and adventure on capitalism's wildest frontier /
Matthew Brzezinski.
    p.   cm.
1. Post-communism—Russia (Federation)   2. Russia (Federation)—Social
conditions—1991–   3. Political corruption—Russia (Federation)
4. Capitalism—Russia (Federation)   I. Title: Tale of greed and adventure
on capitalism's wildest frontier.   II. Title.

HN530.2.A8 B79 2001
306'.0947—dc21   2001031513

ISBN 978-0-684-86977-3

Rule one, on page one of the book of war, is: Do not march on Moscow! Various people have tried it, Napoleon and Hitler, and it is no good. That is the first rule.

—Field Marshal Montgomery, 1962

Contents

To Roberta

Buzz had dreamed up the textbook tactic and rounded up Bun to play the part of a student. They had called days in advance to set up the trap. In American cities, you just got mugged. Here you fell victim to a finely choreographed production, hardly worth the hundred dollars in my wallet. Buzz was going to make damn sure I wasn't holding out on him. That was what frightened me the most.

"Put on some music," Buzz snapped. Bun scurried off to find my portable short-wave radio—set to the BBC World Service, my sole connection to the outside world. "Louder," he said, when she had managed to turn on the unit. "And find another station."

The electronic throb of techno-pop filled the air—some Swedish Eurotrash that had forsaken lyrics in favor of digitally enhanced drumbeats. These would mask Buzz's grunts and muffle the sound of my bones breaking as he pounded me into disclosing the location of my loot.

A gag was thrust into my mouth. My screams would also be insulated. No one would hear me cry. And there was nothing, not a single thing, I could do to save or protect myself. I was utterly at Buzz's mercy. Never had I experienced such a sinking feeling of helplessness.

Nor could I any longer discount the horror stories of similar assaults in Moscow. Would I end up like the British accountant, whose back and chest had been used as an ironing board? The unfortunate bookkeeper had brought two prostitutes home for what he no doubt expected would be a memorable evening. While he was occupied with one of the young ladies, the other let two masked thugs into the apartment. They tied him to the bed and found an iron in his laundry hamper; heated it up; and spent several hours torturing him with it. He survived the attack with severe burns, but suffered a nervous breakdown afterward and spent six months in an English sanitarium.

At least he lived. The body of a former American adviser to the World Bank had just been found in Moscow, gagged and bound and stuffed in a bathtub. The Russian police claimed he had died from heart failure, but the *militsia*'s refusal to release the corpse or allow an autopsy prompted widespread speculation that the consultant had been sliced to pieces and had drowned in his own blood.

Distressingly, Buzz had made no effort to conceal his identity.

This I had taken as a bad omen from the start, and as the minutes passed and his blows rained down on me, I became convinced that he did not intend to leave me alive.

He was perspiring from the exertion, and his face shone with sweat and menace. As he leaned over me, I felt drops of his sweat fall on the nape of my neck. For some reason those droplets stung more than his fists. They landed with a tremendous thud, like Chinese water torture, each one sending wrenching shivers down my spine.

I whimpered into the gag, as frustrated and angry as I was fearful. How could Buzz not believe me? Didn't he realize that I valued my life more than money and would have handed over the cash if I had any?

Buzz halted the interrogation, as if sensing that maybe, just maybe, I was telling the truth. I whimpered some more.

"Shut up," he snarled with a kick, apparently also frustrated with the way things were going. I'm sure he had planned on being out of there by then, on the way to a bar to celebrate his haul. But some forty-five minutes had passed, and he was running out of time. In the interim Bun had torn up the place and found nothing except my office equipment, camera, leather jacket, and favorite pair of jeans.

Buzz decided to go for broke. He hauled me up by the hair and dragged me to the bathtub. He slipped the Makarov into his waistband, ran out of the bathroom, and returned wielding my Swiss Army knife. It had been a gift from a past girlfriend. Was she ever going to feel guilty!

The blade felt cool against my throat. The tub drain, I noticed with almost detached interest, was unplugged; my blood would flow freely into the sewers of Kiev.

"Do you believe in God?" Buzz asked quietly, almost gently.

When I didn't respond, Buzz repeated the question, perhaps in case I hadn't fully understood. I nodded, I don't remember whether in the negative or the affirmative; everything was becoming blurry and my sanity was leaving me.

"Then you'd better start praying."

That's when I thought about all those times I had tried to kick the habit. The misery, the agony of withdrawal. All for nothing. All to end up bludgeoned in a bathtub.

floors. Finnish furniture, French fashions, Italian marble counter-tops, cookware, name-brand jeans, stereos, and household appliances basked under the soft, flattering beams of halogen spotlights.

Though it was almost 9:00 P.M. and the storm was still mercilessly lashing the city, most of the stores were open for business. Shoppers, muffled against the windy deluge, slogged along the slippery concourses, lugging large shopping bags (the kind Kievites dueled over) and scattering out of the way of the miniature snowplows that cleared the sidewalks, leaving narrow trails for people to follow to the next store.

The boulevard teemed with traffic. The buses that plied the route had also gone commercial. One was painted entirely in pink and purple, and advertised Mattel's latest Barbie doll collection. Another flew Pepsi's red-and-navy corporate colors. A third depicted a happy blond kid biting into a giant Kinder-Chokolad egg, the accompanying text promising parents a toy surprise inside every German-trademarked treat.

The Teutonic presence was strong; Mercedes, BMWs, and Audis growled at every traffic light. They were not the second-hand models Eastern Europeans bought in Berlin or Amsterdam; these still had that fresh-from-the-factory look about them. Billboards recommended all sorts of German goods, brands of exercise equipment, and car alarms that boasted of their *nemetskoye kachestvo* (German quality) even as signs for Lufthansa, the German national airline, trumpeted its business class.

The magnitude of Moscow's makeover was overwhelming. It was hard to believe that this was the same city I had seen in 1992, when at this time of the night there had been nothing but darkness and gloom.

We passed a series of modern glass structures with illuminated logos reading Alfa, Most and Inkombank. Roberta volunteered that these were private and hugely powerful new financial giants. Outside one of them, an electronic board flashed the ruble exchange rate in large red digits. The ruble stood at just over 5,200 to the dollar—much battered since the last time I'd been here, when a dollar bought just over two hundred rubles. But after half a decade of decline the Russian currency was now holding steady, Roberta said, so

steady that the Kremlin was considering lopping off all those silly zeroes the ruble had sprouted during the hyperinflation years.

As we approached the city center, and the traffic thinned a little,
I recognized a soaring and unmistakably "Socialist Realist" steel
sculpture memorializing Yuri Gagarin's first space flight. Across the
street, in front of the white marble Central Bank building, a three-
story-high bronze statue of Lenin brooded on its snow-covered
pedestal. Beside the Father of the Revolution, a chrome all-night
diner, ringed in art-deco neon and straight out of an old Route 66
postcard, advertised a special on Philadelphia cheese steak subs.
The diner had come completely preassembled in a cargo container
from Florida, magically appearing one morning at Lenin's foot.

What would *he* make of all this, I wondered? There was an ele-
ment of delicious irony to all the commerce on a street named after
Lenin. Come to think of it, why was his name still on street signs?
Hadn't communism been discredited?

"It's not easy to get rid of a god," Roberta explained. "To many
Russians, Lenin stands for everything that made them proud of the
Soviet Union, like beating the U.S. in the space race. They don't
blame him for what went wrong with communism."

This didn't fully satisfy me. "What does Volodya think?"

At the sound of his name the driver's head popped up attentively.
The International Finance Corporation, or IFC, as it was better
known, like the rest of the World Bank, had diplomatic status in
Russia and kept a fleet of chauffeured vehicles at its staff's disposal.
Volodya had started working for the IFC carpool after many years of
faithful service with the PLO legation in Moscow, where his charges
had included one side-armed passenger by the name of Yassir Arafat.

Volodya listened to the translated question and shrugged noncommittally: "It's difficult enough trying to get around with so many
more cars on the road nowadays. Why make it worse by confusing
people with new street names?"

Traffic, sooner or later, crept into just about every casual conversation in Moscow. The streets, broad as they were, had been designed primarily for public transportation, military parades, and
propaganda marches. Moreover, some maniac at City Hall had
mapped out the traffic patterns so as not to permit any left turns.
The reason, it was said, was that a Politburo member had once been

struck by a vehicle making a left. That had the sound of an urban legend, but there was nothing fanciful about the bottlenecks that brought Moscow traffic to a frustrating standstill. The number of vehicles registered in the capital had more than doubled since the collapse of communism, when waiting lists for new automobiles had stretched so long that people actually paid more for beat-up second-hand models that they could drive home right away.

You can learn a lot about a country from the cars its citizens drive. The makes I saw around me in Moscow fell into two categories: Soviet clunkers—such as boxy Ladas, accident-prone Volgas, and indescribably pathetic little Moskvitches—and top-of-the-line Western imports with sticker prices easily topping a hundred thousand dollars. There was very little resembling the low-end Fords and Fiats and Skodas one saw in Warsaw, Prague, or Budapest to indicate the emergence of a middle class. The streets of the Russian capital spoke only of haves and have-nots.

I was relating this observation to Roberta when the blinding high beams of a convoy pulling up fast behind us forced Volodya to swerve into another lane. A procession roared by at twice the speed limit, sending a wake of slush onto our windshield. The column was led by a black Toyota Land Cruiser filled with large men. Despite the cold, they drove with their back windows open. Directly behind the big SUV, a Mercedes limousine cruised past, a flashing blue police light pinned to its wide, sleek roof. Another Land Cruiser brought up the rear. The three cars were spotless, as though they had just been driven off the showroom floor.

"Look, a minister," I pointed, excited at my first brush with Russian officialdom.

"*Niet, bankir*," corrected Volodya. "It's a banker."

Noting my puzzled expression, Roberta took a few minutes to bring me up to speed on recent events in Russia. This was how I first came to hear of the *bankirshchina:* "The Reign of the Bankers," the period of economic boom Moscow was now experiencing, under the stewardship of a group of powerful business barons. To Russians, who are pessimists by nature, the word's untranslatable root had an unmistakably ominous sound, stemming from Tsar Ivan the Terrible's raping and rampaging Oprichnina and the Soviet secret police chief Ivan Yezhov's purging *Yezhovshchina.*

The message was that no good could come of the *bankirshchina*, which, by the look of things, seemed like Slavic superstitious bunk. Moscow was enjoying unparalleled prosperity; that much was obvious to the naked eye. The city was open to outside influences as never before in its history; satellite dishes, thousands of foreigners, multinational corporations, cultural exchanges, and even the Internet were all bringing in new ideas and money to a society that had long been closed.

The era had its genesis in the economic enfranchisement of the great privatization programs of the early 1990s, during what was probably the largest transfer of property and power in recorded history, when the wealth of Soviet Russia was returned, after seventy years of state control, to the people. The scope of the giveaway was breathtaking, and not only in the form of personal freedoms. No other nation on earth was blessed with Russia's natural resources. She possessed nearly half of the world's supply of natural gas, and almost all of its precious nickel. Her Siberian fields were studded with diamond and gold reserves second only to South Africa's. Only Saudi Arabia produced more crude oil than the USSR's bottomless wells. Russia had vast deposits of copper, magnesium, uranium and virtually every mineral needed in the production of heavy industry. Her mills churned out more aluminum than any country other than the United States and enough rolled steel to flood world markets for a decade. No other nation could boast of more farmland, or bigger fishing fleets, or longer rail systems than Mother Russia.

Almost all of this was put up for grabs in the 1990s, as were the apartments, office buildings, department stores, and restaurants of Moscow, St. Petersburg, and cities across a dozen time zones all the way to the Pacific port of Vladivostok. Factories producing every imaginable widget, rocket or food product also landed on the auction block, as did timber concessions and lucrative export and banking licenses. The sum of the stakes was bigger than anyone's wildest dreams.

Russia's problem was that the scale of the transfer was unprecedented. Poland and the other former satellites in Central and Eastern Europe had had a two-year head start over Moscow in their transition to a market economy, and faced far less daunting obstacles. Before 1989, the People's Republics of Poland and Hungary had tolerated some private enterprise and property ownership (what the Hungarians called "Goulash Capitalism") and thus had already established some free-market traditions. Their economies were more service-oriented and less geared to heavy industry and raw-material production, and thus lent themselves more easily to privatization. And the Central Europeans had the added advantage of bordering the rich European Union. There, soaring labor costs were driving industrial giants east to invest in the Polish and Czech factories whose skilled work forces came cheap and didn't grumble about dental plans and vacation pay.

The task of finding a way to privatize Russia fell to a team of President Boris Yeltsin's advisers led by a portly economist by the name of Yegor Gaidar and his shrewd, self-assured protégé, Anatoly Chubais. It was the brilliant Chubais, the master intriguer, who emerged as Yeltsin's favorite and the gatekeeper to all the riches in Russia.

The dirty details of the privatization scheme would be revealed to me later, but that first evening in Moscow it certainly seemed to be paying dividends for a great many Russians. I had, in the space of an hour, seen more Mercedes and BMWs here than anywhere else in the world.

As we crossed the Kamennyi (Great Stone) Bridge, and the great, heaping ice slabs of the Moskva River slid beneath us, Roberta resumed the history lesson. Though Russia's privatization had been anything but fair, the West, she said, had supported it on the grounds that the sooner Russians owned property the quicker they'd abandon the ghost of communism, turn the moribund economy around, and start acting like civilized Westerners.

The principal beneficiaries of Chubais' privatizations turned out to be a clique of young bankers. Most had been in their late twenties and early thirties when the Soviet Union fell apart; they had moved swiftly to seize opportunity during the very brief window when anything was possible. Banking was a rough business during the early, and violent, days of the transition. During the Great Mob War of 1993–1994, hundreds of gangsters died in spectacular shoot-outs and assassinations. In those days, the lines between legitimate businessmen and the mafia were often too blurry to distinguish. Between 1992 and 1995 car bombs and contract killings had claimed some three hundred bankers' lives, and financial sectors and spheres of influence were disputed with the ferocity of America's bootleggers' battles during Prohibition.

By early 1996 the turf wars had subsided and a league of super-bankers—some more legitimate than others—had emerged from the fray. It was said that this select group held within its ranks the future Kennedys and Bronfmans and Rockefellers of Russia, only with Slavic names—Potanin, Khodorkovsky, Berezovsky, Gusinsky, and so on. Very little was initially known about these new titans of finance, or how they had amassed such vast fortunes in what seemed like a blink of an eye. The presidential race during the summer of 1996 changed everything, though. Yeltsin's miraculous come-from-behind reelection triumph made these entrepreneurs household names in Moscow, because everyone knew they had made the triumph possible and were set to reap the rewards of victory.

Faced with the unappealing prospect of jail and property seizures that would have surely followed a win at the polls by communist challenger Genady Zyuganov, Russia's richest men had decided to rally around the one candidate who could keep their newly-acquired fortunes secure. As much as five hundred million dollars was secretly funneled into Yeltsin's campaign coffers, and the full, fawning force of the nation's newly private newspapers and television networks was forcibly conscripted to shill for him.

Yeltsin boogied with Russia's biggest rock stars at free concerts funded by his contributors, kissed babies and babushkas alike at collective farms and coal mines where months of wage arrears were quietly settled from slush funds, and was careful to have his alcohol-induced heart attacks off camera. Never in the history of Russia had a leader so shamelessly prostrated himself before his people. But it worked. The world held its breath as the final votes were tallied, turned a blind eye to a slew of electoral irregularities, and hailed Russian democracy with expressions of tremendous relief when Yeltsin defeated the unpalatably Red Zyuganov.

Beholden and bedridden after emergency quintuple-bypass heart surgery, the Russian leader gratefully retired soon after the election to a leafy sanitarium on the outskirts of Moscow, and was not seen for months on end, which suited his backers just fine. In his absence, the reins of government were left to his trusted but bland prime minister Viktor Chernomyrdin, the wily technocrat Chubais, and the seven all-powerful men who had bought the president another four years in power.

These bankers, with their private armies, fleets of planes, industrial empires, and media and intelligence-gathering networks, were known as *gruppa semi*, the Group of Seven, and later simply as "the oligarchs." They were Russia's real rulers. And despite some grumbling that they dipped into the State treasury from time to time, their presence reassured the West. After all, went the reasoning in the White House and Whitehall, having a bunch of businessmen in charge of Russia was a big step up from the communists who had stormed around the Kremlin for most of the century.

Such was the state of affairs in Russia in late 1996, as Volodya dropped me off in front of my new home, a tall, granite, slate-gray structure of elegant and imposing design, not too far from Red Square, on stately and sought-after Bryusov Lane.

Bryusov, having recently recovered its old moniker (it was named after a minor communist functionary in Soviet days), took its name from a famous pre-Revolutionary composer. To get there, one turned right off Tverskaya Street, just before the big McDonald's across from the main post office, and drove under the shadow of a large Stalinist arch cut through a spooky building of Gothic inspiration. The street was narrow and crowded owing to its central location and status as home to the Soviet cultural elite, the *narodniye artisti* (People's Artists), who in appreciation of their talents had been awarded the big apartments usually reserved for the Party elite.

Roberta rented our Kremlin-view pad from Nadya Bessmertnova, a prima ballerina whose last name means "immortal," one of the greatest legends in the Bolshoi ballet's storied history. It was said that Brezhnev had been enamored of her, and worried so much about her defecting to the West that he did not allow her to perform abroad. Bessmertnova was married to Mikhail Mikhailovich Gabovich, also a Bolshoi dancer and contemporary of Mikhail Baryshnikov. In the threadbare early nineties, the star couple had moved to their dacha among the silvery beeches of Peredelkino, where Boris Pasternak once wrote, to supplement their meager retirement pensions with a little rent money—four thousand dollars a month to be precise—which Mikhail Mikhailovich requested that Roberta deposit in his London bank account.

Ballerinas and bank accounts in Britain? Mercedes and four-grand-a-month apartments? After the poverty of Ukraine, this was all a bit much to digest.

More surprises followed. Our apartment was nothing like any I'd seen in the former Soviet Union. There was no tattered and mildew-stained red-patterned wallpaper to make you feel that you'd descended into the depths of hell. The windows, unlike those in my pad in Kiev, did not have cardboard blocking broken panes. The kitchen was modern and neatly tiled and included a dishwasher, an appliance I'd almost forgotten existed. Burled-maple Biedermeier antiques glistened in the parlor. These were huge matching pieces, each weighing hundreds of pounds and doubtless worth tens of thousands of dollars, and included a massive beveled mirror that reflected the setting's opulent glory. Mikhail Mikhailovich had proudly informed Roberta that the entire dining-room set had been looted from Austria by the Red Army after World War II and brought to Moscow by a general who later fell out of favor with Stalin.

To help Roberta celebrate my arrival, our chivalrous and irreproachably well-mannered landlord had bestowed upon her two hard-to-come-by tickets to the Bolshoi Ballet.

We went the following evening. *Gisèle* was on the program, the same ballet I'd seen performed five years ago during my first visit to Moscow. At that time the theater had been shabby, with grimy scaffolding from ongoing renovations concealing its fissured neo-Romanesque façade. The work had since been completed, the cast-iron chariot over the portico had been meticulously restored, and the whole majestic front was splashed with cozy pink light.

The audience had also undergone a remarkable transformation. Gone were the graying American retirees in Bermuda shorts and sensible shoes, the camera-clutching tour groups from England, and the prim Muscovite mothers, who had no doubt scrimped so that their daughters could see Russian culture in its highest form. In their stead sat row upon row of American and British bankers, lawyers, and accountants in somber, fashionable suits.

Those Russian daughters, I could not fail to notice, had grown up in all the right places. They snuggled with the emissaries of foreign finance, and shot one another competitive glances. The most beautiful women sat with the beefy Russian businessmen. These pencil-thin molls favored form-fitting body suits patterned like various feline predators. They toted chic Fendi bags from which, with long, painted nails, they plucked tiny cell phones.

Mobile phones chirped, rang, and buzzed incessantly throughout the performance, while hushed conversations in several languages echoed from the four corners of the gallery. I understood now why Mikhail Mikhailovich had told Roberta he never went to the ballet any more. Yet I found this vulgar display tantalizing theater. Even the sinewy ballerinas fluttering about the stage were either too wrapped up in their routines to complain about the ruckus or had long ago realized that the real show at the Bolshoi was now the audience.

After the final curtain, we nipped across the street to the Teatro Mediterraneo restaurant for a midnight snack. This establishment was next to a casino and the security guards who barred its doors eyed us suspiciously, relaxing only when they heard the reassuring sound of our American English. Inside, the clientele was much the same as at the Bolshoi, and the lush decor would not have looked out of place in the better districts of Manhattan or Milan. Roberta ordered the pasta salad. I had a bowl of tomato soup. The soup alone cost seventeen dollars.

I was still reeling from sticker shock when we walked home. What frightened me most was how little the five years I'd lived in Warsaw and Kiev had prepared me for Moscow. Journalism had taken me from the red-light districts of Berlin to the smuggler's corridors of western Bulgaria, from refugee camps in Budapest to U.N. peacekeeping missions near Kosovo. I thought I'd learned something about this region, and I thought this knowledge was transferable. But it was clear to me right from the start that Moscow had its own mysterious rules of engagement.

Outside our *podyezd*, or entrance, a dark-green Cadillac idled. Roberta said it belonged to a gentleman who lived a few floors below us. Actually, she corrected herself, he drove a Mercedes 600. The chauffeured Caddie was for his pretty redheaded wife.

Somehow, I doubted the neighbors here would be rummaging

through my trash. Actually, *I* now felt outclassed. And yet I was secretly pleased with my elevated surroundings, as if they were a just reward for all those the years of sleeping in hovels, working for next to nothing, for the pleasure, really, of witnessing history. But all that amateur stuff was behind me now. Henceforth I would be living large, earning a real salary and hobnobbing with the bright lights of Russia. A self-satisfied glow warmed me as I slid between the crisp sheets of our two-hundred-year-old sleigh bed.

Already Moscow had begun to cast its spell over me.

CHAPTER TWO

Baggage

The soldiers break through the door to our apartment with an ax. They stream into the living room, a blur of green and black and sweaty Slavic faces. Furniture is flying. Boots are stomping.

Someone is screaming. It's me, I notice with detached interest. I'm yelling in Polish. The voices bark at me in Russian, low and throaty as if they're being played at low speed. I don't understand what they are saying, but the tone is imperious, the implication ominous.

Hands are holding me down. They are meaty and strong, and I'm unable to break their grasp. I struggle in vain, watching helplessly as our furniture is being carted off. It takes six conscripts to lift the burled maple dining table. They can't get it through the door, and are hammering away at the wall to create a bigger opening.

It's the Red Army general. He has been rehabilitated and wants his stuff back. He's pointing at the bedroom now, at the antique sleigh bed, where Roberta is sleeping beneath the silk sheets. The conscripts eye her with lewd anticipation. They advance, grinning.

I scream.

Roberta was shaking me. "Are you okay?" she asked. "I think you were having a nightmare." It was only my third night in Moscow, but my unconscious was already acting up, warning me that I was behind enemy lines.

Over a cigarette in the small hours, Roberta counseled me to relax. "The Cold War is over, you know."

"Yeah," I admitted, reluctantly. "I know."

"Try to be open-minded."

43

"Okay," I promised unconvincingly. Roberta pressed on in Russia's defense: "The communists are history. You can't blame the Russian people for Stalin or what happened to your family or Poland."

Secretly I felt I could and would, but I didn't argue, remembering how I had tried to convince my best friend from home, when he had come to visit me in Warsaw, that he was not surrounded by rabid anti-Semites. "Sorry," my friend David had said, after I had exhausted myself defending Polish-Jewish relations. "Poland for me will always be the land of the Holocaust. I can't help it."

And neither could I, when it came to Russia. I worried that no matter what democracy and the market revolution had brought, Moscow, for me, would always be the heart of an evil empire. I suppose I had too much baggage to think otherwise.

A framed photograph hangs in my father's study at our country house in the Laurentian Mountains of southern Quebec. It's a grainy shot, the kind you find dog-eared and yellowed, wedged between sheets of wax paper in old family albums. At the bottom of the photo, in a broad flowing hand, someone has written *Nasz Przyjazd*—Polish for "Our Arrival." There is also a date penned in black ink: 1938.

The picture captures a nautical scene from the age of the great passenger liners. It shows the upper deck of a large ship, the *Batory* of the Gdynia-Amerika Line. The ship is under way; a thin plume can be seen trailing from one of its black-trimmed smokestacks as it clears the cold Baltic waters. The *Batory* is making its regular run to New York, ferrying wealthy Poles and Germans and a few fortunate Jews. My father and his family, the smiling subjects of the photo, are bound for Canada, where my grandfather Tadeusz Brzezinski has just been appointed to serve as Poland's Consul-General. In the shot, Grandfather Tadeusz is serene and elegant in a long coat and fedora. My grandmother is fur-clad and clutches a small bundle: Dad. My father's brothers—uncles George, Adam and Zbigniew—sport knee socks and blazers and wind-swept hair. Off to the side, and a little out of focus, stand a governess and housekeeper who are accompanying the family to the New World. At the front of the group, sprawled regally on the deck, lies John, the family's huge and surly German shepherd.

Everyone looks happy, as if they're going on vacation, leaving Europe's troubles behind for a few years. Grandfather's welcome new post was a reward for back-to-back diplomatic stints in Nazi Germany and the Soviet Union. His appointment to Germany in 1931 had come on the eve of Hitler's ascension to power, at a time when the Nazi brownshirts were just starting to patrol Germany's streets and the first *Juden* signs began appearing on storefront windows. Many of the Jews residing and working in Germany in the early 1930s held Polish passports. So Tadeusz' duties, as Poland's Consul for the Saxony region, revolved increasingly around defending these Polish Jews against Nazi persecution. Two months after Hitler became chancellor in early 1933 and anti-Semitism gained official sanction, my grandmother caused a minor diplomatic scandal by refusing to shake Hitler's hand. Soon after, my grandfather Tadeusz filed the first of a string of formal diplomatic protests on behalf of Polish-Jewish families. Copies of these documents survive today in Jerusalem, as do replies from the Nazi Interior Ministry labeling my Catholic grandfather's petitions as examples of the undue influence exercised by "tightly interlaced international Jewry."

By 1934, Jews across Germany had started disappearing into what the German Interior Ministry delicately referred to in its correspondence with my grandfather as "protective custody." Tadeusz spent the next two years traveling to the Third Reich's swelling network of concentration camps, eventually securing the release and return to Poland of thousands of Jewish prisoners. Whether his actions only delayed their fate is unclear. But as Israeli Prime Minister Menachem Begin put it in a citation awarded forty-three years later, his actions meant a great deal at a time when "so few stood with [the Jews] in their indescribable plight."

After four years in Germany, granddad Tadeusz was transferred in 1936 to the USSR. Stalin, at the time, was embarking on one of his bloodiest rampages yet against the Soviet people—the Yezhovshchina, in which millions of Party officials and innocent civilians were shot or sent to Siberia. Stalin was well known to my grandfather and other Poles from Revolutionary days. It was the

"Georgian butcher's" inept military leadership that in 1920 had turned the Red Army's almost certain capture of Warsaw into a crushing defeat known to Polish defenders as the "Miracle on the Vistula." By the time my grandfather left the Soviet Union in late 1937, Stalin was busily executing most of his army's officer corps and anyone else who might have witnessed his humiliation during that bungled Polish campaign—a move that would cost him dearly when the Nazis invaded in 1941.

So the family posing on the upper deck of the *Batory* steamship had reason to look forward to a few years in the New World, touring Niagara Falls and Manhattan's skyscrapers. It would be a short stint—then back to Warsaw and a desk job in the Ministry of Foreign Affairs, where granddad had high hopes that someday his sons would follow in his footsteps.

But history shouldered its way into the picture. In September 1939, shots rang out at Westerplate, just outside of what is today Gdansk. Hitler marched on Poland, and the world plunged into war. After German Panzer divisions took Warsaw, Tadeusz became the Polish government-in-exile's representative in Canada and keeper of the Wawel Castle National Treasures. The trove had been spirited out of Krakow in September 1939, and shipped along with England's gold reserves via London to Canada for safekeeping from Nazi looters.

The war ended at last, but Poland faced a new trauma as the country fell under Soviet occupation. Stalin installed a puppet government in Warsaw and deported two million Poles to Siberian labor camps. The Russian Iron Curtain raised around Eastern Europe made my family's 1938 Atlantic crossing a one-way trip. To return would have meant imprisonment, possibly even death.

Hardship befell the family in the years following the war. The property and assets left behind in Poland were now confiscated. The funds for the governess and the big stone house in Montreal's posh Westmount hillside district soon ran out. Money for private-school tuition became a problem. Granddad was reduced to selling life insurance, scouring the phone book for listings of Polish immigrants who might buy policies from him.

Another family photograph hangs in my father's study, this one taken at a later and happier time. The setting is a paneled, high-ceilinged room in the White House in Washington, D.C. The occa-

As he fumbled with a lighter, I couldn't help staring. Here stood the enemy personified, a servant of the hated system I had from early childhood been taught to fear and mistrust. He didn't look especially threatening. Short and wiry, the conscript had the pinched, pimply features of an undernourished teenager. His baggy uniform was stained with oil and looked like a hand-me-down from a sloppy older brother. His hair was shorn prison-style, so that his pale scalp shone through wheat-blond bristles. There was a pathetic shabbiness about him reminiscent of a character out of *Oliver Twist*. Even with his hammer-and-sickle brass belt buckle this young kid appeared more victim than conquering warrior. I found it hard to hate him.

"What's your name?" I asked slowly in Polish, hoping he'd understand. Vladimir, he said shyly, after some hesitation. We smoked in silence for a few moments, neither knowing what more to say. Vladimir appraised my Levis and Nike sneakers, looked hungrily at my striped rugby shirt and Tag Heuer wristwatch. His gaze shifted to the rental car, taking in its sleek, sharp lines, and he nodded approvingly. All the while I gawked right back. Finally Vladimir thanked me for the cigarette and made for his decrepit army truck.

"Hey!" I shouted after him. "Wait. Take two more for the road."

The road marker announced POLEN—Poland—5 KM. Impatient, I accelerated, nearly sideswiping a wobbly Trabi, the misbegotten East German offspring of a Fiat and a lawnmower. My stomach cramped. I had grown up speaking the language, listening to the stories. But this would be the first time I saw my "native" land.

Another signpost indicated two kilometers to the frontier. The road was better now, the blacktop smooth and broad, as if drawn with a felt-tip marker. Orange cones marked off one lane, and behind them a paving-company worker painted fresh median lines. The Germans were upgrading the border facilities, widening the artery that the old regime had tightened into a constricting knot. I'd been warned to expect delays at the Polish frontier, which had not been designed to cope with large traffic flows.

I passed a small stream, a tributary of the Oder River, whose muddy banks and swift current form a natural barrier between

Poland and postwar Germany and gave a famous treaty its name. Some kids dangled bamboo fishing rods over an eddy that meandered to the side of the highway, oblivious to history and everything else except the water that licked at their bare feet.

The bottleneck came out of nowhere. One moment, the road had been empty, the grasses on either side swaying lazily; the next second, I found myself staring at a sea of angry red brake lights. Heat waves rose and rippled from hundreds of idling engine blocks.

Minutes passed, then an hour, and still the line barely inched forward. There were hundreds of cars with mean little black license plates. They were attached to old jalopies with outdated designs that one might have found in a 1968 issue of *Car & Driver*. Most were no bigger than British Austin Minis and rode low to the ground. They were weighed down by parcels of all sizes, crammed into back seats and lashed to roofs that appeared on the verge of buckling under the extra load. Cardboard boxes with the logos of German electronic firms like Bosch and Blaupunkt stuck out of trunks tied shut with frayed rope. One ancient Mercedes had been converted into a mobile clothier. Dozens of flower-patterned dresses and loud sports coats hung on makeshift racks suspended over the back seat. Its driver wore a yellow athletic tracksuit and flashed a gold-crowned grimace. Dozens of vehicles towed trailers on which secondhand Audis and BMWs rode piggyback.

The acrid stench of car exhaust hung in the air, enveloping the pasty-faced travelers who peered out from grimy windows. Some milled about, smoking and drinking next to their immobile vehicles. Others had spread out little aprons on the hoods of their dusty cars and were enjoying a picnic of hard-boiled eggs, kielbasa, and ripe red tomatoes, seasoned with carbon monoxide. A few tinkered with their engines. Everyone sweated.

I felt terribly sorry for these motorists, so bedraggled and unwashed in their sweat-stained rayon shirts and gray plastic shoes with velcro straps. They appeared to be petty traders of some sort, economic refugees from some blighted Balkan nation trying to make a little money by buying goods available on the other side of the border to resell at home. Getting out to stretch my legs, I walked past a chatting pair of middle-aged men. Then a familiar sound hit me like a shock wave. These pale, unhealthy people, with their ill-fitting clothes and dirty eating habits, were speaking Polish! Those ugly black tags were Polish license plates!

I hastily retreated to the car to mull all this over. I hadn't pictured Poles looking this grim. Russians, yes. East Germans, naturally. But not my countrymen.

Which brought to mind an uneasy question: What did I really know about this country that I called my ancestral homeland? I had grown up observing Poland from afar, nurtured on a diet of folklore and myth. My earliest lessons came from my maternal grandfather, Jozef Kotanski, a career cavalry officer after whose favorite parade horse I take my legal name—Maciej. I would sit on my granddad's giant lap—he was six feet six—and poke at his scarred torso. Over and over, I would beg to hear how he got the brown, coin-sized shrapnel wounds that dotted his chest like pins on a military map; about the tank battalion he commanded; about the five years he spent in a Nazi POW camp. But I never asked about living in the postwar People's Republic, and he never told me. It was as if history in our house stopped the day the war ended and Poland found itself on the wrong side of Europe's tracks.

I knew that Poland had been a victim of geography through much of her thousand-year history. I knew she had been divvied up on countless occasions by rapacious neighbors to the east and west. I knew Poland had been cruelly occupied by Hitler and then lost, seemingly forever, to Stalin.

Then I drew a blank, as if the place stopped existing after the communist takeover. In my mind, time itself had skipped a beat, as if one day it was 1945 and the next day a mustachioed electrician named Lech Walesa was being sworn in as the first democratically elected Polish leader in half a century.

What had happened to Poland in the interim, when so many Poles became willing accomplices to the communist fraud? I'd never bothered to ask. Or maybe I had never really wanted to know, preferring, like so many other children of émigrés, to forget the old country and focus instead on blending into the great North American melting pot. While Poland was under martial law and tanks patrolled the streets of Gdansk, I was preoccupied with "All-American" pursuits like getting elected captain of the football team and president of the student council. I would cringe and blush crimson whenever my grandparents called out for me in Polish in front of my friends. "Machee! What the hell kind of name is that?" In high school, I even dropped an unpronounceable Z from the back of my football jersey to seem less like a "Polack," and was surprised when my parents shook their heads disapprovingly. And as I watched the familiarly foreign red-on-white Polish flags flutter over the border checkpoint, I wished my grandparents were still alive—because I was about to need the answers to a million questions I had never taken the time to ask.

Something had happened. The mood at the border had suddenly changed from fatigued to fearful. People looked alarmed, running from car to car and congregating in small conspiratorial groups. Some kind of bad news was spreading rapidly down the line of cars.

I rolled down my window. "*Putsch w Moskwie!*" shouted a woman to no one in particular. "A coup in Moscow."

People were rushing to their car radios.

"Tanks on the streets," someone yelled.

"Mass arrests."

"*O Boze*—Oh, God."

Passengers were spilling out of and into their cars, panicked. Several huddled around a blue Opel ahead of me, listening as its driver translated the news broadcast from a German radio station. "They say Gorbachev has stepped down for health reasons," the man interpreted. "A committee for emergencies has taken over. The correspondent says KGB hardliners are behind it."

"Gorbachev is dead," he added sadly, though it was unclear whether he was still translating or now offering his own conclusions.

"No" said a latecomer to the group. "Polish radio says he is under house arrest in Crimea."

"If Gorbie is still alive," interjected a surprisingly well-dressed woman, "then he has fled the country."

No one seemed to know for sure what was going on in Moscow. I fiddled with the dial of my radio but could only catch German stations, which I didn't understand save for the occasional reference to Moskau or Russen.

People were still arguing, breaking off discussions to move their cars a few lengths now that traffic seemed to be flowing faster. Maybe the customs officers were also preoccupied with the news out of the Soviet Union, waving people through without their usual scrutiny (and without the usual demands for a small consideration). A woman in line ahead of me turned to a green-uniformed border guard, her voice trembling as she asked what undoubtedly was on the minds of every Eastern European: "What will happen to Russia?" she wailed. "What will happen to us?"

Up to now, I had viewed events in the Soviet Union as distant rumblings from an inhospitable and faraway planet, reported via satellite in surreal sound bites on the CBS evening news. But the upheavals in the Kremlin suddenly struck uncomfortably close to home, brought to life by the palpable fear of the people around me.

History was being made on that muggy afternoon. And as the border guard stamped the entry date August 19, 1991, in my passport, I turned my back on the West and joined the ranks of Eastern Europeans waiting for their fate to be decided.

Had someone told me that day on the Polish-German border that within a few years Gorbachev would be flogging Pizza Hut on American television, or that I would be dissecting the yield curves of Russian Treasury bills for the *Wall Street Journal*, I think I would have died laughing.

Yet all this had come to pass, and at unimaginably high speed. Moscow—in the eyes of all but the most hardened skeptics—was no longer the heart of an evil empire, but a promising profit center whose growing importance was duly noted in the financial statements of multinational corporations. Russia was no longer an imperialist power bent on expansion and the enslavement of Poland, but an emerging market with duly elected democratic leaders. Even the Russians were now "New Russians," capitalist converts, absolved of past sins.

Meanwhile in North America a new breed of Russia experts had emerged with the changing times, and these men and women now focused more on Russian bonds than on nuclear bombs. The Cold Warriors had been shouted down by the money managers, and the veterans of countless covert campaigns against the Kremlin had retired bitterly to their conservative think tanks, or to Florida. Russia, it was now said, had abandoned a thousand-year tradition of autocracy and aggression, and was entering the Western orbit, at least in the sphere of high finance and banking, which recognized no boundaries or frontiers, only profit margins and stable growth.

Yet all these hosannas flew in the face of everything I had heard in five years of traveling through Moscow's old dominions. In Warsaw and Prague, Vilnius and Tallinn, Lvov and Budapest, everyone was still suspicious of the Kremlin to the point of paranoia. Almost no one bought the story of the New Russia. And my relatives in Poland were no exception.

My relatives lived next to Warsaw's *Stare Miasto* (Old Town) historic district, in a gloomy two-room apartment crammed to the rafters with old furniture, dusty family heirlooms, and tarnished silverware.

To get to their place, you walked through musty courtyards and along cobblestoned lanes, passed under the echoing belfries of fourteenth-century cathedrals, and ducked through turreted brick ramparts originally erected to fend off the Tartar hordes that threatened from the east.

The entire old quarter, with its whimsical peach and lavender townhouses, slanted red-tiled roofs, and weathered bronze door knockers, had been blown to smithereens by the Nazis after the failed Warsaw Uprising in 1944. Hitler was so outraged at the insurrection that he ordered Poland's capital wiped off the map. The Nazis systematically razed 90 percent of Warsaw to the ground while the Red Army, camped just a few miles away across the Vistula, watched and did nothing. The Russians, having sent the prearranged signal for the partisans to rise, picnicked instead of joining the battle as promised, and so allowed the Nazis to finish off any armed resisters who might have later opposed the Soviet takeover of the ruined city.

Because of this betrayal, the SS were left free to methodically murder more than two hundred thousand civilians in the bombings and mass executions that almost cost my mother her life. She and my grandmother had been caught in one of the Nazis' deadly street roundups and lined up against the wall in front of a firing squad. Only the intervention of a passing Wehrmacht officer, who apparently took pity on a freckled four-year-old, spared their lives. Fifty of their neighbors that day were not so lucky.

After the war, Poland's communist puppet government painstakingly rebuilt the old aristocratic quarter—a way, some say, of subtly giving the new/old overlords in Moscow the middle finger. The detailed restoration was one of the few things the Polish Reds managed not to bungle, making it a national effort that drew skilled tinsmiths and masons from all over the country. The government was also busy rebuilding the rest of Warsaw. My mother, like all elementary-school children in Warsaw in the late 1940s, spent one school day a week picking bricks from the rubble for reuse in the reconstruction of the capital. "We got to miss class, so we thought it was wonderful," Mom chuckled when I asked her about the city-wide program. (Unfortunately the children's handiwork was glaringly apparent in most sections of the capital, whose slapped-together, crumbling apartment blocks virtually begged for another *Blitzkrieg*.)

My relatives, the Romans, lived on the ground floor of a drafty edifice of the mass-produced matchbox design exported by the Soviets to all their colonies. The first time I showed up at their doorstep in 1991, my aunt Dagmara greeted me with an uneasy blush. "We know you don't have to live like this in the West," she apologized, ushering me into a narrow, wood-paneled hall where threadbare coats drooped five to a hook. "Please forgive our circumstances. We must seem very primitive to you."

It did take some effort on that first visit to mask my shock that four people and two dogs could share an area that was not much bigger than my bedroom in Montreal. The kitchen, with its rattling old appliances and eight square feet of yellowed linoleum, could have easily fit in my closet at home.

My distress grew when I learned that uncle Andrzej had to stay in a separate one-room bachelor efficiency down the corridor from the rest of the Roman family, an illogical arrangement possible only under communism and a big step down from the circumstances into which he had been born.

Andrzej (Polish for Andrew) was my dad's first cousin. I often saw him as a reminder of how different my life would have been had my own father also been stranded behind the Iron Curtain. Andrzej had been in his early teens when one morning in 1946 Stalin's peasant henchmen burst into the Romans' villa and started knocking over furniture. "Pack your bags, swine," they ordered, herding the family onto a flatbed truck. The Romans' property was seized for "crimes against the people," Andrzej's father was interrogated for several days, and the Romans were relocated into a communal apartment they had to share with three other displaced families. Unable to get jobs because of their bourgeois roots, the Romans survived the postwar Stalinist years by hawking family heirlooms.

A tall, rakish man in his mid-sixties, Andrzej had thinning hair, expressive eyes, and the trim, sinewy build of an athlete at rest. He looked like the sort of gentleman born to wear a tuxedo, sip champagne cocktails, and flick scented ashes from an ivory cigarette holder. A lawyer who never practiced law, he had long ago opted to become a sports columnist on the grounds that under communism, sportswriting was the only form of journalism that allowed one to actually tell the truth, not overexert oneself at the office, and travel abroad. Andrzej's chosen profession meshed well with his two true passions—tennis and high-stakes bridge.

During the eighties, Andrzej, like half his fellow Poles, became a dissident. The hours were short and the risk appealed to the gambler in him. Sometimes he and his colleagues snuck up on rooftops with homemade radio transponders to jam the government's sanitized nightly news broadcasts; anyone within a one-mile radius heard Solidarity's voice-over instead of the Politburo's propaganda. "It used to drive the commies crazy," he laughed, whenever he told the story, which was often. "The army had triangulation trucks trying to track us down. We would have two minutes to beam our signal and pack up before the militia zeroed in on us." Andrzej also wrote articles under a pseudonym for the underground papers that Solidarity published with CIA-funded printing presses.

After the fall of communism, Andrzej served briefly as the press spokesman for the Solidarity parliamentary caucus in 1991. But he quickly distanced himself from the union over its opposition to economic reform. Solidarity by that time was a shadow of itself. No longer the powerful movement that had counted a member in virtually every Polish household in the 1980s, it had splintered into a half-dozen quarrelsome parties, many of which lobbied to preserve the wasteful subsidies that had kept communist industry afloat.

"Such short memories," Andrzej muttered one night, as we crowded around the Romans' old television to watch coverage of the nationwide strikes against the economic austerity program, which became known as Shock Therapy. "People have such short and selective memories."

"They've conveniently forgotten the bread lines," he went on, as Dagmara brought tea, which we drank Russian-style, scalding hot and in a tall glass. "Or the days when the only things on store shelves were jugs of vinegar. They've forgotten the lies, and the midnight visits by the secret police. All they remember is that they had money—useless play money that they couldn't buy anything with anyway."

Despite benefiting from communism's lax work ethic—Dagmara retired from the national ballet on full pension in her late thirties, and Andrzej bragged that he never did an honest day's work for the Reds—the Romans supported Walesa's tough economic policies. Andrzej maintained that no matter how painful, the sacrifices would be worth it if they helped shift Poland into the Western camp and away from Moscow's clutches. "Whatever it takes to get free of those bastards," Andrzej would often growl. His paranoia about Russian imperialism bordered on religious fervor. He distrusted Moscow's new masters almost as much as the old guard and fretted that until Poland entered the NATO alliance, she would be a sitting duck for the endlessly expansionist machinations of the Kremlin.

Though now approaching middle age, my Aunt Dagmara still had a dancer's figure and a dainty, upturned nose that wrinkled disapprovingly whenever I blundered with some off-the-mark comment on Polish politics, which was often. It was remarkable how politicized Eastern Europe was in the early 1990s; people were making up for all those decades when they hadn't been free to talk, choose, vote.

Politics was in Dagmara's blood. Her grandfather had been a well-to-do general, serving during the 1930s as military governor of what is today western Ukraine. Portraits of Poland's prewar horsey set competed for space on the Romans' crowded walls, recalling happier days when Dagmara's mother, Pani Albrecht, rode with the country's ruling aristocracy. (Pani means Madam, and is the formal manner of addressing female strangers and old ladies in title-conscious Poland.) Pani Albrecht was an elegant grand dame in the old European tradition. Blessed with regal snowy curls and the clipped upper-crust British accent that young Polish ladies in good society once learned at Swiss boarding schools, she now slept on the Romans' stained couch with the family's two drooling boxers, Lola and Pola. She had moved in shortly after the Shock Therapy reform programs were introduced in 1990, when it became apparent that Andrzej, Dagmara, and their son could not make it on the two-hundred-dollar-a-month pension they received from the new Solidarity government. Renting out her own apartment to an American accountant, Pani Albrecht brought an additional five hundred dollars of monthly income into the Romans' coffers and thus secured the family's survival through the lean years of austerity.

At seventy-eight, an age where most elderly people in North America are sent to rot away in retirement homes, Dagmara's spirited mom did just about everything around the Roman household, from cooking and cleaning to walking the ferociously rambunctious Lola and Pola. Although I weighed more than two hundred pounds, I could barely control the boisterous beasts. So it was with some awe that I watched Pani Albrecht wrap their leashes around her frail wrists, lock her septuagenarian knees and sail out the door like a white-haired rodeo rider. She didn't so much walk the dogs as dig her heels into the pavement and double over at a ninety-degree angle, slowing them down just enough for the neighbor's terror-stricken cats to scamper safely up a tree.

Pani Albrecht, like many Poles during the early 1990s, was wont to groan and complain incessantly about the tough times. If it wasn't the price hikes or the family's hyper mutts turning the place upside down, it was Andrzej out with his card buddies until three in the morning. Maybe the griping kept her young; without the family to care for, I think she would have withered away.

Pani Albrecht's most fervent complaints were reserved for Zbigniew Junior. Zbig was the Romans' deceptively angelic-looking thirteen-year-old son. Dagmara and Zbig shared the apartment's single small bedroom, his posters of Arnold Schwarzenegger adorning one wall, her antique oil paintings tacked to the other.

Zbig was among the most inventive people I've ever met—a polite way of saying that he was an adorable little bullshitter. He always had a ready excuse to explain neglected homework and could be relentlessly thoughtful in the solicitation of presents for obscure Polish holidays, of which he always gave me ample notice. "You don't have to bring a gift," he would insist with studied insincerity. "It would be enough just for you to come."

Zbig Junior wanted to be a lawyer, because, as he perceptively put it, that was where the money would be. (Indeed, even as enrollment in sciences and humanities at the University of Warsaw plummeted as students dropped out in droves to become petty traders, applications for the law faculty and the new business administration program soared to a point where bribes were openly offered to gain admission.) I sided with Pani Albrecht's view that Zbig's less-than-stellar grades could preclude a career in law, and suspected that he might even require the services of a skilled attorney himself some day. His ploys to separate Andrzej from his spare change were very creative, usually achieved by overstating the rate of inflation so that whenever Andrzej sent his son to the store on an errand, he unwittingly paid next month's prices that day.

Zbig Junior's biggest scam involved flowers. He would appropriate them at Warsaw's Public Gardens and sell them to patrons of the outdoor cafes in Old Town Square. "Would you like to buy tulips for the beautiful lady?" he would ask a couple, proffering a scraggly bouquet. Only after the victim had taken the bait and presented his date with the flowers would Zbig innocently drop the hammer; "That will be 80,000 zlotys please." The man would choke, his bile rising at the exorbitant sum—about six dollars, or a day's salary for the average worker at the time. But not wanting to look cheap in front of his girlfriend, the mark would invariably pony up.

Andrzej, naturally, was horrified to learn about this commercial activity. "You can't run around like a peddler," he would splutter, for once at a loss for words. "Like—like—like some Gypsy. I forbid it."

The ever-pragmatic Dagmara invariably intervened. She herself traded on the side to plug the family's budget shortfalls, buying smuggled caviar and icons from the Russians at Warsaw's soccer stadium-cum-flea market and giving them to her husband for resale in Paris (at massive markups) during his annual pilgrimage to the Roland Garos French Tennis Open.

"How much money did you make?" she would ask her equally enterprising son.

"Eight hundred thou," Zbig would beam.

"Andrzej," Dagmara would then turn to her husband. "How much did you lose at bridge last night?"

As the weeks passed in Moscow and I was neither lynched by street mobs nor hounded by the government, my Polish paranoia faded. The city's big streets became less intimidating, and some of the strange faces around me grew more familiar. I became friendly with the *Journal*'s driver at the office, and learned of his love for jazz. I got to know the name of our ancient elevator woman, and heard her tell how, for the past thirty-six years, she had guarded the entrance of our apartment building.

A holdover from the old "full-employment" days—when central planners created such exciting career opportunities as department store escalator watcher (job description: press the emergency-stop button if someone's coat gets caught in the moving stairs)—she carried herself with dignity. As the official gatekeeper of our building, our elevator woman acted more like the imperious president of a Manhattan co-op board than a lowly doorperson. Though she probably couldn't have offered much resistance to an intruder, she was fiercely protective of the tenants, many of whom she had watched grow up. It took some doing for her to accept the notion of newcomers, much less foreigners, moving into her building. But with time, the curt nods she initially accorded us softened to weak smiles, and then polite greetings, until one morning she inquired with matronly concern about my health.

At first, it was almost disappointing to discover that the Russians were no longer hell-bent on territorial conquest or mischief. Roberta joked that I was undergoing my own form of Shock Therapy: curing myself of the post-colonial complex that ailed all the old satellite states. But the truth of the matter was that no one in Moscow seemed to care one iota about reclaiming Poland and the former dominions. Everybody was way too busy making money.

CHAPTER THREE

Renaissance

The *Wall Street Journal*'s Moscow bureau was on the top floor of a sixteen-story structure off the busy Garden Ring Road. The building stood next to one of Stalin's sinister wedding-cake skyscrapers and was of the prefabricated matchbox variety favored by Khrushchev's quota-driven builders. It had ten thousand clones in Moscow, and countless identical siblings blighting urban landscapes from Kamchatka to Krakow.

In spite of its unappealing façade, this particular building had a number of things to recommend it. It belonged to the Ministry of Foreign Affairs, and was thus safe and relatively cheap. Real estate prices in Moscow had gone berserk with the influx of foreigners in the mid-1990s, the demand for modern office space so outpacing the city's shabby Soviet-era supply that Turkish and Austrian property developers charged Tokyo-level rents for space in the glass boxes they were slapping up on every second block.

The *Journal*'s address also benefited from proximity to Moscow's Wall Street, a road occupied by three massive modern moon-shaped structures that housed Russia's biggest banks and their oligarch masters. Our balcony afforded a bird's-eye view of the comings and goings at Oneximbank, Alfabank, and Menatep Bank. The bureau also overlooked Oneximbank's executive rear parking lot, which resembled a well-stocked Mercedes dealership that specialized only in armored, navy blue 600-series sedans, or *shestsotki*, as the top-of-the-line models were affectionately known—as in "My *shestsotka*'s just been blown up, can I borrow yours?"

The bankers were Ivan-come-latelys compared to the *Journal*, which had inhabited the gated complex since before Gorbachev; the Soviets, following tsarist tradition, had isolated foreigners in special compounds lest they spread mischief by mingling with the general population. These guarded compounds, which also afforded the KGB's eavesdropping teams economies of scale, were managed by a branch of the Ministry known under the Russian acronym of UPDK (Administration of Diplomatic Personnel). After 1991, when Yeltsin's government lifted housing restrictions on foreigners, the vast majority of budget-conscious media organizations opted to remain in their bugged UPDK quarters, where inexpensive leases offset any inconvenience posed by the old and probably inoperative listening devices embedded in the walls.

The *Journal* shared its humble home on Bolshaya Spasskaya Street with a motley assortment of expatriates. Our neighbors included North African diplomats who warded off the Eurasian chill by throwing parties nightly; a taciturn Portuguese television crew who always tied up the elevator with their equipment; the lone *Newsday* correspondent; several French trade representatives whose wives back in Paris had ample grounds for divorce; and a local travel agency, run by a morose Russian woman who had managed to sneak in despite the foreigners-only rule.

Our bureau was a converted residential apartment, with low ceilings, scuffed hardwood floors, and whitewashed walls in dire need of freshening. It had a harried and unkempt look, like a group house or college dorm in the waning days of the semester, and reminded me of the *New York Times'* tiny office in Warsaw, where I had started my career as a glorified gofer and cub reporter. Whoever said being a foreign correspondent was glamorous had obviously never set foot in one of these Spartan outposts of American journalism.

While the *Journal* had skimped on furnishings, it had spent lavishly on state-of-the-art computers and communications equipment. Banks of shiny new terminals squawked and beeped throughout the bureau, connected via a satellite phone system to a central server that was housed next to the moldy bathroom in a refrigerated glass cabinet about the size of a Coke machine. I had no idea what 90 percent of these costly machines did, a sad fact that would remain one of the ten true constants of my tenure in Moscow.

Three full-time correspondents worked out of the Moscow bureau, along with support staff: a driver, an interpreter, and Nonna, the towering office manager. Like a great many Russians in the employ of foreign firms, Nonna was vastly overqualified. She had been polishing her Ph.D. dissertation when communism collapsed, and the depression that followed had forced her to abandon academia for the relative security of secretarial work. Wasted brainpower was one of the postcommunist East's great tragedies. The first McDonald's to open in Warsaw (the very outlet on Marshalkowska Street where young Zbig would always slyly suggest that we meet and then let slip that he had missed lunch) had drawn twenty thousand job applications, almost all from college graduates. A new Ford assembly plant I had visited in Minsk had engineers with master's degrees manning the assembly line and Ph.D.s bolting seats into the chassis of Escorts. So perhaps it was not surprising that Nonna was the best educated person at the bureau. She could have easily been resentful of her situation, but instead was perennially cheerful, even while suffering the indignities of ordering ballpoint pens.

My new office looked out onto a dreary hospital and the soaring globe-tipped needle of the Ostankino TV tower, which had briefly been the world's tallest structure until the Canadians one-upped the Politburo with Toronto's CN Tower. The Ostankino tower had been the site of a bloody confrontation during Yeltsin's 1993 coup against the Duma, or parliament, where one American had been killed and a *New York Times* photographer had been shot. Even without ricocheting bullets, the tower provided a picturesque distraction from the mind-numbing bond stories I was assigned upon arrival. I had dreaded the prospect of writing financial stories from the time I accepted the *Journal*'s stringer gig in Kiev, for the simple reason that I didn't know the first thing about capital markets. To me, GDRs were East Germans, not Global Depository Receipts; you launched ICBMs, not IPOs; and a spreadsheet was something a bookie gave you. I was certain the editors would rip my copy to shreds.

The only comfort I had was that most people in this part of the world knew even less about markets than I did, as had been comically evident during my first visit to the Kiev stock exchange. My editors had made disappointed noises about the lack of business stories out of Ukraine, and suggested a piece about the new stock exchange. It had been one of those "suggestions" that you ignored on pain of banishment, though I didn't know any place further off the beaten path I could have been demoted to, except maybe Moldova.

Finding the Ukrainian bourse was easier said than done. It was housed in a small nondescript brick building whose address plate had either been stolen or never installed. The place was deserted, save for an old babushka cleaning the floor, who, when I asked about the exchange, wordlessly pointed her mop at the staircase. On the second-floor landing I was greeted by an elderly gentleman in a tweed jacket. This turned out to be Vladimir Vasilenko, the chairman of the Kiev stock exchange.

"The *World Street Journal?*" he frowned, when I introduced myself. "What country do you represent?"

"No, no," I corrected. "*Wall* Street, you know, like in New York."

"Ahh," he said brightening. "So you're American."

"Canadian, actually."

This revelation produced more frowning, and further explanations were required. When at last all was clear, Vasilenko led me to the trading floor. It occupied a quiet hall with the rough dimensions of an elementary-school gymnasium. Neat rows of computer terminals sat on fold-up tables, and behind each terminal sat a floor trader. There were about thirty of them, ten if you only counted those who were awake.

By now, I had surmised that this was not the New York Stock Exchange. Not only were there no clanging bells, mad shouts, flailing arms, or other signs of controlled pandemonium, there weren't even that many visible signs of life. I assumed it was lunchtime, and turned my attention to Vasilenko. "What is the market capitalization of your exchange?" I inquired, mentally ticking off the first of the buzzwords I had memorized so as to sound like less of an impostor.

"Market capitalization?" Vasilenko repeated, eyes glazed.

I had used the term in English, presuming it universal. But while Vasilenko had a smattering of the language, he had never heard of capitalization. I tried explaining in Russian, which only seemed to confuse matters further. An interpreter was sent for. His English turned out to be worse than my Russian.

Nonetheless, we tried again. What was the total value of all the stock listed on the Kiev exchange? This, I had been told recently, was the standard measure of the size of any given market. In Ukraine's case, it couldn't have been that complicated a question. There were only a dozen companies trading on the bourse, mainly because the government was reluctant to privatize its State enterprises; Ukraine's moldering chocolate and glass factories were deemed too "strategically important" to be allowed to fall into private hands.

"Ahh," said Vasilenko finally, a flicker of understanding in his gray eyes. A calculator and two assistants were called for. Vasilenko and his two aides huddled over the machine, pecking and mumbling. Five minutes passed, punctuated by a good deal of sighing. There were disagreements among the aides, and a hushed, spirited discussion.

Finally, the tally was read. "Two trillion dollars."

Come again?

"It is impossible to know precisely," one of the aides hesitated, seeing my jaw slowly drop at the figure. "It is our best estimate."

"For your listed companies?" I asked, still stunned.

"Oh, no, no," came the shocked response. "For all of Ukraine."

After that edifying exchange, my fear of being outed as a fraud evaporated. These guys couldn't tell the difference between a stock and an option, much less spot that I was not a seasoned financial reporter. Emboldened and somewhat amused, I made for the lifeless trading floor. After some fifteen minutes of total silence, during which Vasilenko respectfully asked after my famous uncle's health, an order to sell several hundred shares of a river-shipping company came through, and the somnolent traders stirred. Newspapers were put away, yawns were stifled, someone stretched. The bourse was ready for action. Someone called for bids, and capitalism was set in motion. Languidly, almost reluctantly, several traders raised little yellow cardboard sheets. The laws of supply and demand were taking control. Not much happened for a few minutes. Then, anticlimactically, a gavel slammed, announcing the day's first, and as it turned out, only trade. The Ukrainian stock exchange's total volume on that Thursday: $7,340.

"Why do you need all the fancy computers?" I later asked Vasilenko, thinking that an abacus would have been better suited to tally the paltry sums.

"Oh," he replied airily, "they were a gift from the French government."

All of Eastern Europe's bourses had had similarly humble beginnings. I remember when the Poles opened their exchange in 1991— on the top floor of the old Communist Party Central Committee Headquarters, in a gesture of delicious irony; they too started small, with six listings and two hours a week of trading. By 1993, the throngs outside brokerages and banks stretched round the block, so great was the market frenzy, and people paid pensioners and students to wait in line for them, just like in the socialist days of shortages, except that they were lining up to buy shares, not bread. No one, back then, had a clue about price-to-earnings ratios or the mechanics of a market; the average Pole only knew that his neighbor had bought a new Fiat with stock gains, and he wanted one too. As a result, the Warsaw stock exchange index, or the WIG composite as it became better known, rose over a thousand percent that year, spurred by what can only be described as a national gambling fever, and set the record as the world's best-performing market.

By 1995, Westerners had gotten in on the action, the bourse boasted over a hundred listings with daily volumes topping a hundred million dollars, and Warsaw offered such sophisticated financial instruments as derivatives, options, and warrants. By then, of course, I'd missed the boat. A stringer's salary left little disposable income for playing the markets, and besides, the fortunes had already been made.

That brief window of opportunity, that fleeting moment when time and place align so profitably, had now opened in Moscow. Unfortunately, I was destined to miss this one too. One of the appendices to my employment contract with Dow Jones, the *Journal*'s publisher, was a lengthy and detailed form requiring disclosure of all stocks, bonds, and other securities owned by reporters. This was meant to forestall the sort of embarrassing incidents in which financial journalists wrote glowing reports about companies whose stock they owned. For me, filling out the form was a little like responding to those questionnaires handed out by the U.S. Immigration and Naturalization Service: Have you ever participated in war crimes or genocide? Have you ever been convicted of selling narcotics or trafficking in nuclear-grade materials? I just checked No for every question and counted myself the perfectly impartial business journalist.

To better prepare myself for the market bonanza I would have to chronicle, I had also made sincere, if desultory, efforts since my arrival to better educate myself as to the mysterious ways of high finance. I rented *Wall Street* from Moscow's lone English-language video store, where it seemed that the entire expat community congregated nightly, and watched a young and still sober Charlie Sheen grow disillusioned. Roberta lent me her copy of Michael Lewis' *Liar's Poker*, and I noted with keen interest the young author's gradual disaffection with the bull markets of the 1980s. *American Psycho* rounded out my instructional reading list, and by the time I had digested the gory parts, I thought I had a fair understanding of the underlying principles of a boom market: You made a ton of money, and then mused about the injustice of it all, preferably from the aft deck of your fifty-foot yacht.

I was ready to become a business reporter.

My first major assignment took me to the plush offices of an outfit called Renaissance Capital. Renaissance Capital was an American investment bank, which I (incorrectly) assumed meant that it made investments instead of loans.

My first impression of the place was that bankers had decidedly nicer digs than journalists. Renaissance occupied several swanky floors of a brand-new glass and granite tower that perched expensively on the frozen banks of the Moskva. The building looked out on a steaming municipal heating plant across the icy river and was not too far from the famous Novodevichy Convent, where Peter the Great had locked up his scheming half-sister Sofia.

The second thing that struck me was that investment bankers really did wear those striped shirts and silly suspenders, just like in the movies. A good number of them also slicked their hair back like the evil Gordon Gecko.

Everyone at Renaissance was very young, in their mid-twenties at most, and purposeful, seeming to be in a hurry to cash out before the window slammed shut. The offices had an open floor plan that reminded me of a casino floor, with different gaming tables scattered throughout: Fixed-Income Securities to the left, Funds to the right, Equities in the middle. The croupiers manning the terminals were fast-fingered Russians, while the pacing pit bosses were all gimlet-eyed Americans.

I was there to meet Renaissance's boyish founder and nose around for material for a story about bonds, though what exactly a story on bonds entailed, I did not yet know. Still, I was curious about Renaissance's CEO, the *Wunderkind* who was probably the most influential and plugged-in Westerner in Russia amid more than 100,000 foreigners mining the Moscow gold rush.

Boris Jordan made interesting copy. He was the poster child of the Russian market boom, both symbol and chief salesman of the overnight wealth and power that awaited those bold and prescient enough to have risked it all in Moscow. A New Yorker of Russian extraction, Jordan had been a bit player on Wall Street when the Soviet Union collapsed. Though only in his mid-twenties at the time, with an earnest face still ringed in baby fat, he had persuaded his employers at the venerable firm of Credit Suisse First Boston to send him to Moscow to ride the privatization wave of the early nineties. At the urging of Western advisers, the new post-communist government had launched a "mass privatization" program: every Russian citizen received a voucher that could be traded for shares in various State enterprises. Practically the whole economy was going on the block—the Soviet communists had controlled everything from tractor factories to hairdressing shops to grocery stores. There were a lot of dogs, but a savvy voucher-holder could pick up shares in some real jewels— oil companies, aluminum smelters, airlines— all valued at ridiculously low prices. Most Russians, especially outside of Moscow, had little use for the voucher scrip, which to their inexperienced eyes was just a piece of paper, and they were only too happy to part with their vouchers for a few dollars or a bottle of vodka.

Seeing the potential value of the vouchers, Jordan sent out a small army of purchasing agents, who, escorted by armed guards, traveled the provinces, setting up shop outside the gates of factories and offering workers a few rubles for their scrip. Then the young entrepreneur used his vouchers to buy up shares in potentially juicy enterprises that were coming under the auctioneer's gavel. In this way, Jordan became the biggest buyer of Russian shares even before the country had a stock exchange. After a bourse was founded in 1994, Jordan saw his gamble net $150 million in profits for CS First Boston and a tidy $9 million bonus for himself. But he thought he deserved more, and when his bosses balked at upping his compensation, he quit and in 1995 started up his own investment house, which he romantically christened Renaissance.

Renaissance was growing exponentially. Jordan had charmed the philanthropist-financier George Soros (the man who had famously made a billion dollars in one day by betting against the British pound) into backing him, and had hired away many of his former colleagues at CSFB. In less than two years his bank had amassed a two-billion-dollar management portfolio and a staff of over two hundred. At the same time Jordan had married a Russian beauty, allied himself with Vladimir Potanin, the powerful oligarch who headed the giant Oneximbank group, and set up residence in a palatial apartment that was swept monthly for bugs by his security chief, a former KGB colonel.

Jordan's mind was not fully on work when I was ushered into his elegant office. The week before, his infant son had fallen ill and almost died in the same elite government hospital where Yeltsin had undergone open-heart surgery. The child's blood pressure had been so high that Jordan had needed special authorization from the Ministry of Defense for a low-flying air ambulance to medevac him to Germany. As he related the story of his son's recovery, I wondered what I would have done if nine million dollars had landed in my bank account. Would have I stayed in Moscow, hired bodyguards to protect me from grasping mobsters, and kept a plane on standby to whisk my child to medical safety? Or would have I gotten the hell out of Dodge and lived happily in California off the interest?

The very rich say that after a point, money becomes secondary, just a way of keeping tabs, and that it is power that is the real aphrodisiac. As Russia's biggest pitchman to the West, the principal intermediary between Moscow and the world of international high finance, Jordan enjoyed far greater influence than the American ambassador. Jordan was, in fact, Moscow's unofficial ambassador to Wall Street. It was because of him that billions of dollars were pouring into Russia's capital markets, and he seemed to derive a quiet confidence from his unique position. His sales pitch was always the same: the vague but alluring promise of limitless growth.

"The beauty of Russia," he enthused to me, "is that everything is so wide open. The country is starting over from scratch, and if you get in on the ground floor, there is no ceiling, no limit to how far you can go."

As for me, with the arrogance of the uninitiated, I found the boom utterly mystifying. It made no sense that although Russia's economy had shrunk by nearly half during the 1990s, capital investment in the industrial sector had sunk 90 percent, and life expectancy itself had plunged alarmingly to third-world levels, the stock exchange should have risen tenfold. Plus, it seemed as if the more money a Russian company lost, the higher its stock price rose. Shares, for instance, in the auto plant that assembled the dreadful Lada Zhiguli (a box-shaped compact based on a 1970s Fiat design that made a Yugo look like a Porsche) had just doubled, even though the factory, Avtovaz, had amassed a stockpile of 740,000 unsold and unwanted cars.

Despite its shoddy reputation, the Zhiguli, priced at around four thousand dollars, was still the only car ordinary Russians could ever hope to afford, and millions of Zhigulis plied the country's roads. This naturally made the plant a favored target of organized crime. According to a 1997 police survey, 65 Avtovaz executives and dealers had fallen victims to contract killings. Mafia gangs so brazenly stole from the assembly line that, State television claimed, each gang affixed its own identifying stickers on the windshields of the cars it earmarked for the lucrative spare-parts markets. Factory bosses added to Avtovaz's woes by signing a cozy arrangement in 1990 with the billionaire bureaucrat Boris Berezovsky. Under the terms of the deal, Avtovaz sold Berezovsky its clunkers at well below cost; he then resold them at fair market value, pocketing the difference. The practice had left Avtovaz a billion dollars in debt, and technically bankrupt.

Avtovaz was just about the biggest aberration in automotive history. Yet brokerages were all breathlessly rating it a "Buy" and Western investors were obligingly driving up the price to insane valuations. Frankly, no one cared what happened at the plant; the only thing that mattered was the steady stock climb.

A similarly baffling frenzy was taking place in the bond markets. Jordan's bank was also tapping that gold mine, packaging, underwriting, and buying—on behalf of American clients—the bonds that Russian companies and federal, provincial, and municipal governments were issuing as if there was no tomorrow. The biggest of the bond plays was the Russian Treasury bill, which offered the sort of sky-high yields that made Michael Milken's notorious "junk bonds" seem like CD deposits. The history of these T-bills, known locally as GKOs, dated back to pre-Revolutionary days, when Tsar Nicholas II issued Imperial bonds to help pay for plumbing repairs in the Winter Palace (or whatever tsars needed money for). The Bolsheviks cheerfully defaulted on those loans, and Russia stayed out of the global T-bill market until 1993, when the Kremlin rediscovered borrowing as a way to cover its budget deficits.

This marked a significant break from the days of the command economy, when the Politburo covered shortfalls by simply ordering more money printed. But now that price controls had been lifted, printing money could land you in a Ukrainian-type pickle. In the early 1990s, the Ukrainians had remedied chronic deficits by printing so much money that it devalued before the ink was dry. As a consequence, Ukraine's annual inflation spiked at 10,000 percent in 1993–94, which meant that the price of a loaf of bread sometimes doubled daily, and that the country no longer had any semblance of a working economy.

So Moscow consulted with the World Bank and the International Monetary Fund—and hit upon the idea of borrowing the extra money it needed, just like the United States or Canada or Japan. But according to the risk-and-reward profile that determines interest rates on bonds, Russia was on the opposite end of the curve from the West. People willing to lend it money expected to be handsomely compensated for the chance they were taking. The wobblier Russia was, the more she paid to borrow, as evidenced in the presidential election of 1996, when Yeltsin was trailing the communist Zyuganov and yields on 90-day GKOs shot to 220 percent. Investors who bet on

Yeltsin doubled their money in a few months, fueling a stampede to get in on the action. When word spread that you could earn the same gains lending Russia money for three months as you would sitting on U.S. T-bills for more than a decade, a new Klondike was born.

Renaissance was at the forefront of the frenzy. Its bustling bond department was run by a reedy young man in his late twenties by the name of Richard Dietz. Dietz wore blue suspenders over his tailored dress shirt. He wordlessly pointed to a chair when I entered his office, lifting a bony hand to indicate I should be patient as he spent the next five minutes barking instructions into the telephone, peppering his commands with frequent references to procreative organs. The guy was straight out of "Big Swinging Dick" central casting, right down to the oversized red boxing gloves prominently displayed on his desk.

"You box?" I asked, when he finally got off the phone, to break the ice.

Dietz ignored the question. "What can I do for you?" he said, impatiently.

Taken aback, I got down to business and asked him to bring me up to speed on the GKO market. With that he went into salesman mode. The bond market was now worth about forty-five billion dollars, he said, and Westerners held about a third of the paper, the Russian Central Bank's limit for foreign participation. The real beauty of the bonds, Dietz chummily intimated, was that they were a safe bet: "The IMF will never let Russia fail. Russian is too nuclear for that to happen."

The other good news was that the Central Bank (equivalent to the U.S. Federal Reserve) was probably going to lift restrictions, allowing foreigners to buy more GKOs. Yields were going to come down in the near future, he added, for the benefit of the two million potential investors he was addressing through me, what with Russia's growing recovery and increased stability. Now was a good time to get in, while the interest rates were still sky-high.

It certainly did seem to be a good time to be in Russia. Numbers never lie, or so they say, and the results posted by some of the big American players in Moscow were nothing short of astonishing. The billion-dollar Hermitage Fund, for instance, run by a former Salomon Brothers trader by the name of Bill Browder (no suspenders, but solid-gold dollar-sign cufflinks) had soared over 700 percent in its first year, billing itself in half-page ads in the *Journal* as the "world's best performing fund." Browder, like Jordan, was a star, and I, like the other business reporters, leapt at the opportunity to grill him over lobster tails at the Gastronom, a place so conspicuously splendid that the toilet stalls were carved out of solid black marble.

Browder's and Jordan's billions notwithstanding, Russia's was indeed an odd renaissance. The resurrection seemed to begin and end almost entirely within the relatively narrow confines of the MKAD, the seventy-mile beltway that ringed Moscow and concentrated the country's wealth. Outside the MKAD lurked an entirely different Russia, one that Jordan and the legion of other investment bankers who had descended on Moscow did not hype in their glossy promotional brochures. One had only to travel to Russia's storied second city, St. Petersburg—or Piter, as Russians affectionately call it—for a reality check.

There had been a snowstorm on the February night when I first flew into St. Petersburg in 1997, and morning saw the old capital covered by a thick blanket of white powder. At dawn flurries swirled around the gilded dome of St. Isaac's Cathedral, licked the pale blue colonnades of the Winter Palace, and danced around the battlements of the Peter and Paul Fortress across the Neva River. Half hidden by fog and falling snow, the island fort was like a hazy vision from an old silent movie. Beyond stretched the Gulf of Finland, which lay flat and frozen as far as the eye could see.

At 10:00 A.M. the thermometer outside City Hall—once the infamous Smolny School for Girls, from which Lenin had led the Revolution—read minus 15 Fahrenheit, and I stamped my feet on the icy cobblestones to ward off the cold while a uniformed guard checked my documents.

"You're not on the list," the guard declared, with imperious finality. I had been so enthralled with Petersburg's faded glory and fairytale skyline, and now he was ruining the moment.

"Call inside." I shivered impatiently. "I have an appointment to meet the deputy mayor."

The guard scowled, ready to dismiss me. If I wasn't on his list I didn't exist. This sort of thing had happened to me all too frequently in Ukraine, some petty official and his stupid stamps bringing my world to a frustrating halt.

"Call," I repeated. "It's about the Olympics," I added importantly, in hope that this might spur him into doing his job.

At the mention of St. Petersburg's bid to host the 2004 Olympiad, the guard was galvanized into action. The passions surrounding St. Petersburg's bid were nothing short of a matter of national pride in Russia. And the propaganda value of landing the Summer Games was not lost on top politicians, who were desperately seeking to unite their vast and troubled land.

Ever since the USSR had been broken up into fifteen pieces, Russia had suffered a severe identity crisis. The majority of Russians had grown up believing that to be Russian was to be part of a great and lasting tradition of empire. Ordinary Russians always harped on the symbols of conquest: Peter and Catherine the Great, Gagarin, Sevastopol, Sputnik. Even Stalin was praised for expanding the empire's borders all the way to Berlin. To be a Russian was to be a lord and master, even if you lived like a pauper. It wasn't all that different from the way the British or French must have felt about themselves at the turn of the last century, a type of opiate for the masses.

The breakup of the Soviet Union changed all that. Many Russians no longer knew who they were. After all, their way of life had been turned upside down. Their old Western enemies were now their benefactors; their ideology was discredited, and their former satellites were suddenly uppity and inhospitable.

Ordinary residents of St. Petersburg felt this as keenly as anyone. When, for example, they now traveled to Tallinn, just across the new Estonian border, they mostly went as beggars. Unable to afford the Scandinavian prices charged in the liberated city now that it had rid itself of Moscow and reverted to its rich and conservative Nordic roots, the Russians found themselves discriminated against by the angry Estonians, who were now free to tell their struggling former overlords just where to go.

But the Games would show the world that Russia was back from the brink, that it had been resurrected from the ashes of communism and was a nation to be reckoned with once more. At least that was the thinking.

There was only one problem. Moscow had held the Games in 1980, when athletes from the United States and most other Western nations had stayed home to boycott the Soviet invasion of Afghanistan, and thus the capital could not enter another bid so soon. That left St. Petersburg. And St. Petersburg was woefully unprepared. Seven decades of socialism had wrought unimaginable devastation on this magnificent city. Built nearly three hundred years ago on oak piles driven into the coastal marshland, this town of canals and cathedrals became known as the Venice of the North. But this symbol of tsarist might had fallen out of favor with the communists, who allowed its ornate palaces—and virtually everything else—to fall into lamentable disrepair.

The snow helped conceal the carnage, but couldn't erase the fact that the city was literally falling apart. Ancient trolley-buses with broken axles listed, abandoned, on the roadsides. The gaping streets looked as if they hadn't been patched since the *Aurora* fired its shots. The sidewalks were littered with slabs of brick that, along with jagged icicles, had plummeted murderously from once-elegant façades. The city's underground heating ducts were so corroded that the ground above them had melted, leaving strange, unseasonable grassy lanes in the snow. In some parts of town, the water mains had rusted through so badly that orange slime trickled out of the taps. The phone system was possibly even creakier than Kiev's. If you tried calling St. Petersburg's official Olympic hotline, you were just as likely to reach a puzzled receptionist at a Siberian steel mill.

Strolling down Nevsky Prospekt it was, frankly, hard to imagine St. Petersburg hosting the 2004 Games. What came to mind was Olympic cyclists careering into career-ending potholes, plaster from crumbling balconies raining down on spectators, and divers leaping into murky, leaking pools as legions of disgruntled tourists who had paid top dollar were crammed six to a room in dingy Soviet-era dormitories.

It was not by chance that when International Olympic Committee President Juan Antonio Samaranch was invited to Russia by Prime Minister Chernomyrdin, he was given the red-carpet tour of Moscow, but returned to Switzerland without ever being shown sleepy St. Petersburg. Moscow was the West's window on Russia, the country's newly-refurbished parlor room, where honored guests were invited to gawk at the gilded furniture. St. Petersburg had been relegated to attic duty, where the in-laws were sent to sleep on dusty, broken-down antiques.

It was heartbreaking that St. Petersburg had been so mistreated. Yet even in its state of decay, I still preferred its shabby elegance to Moscow's new-money makeover. In St. Petersburg you lived for the past; Moscow lived only for the day.

I soon discovered why my name had not been left with the guard. City Hall was in shambles. The ex-mayor had recently fled to Paris, purportedly for medical treatment, but hounded by allegations of impropriety. The head of the city's privatization board had just been shot. And the deputy mayor I was supposed to meet was just moving into his office—his predecessor, some guy named Putin, having a few months before been called up for duty in Moscow.

Deputy Mayor Valery Malyshev was a big man with a barrel chest. He wore number 7 on the City Hall soccer team, I noticed from a framed photograph that sat proudly on his large desk.

"How do you like our fair city?" he asked, after I gratefully accepted tea.

I told him I loved it, wrinkles and all. He smiled sorrowfully. "Moscow almost ruined Piter," he said. "The Kremlin wanted to make us forget the Winter Palace was ever built." Everyone always blamed everyone else in this part of the world. The residents of St. Petersburg faulted their rivals in Moscow for communism's legacy. Muscovites, in turn, faulted the Bolsheviks, who—as one of our interpreters at the office once angrily complained—were not Russians, but those time-honored villains, the Jews. That Malyshev and Yeltsin and most of the "new" Russia's leaders had been Party functionaries was conveniently forgotten.

"Moscow can never match our unique history and culture," Malyshev agreed, as we discussed the traditional Moscow–St. Petersburg rivalry. "Even with all of Luzhkov's money," he added, somewhat bitterly.

Yuri Luzhkov was the mayor of Moscow, a modern-day Richard Daley who ran perhaps the best-oiled political machine in Russia. If you wanted to do business in the capital, you cut Luzhkov in. Muscovites adored him for cleaning up the city and making its buses run on time. Other city leaders were openly jealous.

Even though he had fewer resources, Malyshev had grandiose

plans for St. Petersburg. They were detailed in larger-than-life print on an enormous city map that occupied the entire back wall of his office. The map outlined the location of thirty-eight new sports venues, an Olympic village, twenty luxury hotels, an eight-lane super-highway, and two additional terminals for the town's airport. The total tab for the planned projects topped nine billion dollars, which might as well have been nine trillion because St. Petersburg plainly couldn't afford it.

For that matter, Russia couldn't afford it. With most of the country in ruins, hospitals reusing needles, and pensioners going unpaid, to spend nine billion dollars to assuage your bruised ego seemed at best irresponsible. Besides, where would the perennially cash-strapped Kremlin get that kind of money?

Back in Moscow a few days later, I went to see the head of Russia's Olympic Committee, an elegantly attired Kremlin official by the name of Alexander Kozlovsky. We met at Committee headquarters, a pale brick building not too far from the huge Luzhniki Stadium that Mayor Luzhkov was renovating at great taxpayer expense. (A plastics company partly owned by Mrs. Luzhkov had just won the tender to replace the arena's eighty thousand seats.)

Security was oppressively tight outside Kozlovsky's office; there were police everywhere, and the street was closed to traffic. The precautions had nothing to do with the Olympics, however. The beating and stabbing of several Armenian traders at a nearby open-air market had sparked protest rallies by the Armenian community in Moscow, and the police were taking no chances.

When I finally got through the cordon and put the question of financing the Olympics to Kozlovsky, he shot me an icy glance. Plainly he had heard the skepticism too many times already and was growing tired of pesky Western reporters.

"It's disgraceful and humiliating," he fumed in faultless English. "When other world leaders make similar pledges, they are taken at their word. But not so for the guarantees of our government. If the world is interested in a peaceful Russia," he went on, adopting the saber-rattling tone Moscow frequently used to advantage in negotiations with the World Bank and the International Monetary Fund, "then it will press the International Olympic Committee to give us the Games."

The Games, of course, did not go to St. Petersburg, the Olympic organizers ruling wisely that postcommunist Russia was not yet ready to put on such an expensive and elaborate show. Luckily for Kozlovsky, times had changed enough at the Kremlin so that he and his colleagues were not exiled to Siberia over the failure.

"It's not like the old days," he deadpanned, when I called him a couple of months later for comment. "Fortunately, we no longer have to explain to the Central Committee how it's possible that some crazy Norwegian beat us to the gold medal."

CHAPTER FOUR

Wedded to Reform

There were one hundred forty thousand cops in Moscow, and every one of them seemed to be giving me a ticket. Sometimes I got pulled over twice on my way to work. Did I have a bumper sticker I didn't know about that read PROUD TO BE POLISH? Had word of my skepticism about the Russian renaissance spread throughout the precincts?

It took me a few weeks to realize that the ticketing was not personal, that every motorist in Moscow got shaken down and that it was simply the way patrolmen supplemented their meager wages. The staggering number of uniformed cops patrolling the Russian capital—four for every one in New York City—was a legacy of the police state. The heavy police presence offered a poignant insight into the state of Russian reforms. While the country had made quantum leaps from Soviet times its government structures remained surprisingly unchanged, with millions of underpaid bureaucrats still employed by dozens upon dozens of dubious ministries.

With all the brazen ticketing going on—payment of fines was always in cash and on the spot—you got the feeling that Moscow's police force was designed to live off the people rather than protect them. The police themselves were not entirely to blame. It was the system. The average cop's salary was about $150 a month—a laughable amount. The average expat had trouble surviving on less than $100,000 a year in Moscow, which was ranked in surveys as the world's second most expensive city to live in after Tokyo. So, for a beat cop, the only way to make ends meet was to extract bribes.

Peak ticketing hours coincided with mealtimes, when the gray-clad GAI officers—as the hated traffic police were known—needed lunch or dinner money. They could be quite inventive in identifying real or imagined infractions, my favorite being the fifty-thousand-ruble fine for "an improperly stored tool kit" that the GAI resorted to when they could find nothing else wrong with your car.

The GAI could also be hired as freelancers to lend a stamp of authority to private proceedings. One such group of rent-a-cops had been employed for the wedding of a colleague of Roberta's, which happened to be taking place next door to our apartment. Inconveniently, the GAI had cordoned off our street. Three slush-splattered Lada cruisers, blue lights silently swirling, and a foot patrol cocooned in bulky gray winter parkas diverted traffic. Naturally they made a fuss about letting us through, since we had left our invitations up in the apartment. In Moscow, you couldn't even go home without the proper documents.

Our parking attendant had watched with visible distaste as the patrolmen finally let us through, swaggering self-importantly and pointing now and then with their white nightsticks at other offending vehicles. They shot hostile glances in our direction, like toughs in a youth gang daring you to look them in the eye. The attendant lowered his gaze and muttered something under his breath. He was one of three security guards who rotated round the clock, watching over the Jeeps, BMWs, and Audis parked in the brick courtyard across the street from our building. They had been hired after a rash of car thefts depleted several lots in the neighborhood, an affront made all the more painful since no one carried auto insurance in Russia.

The attendant rooted in his military fatigues and dug out a large key ring. "Must be another big shot getting married," he remarked, nodding toward the cops milling around the ancient, cheery little orange church across the street as he tugged the iron gate shut behind Roberta's new Toyota Land Cruiser. She'd just shipped it in from Washington and paid someone to drive it down from St. Petersburg; the carjacking gangs that routinely cased the port made it inadvisable for foreigners to pick up their own vehicles.

Across the plowed road, the first limousine pulled up in front of the old church. It was a shiny black Chaika of the sort once favored by Politburo members and ministers. These bulky sedans, with their nicotine-yellowed curtains and faded walnut paneling, now mostly saw service ferrying tourists to casinos and newlyweds to receptions, the Kremlin having opted to modernize its fleet with sleeker vehicles of German manufacture. A distinguished-looking couple emerged from the big car. The pair gingerly skittered along a corridor that had been neatly swept through the dirty snow, and carefully made their way up the chapel's stone steps.

"We'd better hurry," said Roberta, and turning to the parking lot attendant, "A friend of ours is getting married this evening."

"Really?" He paused, genuinely surprised. "I thought only gangsters and government officials got married there."

By there, he meant the Jerusalem Church of the Resurrection of Christ, one of the oldest chapels in Moscow and one of the precious few houses of prayer in all of Russia that had stayed open during the Soviet period. This distinction ensured its enduring popularity with superstitious Muscovites, who reasoned that if the chapel had withstood communism, any union blessed within its walls was bound to survive the vicissitudes of marriage. It was a good omen and a mark of prestige to be joined in matrimony there, an honor best attained through a hefty donation to the diocese or a call from a political higher-up to the Metropolitan, the head of Moscow's Orthodox Church hierarchy.

The ceremony was set for six o'clock, but since we had budgeted our time poorly, we had missed the opening prayers by the time we changed into more formal attire and returned. The small church was packed, and several Intourist buses and television camera crews idled outside its sloping battlements. Inside the stout little building (circa 1629) there were no pews and no discernible heat. It was dark, damp and shadowy, and I could see people's breath rising in the chilly confines. The gilded baroque altars and richly lacquered iconostases glimmered with the reflection of hundreds of votive candles. Every time the doors opened and a draft licked the flames, the walls came to life, and the lance in the icon of St. George and the Dragon seemed to dance.

Scented smoke streamed from a bejeweled gold censer waved by a young novice dressed in the coarse brown cassock of the Russian Orthodox monastic order. Another priest, his robes more stately, his girth more ample, and his beard tinged with gray, stood before the bride and groom, chanting in Old Church Slavonic.

"Doesn't she look like a Russian princess," someone sighed, pointing to the bride, who wore a crown over her flaxen hair and stood majestic, tall, and slender in a silk shantung gown exquisitely trimmed at the neckline and cuffs with white mink.

"Right out of a fairy tale," volunteered Roberta, a little too loudly, so that a few heads turned disapprovingly.

"Shhh!" admonished a dark-haired woman in pink standing next to us. This was the wife of Russia's first deputy prime minister. Her eyes were misty and she appeared to be looking forward to a good cry, so we fell silent, let her enjoy the tearful moment, and craned our necks for a better view of the bride.

Her name was Gretchen Wilson; she was a Southern belle with a horse-racing pedigree, who since her days as Vanderbilt University's homecoming queen had been accustomed to drawing the enraptured attention and envy of her peers. At World Bank headquarters in Washington, D.C., where she had begun her international career as an investment banker, Gretchen had been a star, rising through the ranks and conquering Georgetown in her Saab convertible as flowers from admirers piled high on her desk. Reform had brought her to Russia in 1992, the earliest, most hopeful days, and when she moved several of her suitors had followed, setting up businesses in Moscow in the hope of winning her heart. There were no less than four men in the nave of this smoky little Russian church who had asked, and not received, her hand in marriage. They were all handsome and wealthy, and had come from New York, London, and various other high perches of society to see who had finally managed to snag the unassailable beauty queen with a Harvard MBA.

"The guy must be something else," whistled an erstwhile suitor standing near us, his tone a broody mix of regret and admiration.

And who was the lucky guy, *tout* Moscow wanted to know? Very little was known about him, other than the facts that he was a Russian from the provincial town of Nizhny Novgorod, eight years younger than Gretchen, and not, by all accounts, very well traveled. This triple whammy naturally had tongues wagging furiously at the Gastronom and other gossipy expat hangouts.

Gretchen was indeed bucking local tradition and standing gender stereotypes on their head. It was usually American men, gents
whose charms, for one reason or another, had been found lacking
back home, who hunted for eager young wives in Moscow. There
were even dozens of so-called "mail-order bride" services that specialized in introducing America's leering gargoyles to Eastern European
beauties willing to trade love for a ticket to the States. Unsurprisingly, most of these hastily arranged marriages came to an abrupt
end the moment the bride's naturalization papers came through.

But enough about that; it's bad luck to speak of divorce at wed-
dings. The priest had suddenly switched into heavily accented English and was muttering incomprehensibly, as if reading from a
phonetically rehearsed text. Half the congregation pressed forward
to better understand; the other half shrank back at the sound of a
foreign tongue.

While the priest stumbled through his speech—something, I
think, about cultures coming together, and the standard post-Soviet
platitudes about world peace—I tried to sneak a peek at the groom.
All I could see over the bundled-up crowd was the back of his head,
a curly brown mop that at once evoked youth and the fashions of the
1970s. The seventies had probably just hit the wheatfields of Southern Russia. Change, I mused (incorrectly, as it turned out), probably
came slowly to Nizhny Novgorod. During Soviet times it had been
known as Gorky, and the Nobel laureate dissident Andrei Sakharov
had been banished to internal exile there.

Would the worldly Gretchen live out her days in this sleepy
province? Would she become a good, docile little Russian housewife? And who was this country bumpkin she was giving it all up for,
anyway? Was he a drunken wife-beater, like far too many of Russia's
rural males? A womanizer? A Mafia man?

The questions were reflected in the perplexed looks Gretchen's
friends shot one another as the priest pronounced the bride and
groom man and wife. It was only then, and fleetingly, that I caught a
glimpse of the mysterious groom. The thing that struck you about
Boris Brevnov was his confidence; it far surpassed his twenty-nine
years. His eyes were so purposeful as to be almost cold, and his
measured smile radiated intelligence. He was a good-looking guy,

trim and of medium height, obviously at ease with himself, and he wore his dinner jacket well.

He led Gretchen away proudly as the Wilsons of Kentucky and the Brevnovs of Nizhny bear-hugged and congratulated one another—through an interpreter. One could only wonder what the families made of each other.

Outside, a gaggle of photographers and camera operators from Nizhny's evening news pounced on the happy couple. It seemed Boris was a big wheel in his home town, a politically connected banker, rich and influential, and the newlyweds were being celebrated as local royalty. Gretchen and Boris dutifully posed with a slew of thickset men in ill-fitting suits and *ushanky* (fur caps with earflaps). These were the leading lights of Nizhny, envoys of the municipal, regional, and federal governments come to pay their respects. The business community was also represented in the form of half a dozen factory bosses from the city's big employers, including the sprawling GAZ automobile-assembly plant that made those godawful Volgas and a huge paper mill that Gretchen had helped to privatize.

Nizhny Novgorod's star was rising because Yeltsin had just appointed the province's progressive and photogenic governor, Boris Nemtsov, his first deputy prime minister. Nemtsov, I was told, had been at the rehearsal dinner but had been called away on State business just before the wedding. He was Boris's good buddy, mentor, and look-alike. Nemtsov, one of the guests further informed me, had introduced Boris to Gretchen, and it was said that his ascension to the supreme heights of Kremlin power would almost certainly bring great things for the newlyweds.

The reception was held at an old private Politburo haunt that was decorated like a hunting lodge, with warm wood-paneled walls, sweeping staircases, and antlers everywhere. The guests were bussed in under police escort lest the in-laws from Kentucky take a wrong turn on New Arbat Street. Gretchen greeted everyone with a dazzling smile and display of Southern charm: "Mah, don't you look cute as a button. Y'all get something to drink?"

The Russian contingent did not need to be asked twice, and soon the party was in full swing. It was being catered, as a wedding gift, by one of Gretchen's former paramours, a dashing Texas millionaire by the name of Preston. Preston had presciently gone into real estate in Moscow before the office-space boom and had recently opened a hugely successful eatery, the Brasserie du Soleil. Just to prove that he was over Gretchen, he showed up with a spectacular six-foot-tall redhead draped on each arm.

Most of the guests on the bride's side of the dance floor were members of what was known in Moscow as the IFC Mafia, and Roberta knew many of them well. In the early 1990s the World Bank's International Finance Corporation had sent hundreds of young professionals to the former Soviet Union to lend a hand with economic reform and privatization planning. That was how Gretchen had landed in Nizhny Novgorod, which, thanks to Nemtsov's liberal leanings, pioneered the politically explosive dismemberment of the beloved but bankrupt Soviet collective-farming system. When the big privatization push ended around 1996, many of the idealistic IFC staffers found their inside knowledge of post-Soviet capitalism and personal ties to leading officials suddenly worth a small fortune in the burgeoning job market for expats in Moscow.

A group of these lottery winners chewed contentedly on Cuban cigars at our table. Roger Gale, the eldest at around fifty, was holding forth on an artist's colony that he and his wife, a former ambassador from the Philippines, supported financially. He was a kind and soft-spoken man who ran a big private equity fund, collected Russian oil paintings and lived in a fifteen-thousand-dollar-a-month apartment in Brezhnev's old building. Victor Paul sat next to him. He was in the throes of a discourse on deep-sea fishing and the big cruiser he was building. Victor—whom my cousin had known at Dartmouth and predicted would either become a millionaire or land in jail or both—had just been featured on a segment of CBS's *60 Minutes* on young Americans getting rich in Russia. His business was selling restricted shares in Gazprom, the mammoth Soviet gas monopoly that supplied half of Western Europe's natural gas and was technically off limits to foreigners. Lots of shares, apparently, because when he, his Finnish ex-model wife, and their newborn vacationed abroad they brought along their governess and cook.

"Couple of more years like this and I'm going to retire on my boat," he crowed. "You suckers can work for a living." The sad thing was that shares in Gazprom had soared 1000 percent over the previous few years and, if they continued to climb at that rate, Victor probably would in fact get to live out his days trawling the Florida Keys for marlin. No one said life was fair.

Alan Bigman rounded out the happy triumvirate. He and Roberta were needling Victor where it hurt most. "I heard you bought your Land Rover second-hand."

"That's just my Moscow car," Victor snapped. "You still peddling coal?" he asked Bigman.

"Sure am," said Alan, without missing a beat. "You need a few trainloads?"

Alan was Roberta's favorite reclamation project, someone who she thought needed to be brought back into the fold. He suffered from an ailment known in expatriate circles as going native. Going native was at once the highest compliment and lowest insult you could fling at an expat. On the one hand, it acknowledged the extraordinary linguistic and social skills required for a foreigner to be accepted by the "locals." (Alan, for instance, spoke Russian so well that once, on a flight to New York, his seatmate, a Moscow businessman, inquired after several hours of conversation if it was Alan's first trip to the States. The man was dumbfounded to discover that Alan was actually from Long Island and from not central Russia, as his vowel intonations led many Muscovites to believe.) On the other hand, it implied a certain impressionability, a willingness to blindly adopt local customs, which, in the case of Muscovites, ranged from the benign (forcing guests to wear slippers in your apartment) to the downright unsavory (putting out a contract on them if they didn't).

Alan had fallen in love with Russia after a semester abroad at Leningrad State University during his junior year of studying Russian at Yale. He had originally moved to Nizhny with Gretchen and the rest of the IFC crew, slogging through the muddy collectives with the intrepid Nemtsov, badgering reluctant peasants to give private enterprise a chance. Nemtsov and Alan became good friends, and the governor used to regularly crash on his couch after animated drinking sessions, during which a better future for the country was romantically discussed. The rapport the two established in those heady days was now paying off for Alan. Knowing what the newly appointed deputy prime minister of Russia looked like hung over in his underwear was worth millions in Moscow, where politi-

cal connections were prized above all. Alan had gotten his Harvard
MBA and gone to work for a mysterious Russian investment company
aptly named Access Industries, which seemed exceedingly flush, was
allied with one of the big oligarchs, and had broad interests in the
energy sector. The job lent him the trappings of a successful Russian
businessman: loud suits, gold watches, two full-time drivers working
round the clock, as well as two cell phones (to make sure he always
had a free line).

"Alan," Roberta would frequently chide, "you'd better watch it or
you'll end up a New Russian."

"There are worse fates," he would shrug, "than being a *novy
russky.*"

The *novyye ruskiye* were the new rich, the ones who roared
around town with carloads of bodyguards in tow and dished out bags
of dough to have their toilet fixtures gold-plated on the off chance
that a neighbor might need to use the loo. While the recently moneyed are an odd breed the world over, in Russia their unabashed
spending redefined the boundaries of taste and excess. Moscow was
probably the only place on earth where Ferraris slogged through the
snow in the dead of winter, lasting perhaps two seasons before being
scrapped. Before Japanese restaurants opened in town, residents
had had sushi flown in from Paris by private jet. In the new Moscow,
vintage Dom Pérignon was poured as a chaser for vodka shots. My
colleague Betsy McKay at the *Journal* had done a story on nightlife
in Moscow starring an oil baron from Siberia who had popped into
the Up and Down Club, a glitzy strip joint next the Foreign Ministry
building, and run up a bar bill of seventeen thousand dollars in three
hours. At our corner grocery store, thirty-two-hundred-dollar bottles
of cognac in etched crystal decanters were displayed near the meat
counter. A cashier told me they sold two or three of them a week.

The New Russians spent their money as though they were worried someone would take it away from them if they didn't. They
would not be denied anything, which I thought understandable,
given how long they had been denied everything. What puzzled me
was the pride wealthy Muscovites seemed to derive from grossly
overpaying. This wasn't lost on the people who catered to them.
Gretchen's ex-boyfriend, the restaurateur Preston, explained how he
had exploited their need to spend to unload a dud shipment of Span-

ish wine. The stuff wasn't moving at twenty dollars a bottle, no matter how much he pushed it. So he jacked up the price fivefold—and it sold out immediately! On a more ambitious scale, the importers of Parliament cigarettes, a discount brand favored strictly by the downwardly mobile in the States, set the price in Russia to twice that of Marlboros—and instantly captured the loyalty of the newly moneyed. Price defined quality for Russia's novice consumers, who had not yet learned to discriminate by any other yardstick.

We all had our own stories about the limitless New Russian appetite for excess. Alan—who always ordered the costliest items on the menu, and, generous to a fault, always insisted on picking up the tab—was a fount of New Russian jokes, like the one where two *novyye ruskiye* run into another at a Moscow restaurant. "Igor Stepanovich," says one, "what do you think of my new Hermès tie? I paid nine hundred dollars for it in Paris."

"You fool!" cries Igor. "You could have got the exact same tie down the street for fifteen hundred dollars."

In the New Russia there was no higher authority, no better barometer, than money. It mattered not one iota how one got it, as long as one had it. And we Westerners in Moscow—once considered so wealthy but lately the "New Poor," as Muscovites relished calling us now—were starting to develop inferiority complexes about not having enough of it. In that respect, we were all going a little native.

Money was indeed the great divider in postcommunist lands, a far greater source of friction than in the West, for until recently everyone in the former Soviet bloc had been more or less equal. Alan lamented that the professors and postgraduate students he had befriended during his year of study at Leningrad State University had fallen on such hard times in the free-market era that many of them were too embarrassed by their living conditions—as had been my Polish relatives, when I first met them—to invite him over. The same financial wedge had driven apart my Aunt Dagmara and one of her best friends and neighbors. The friend's husband had struck it rich in construction, and Dagmara's friend moved from her dreary apartment next door to a spacious new villa in a tony suburb of Warsaw. "We no longer had anything in common," Dagmara had said sadly. "She worried about which Club Med to vacation at, and I worried that Zbig had outgrown his shoes. Every time she boasted of a new fur it was a painful reminder of how much our lives had gone in different directions."

Alan clambered up on stage and began acting the emcee, translating toasts and telling the customary anecdotes about Gretchen and Boris's courtship. The happy couple shared their first kiss, we were informed, in a cornfield on the banks of the Volga River. Boris, we were further informed, was rather shy about it. Later he proposed the traditional way, by formally asking Gretchen's bemused father for his daughter's hand in marriage.

Alan rattled off a few jokes in Russian that brought half the house down—for the banquet room was very much divided along linguistic lines. Gretchen's family and friends occupied one side of the hall, while Boris's guests congregated near the stage and bar. The Russians smoked cigarettes, while the Americans puffed cigars. The Russians did vodka shots while the Kentucky contingent sipped bourbon and soda. Gretchen's family had brought cute but hyper kids; Boris' banker friends had brought slinky but sullen girlfriends. The Russians huddled together to talk business and politics, while the expats networked. The foreigners danced; the Russians sulked at their tables. Few people outside of Alan transcended the cultural divide, and there was little intermingling. At one point I ventured over to two young Russians in mauve Hugo Boss suits to bum a smoke. We were near a service entrance that opened out onto a side alley.

"You want a cigarette?" asked one, glancing toward his buddy. "Okay, come on, then," he said, starting for the side door.

I hesitated, some instinct telling me not to follow. "Come, come," he beckoned. "We smoke outside."

His friend was taking me by the elbow now, guiding me gently toward the exit.

"That's all right," I said, suddenly realizing the two were drunk and looking for trouble.

"No," insisted the one with the pack of Parliaments, his tone changing abruptly. "You come outside with us."

I definitely didn't need a cigarette that badly, and beat a hasty retreat to the American sector. I still don't know whether those two had intended to wipe the sidewalk with me or whether I was just overreacting. But one got the impression that some of the Russians at the reception resented or were intimidated by the large foreign presence on their turf. We were cramping their style and taking over their country, as a slew of indignant post-wedding editorials in Nizhny's communist newspapers warned, one going so far as to accuse the temptress Gretchen of ensnaring poor Boris on the instructions of the CIA. I imagine that if the Soviets had won the Cold War, and Boris had been sent to Kentucky as a commissar and married the local belle, some good old boy loaded with whiskey would probably have wanted to take a swing at the arrogant commie invaders.

In the early days of March 1997, some weeks after Gretchen's surreal wedding, Roberta called me at the office, her voice brimming with excitement. "Guess what?" she blurted. "Remember how our parking-lot attendant said only gangsters and government officials got married at Gretchen's church? Well, he was right. Boris has been called to the Kremlin to meet Nemtsov. He's going to get some important appointment in the new government. "

The precise nature of Boris's post was not yet known, or at least Gretchen was keeping that information to herself until Nemtsov made the formal announcement. What was clear, however, was that Gretchen's husband would now play some role in the big reform drive that was auguring President Yeltsin's return from near death.

The Russian leader had finally stirred from the secluded sanatarium outside Moscow, where he had spent the better part of the year after his reelection convalescing after quintuple-bypass heart surgery, double pneumonia, laryngitis, flu, and, if the rumors were correct, early signs of dementia. And, like a bear waking after months of hibernation, Yeltsin was in a foul temper and hungry for action. Apparently he was dissatisfied with the way Russia had been run in his absence. Reforms had lagged. Cronyism was up. Tax collection was down. Wage arrears were increasing and the export surplus was decreasing. To top it off, it seemed that some individuals, who in typical Russian fashion remained conspicuously nameless, had taken liberties with the keys to the State treasury he had left in their care.

Yeltsin was not at all pleased with the state of affairs. "*Khvatit!* (Enough!)" he growled for the television cameras. "There are going to be some changes around here, and fast." And to show that he meant business, he pounded his fist on the desk. Not once, but twice. It was shortly after this tirade that the rejuvenated Yeltsin had summoned then-Governor Nemtsov to the White House. Not to be confused with Washington's presidential headquarters, this was the old parliament building on the banks of the Moskva River, which had been shelled by Yeltsin's tanks during his bloody 1993 standoff with the mutinous legislature. Following the revolt, which started when the speaker of the lower house tried to have Yeltsin deposed, the president had taken over and rebuilt the battered Duma building, and had relocated the uppity parliamentarians to lesser digs next to the Bolshoi as a standing reminder of who was in charge.

"Boris Nikolayevich," Nemtsov later recalled addressing the president at that fateful meeting. "How would you like to be remembered in the history books? As a good tsar?"

At the sound of that hallowed title, said Nemtsov, the Russian leader struck a pose of exalted dignity. His chest barreled out with pride, and his chin jutted with rekindled vigor. The answer, apparently, was yes.

In this way, Boris the Bedridden rechristened himself Boris the Good and was inspired to replace his stodgy, corrupt cabinet with a collection of young reformers such as had not been seen in the Kremlin since the days of Peter the Great. This team was anchored by two English-speaking, Western-oriented deputy prime ministers: the matinee-idol handsome Nemtsov and the wily financial genius Anatoly Chubais, who had previously been relegated to behind-the-scenes duties because of the unpopularity of his inequitable privatization program. According to Yeltsin's plan, Chubais would repair the government's patchy finances and watch over the monetary system, while Nemtsov oversaw privatization and reined in the country's runaway monopolies.

Word of Yeltsin's new "dream team" of reformers quickly spread throughout the expatriate community. The Russian stock exchange index shot up in late-afternoon trading and discounts on T-bills in the secondary markets tightened considerably. Messrs. Chubais and Nemtsov's mission had been heartily endorsed by the money managers.

Being the new boy, I wasn't quite sure what the fuss was all about and made a mental note to get down to Nizhny as soon as our coverage of the market rallies permitted. Maybe after seeing Nemtsov's handiwork I'd have a better idea why everyone was betting the farm on the guy.

Nizhny turned out to be a miserable overnight train ride 280 miles southeast of Moscow. I had booked a first-class sleeping compartment, not that anyone can be expected to sleep on a Russian train. The heat in the two-bunk compartment was jammed on Off, so that the frilly curtain in the window quickly froze to the pane and I could see my breath rise like cigarette smoke in the dim glow of the reading lights. The loudspeaker, on the other hand, was perversely stuck in the On position, so that not even my earmuffs muffled the racket that passed for Russian Muzak. The conductor was unsympathetic, offering one extra blanket on the condition that I leave a ten-thousand-ruble security deposit.

The train pulled into Nizhny at dawn, just as I felt I might succumb to hypothermia. The first weak rays of light fell on the frozen Volga River, illuminating smokestacks and old wooden warehouses on the far bank and a little black tugboat that bumped precariously through a seam in the river's thick, gray sheet of ice.

Nizhny was an inland port city, connected to both the White and Black seas through an intricate system of canals dug first by the tsars and later by Stalin's political prisoners. The canal links had permitted the Soviets to build attack submarines in these shallow, sheltered waters, and several large shipyards and dry docks still operated just a few miles downstream of Nizhny, near an oil refinery that took delivery of crude by barge. The waterway network had, over the centuries, turned the town into a commercial hub, Russia's third largest after Moscow and St. Petersburg, and an important center for agriculture and light industry.

A large electronic clock outside the station announced that it was 7:00 A.M. and minus 35 centigrade. My traveling companion, a big Pole by the name of Rafal, stretched his stiff limbs and shivered. "You've picked one hell of a day for sightseeing," he commented. "It's going to be around minus fifty in the farm fields, what with the wind chill."

I had asked Rafal to show me around the farms he had helped to privatize in Nizhny. Like a great many young Poles I'd met in Ukraine and Belarus, he worked as a consultant for the IFC's privatization teams. In many respects Poles like him were more effective ambassadors of private enterprise than Americans, because they hailed from a formerly fraternal nation that had managed to make it through a transition similar to the one Russia was now undergoing. So while U.S. advisers could be warded off by recalcitrant government officials with protestations that such-and-such a reform could never work in a place like Russia, the Poles could tell their Slavic cousins: "Bullshit! We did it and it works."

Rafal had arranged for a car (with, thankfully, a working heater) to take us to the countryside, and as we drove out of the still-sleeping city I saw dozens of middle-aged women in navy pea jackets sweeping snow off the sidewalks with brooms made of twigs. Amazingly, many of them worked without gloves.

"I know," said Rafal with a shudder, when I pointed out the bare-handed street cleaners. "Wait till you see how they live out on the farms. It's pathetic, like they get off on licking their self-inflicted wounds," he added, speaking in Polish lest the driver take offense. Despite the harsh words, Rafal, unlike most Poles, was genuinely fond of Russians. He reserved particular affection for the downtrodden peasants, who he said had been exploited since time immemorial, and always took it on the nose—not like Poles, who were unruly by nature and quick to rise against perceived injustices.

We skirted Nizhny's smoky industrial belt, drove past the endless hangars of the Volga car plant and a glass factory in which the IFC was preparing to invest $100 million, and emerged on a quiet two-lane road. The rutted road wound its way through clapboard villages clustered around weathered general stores that had Coca-Cola and Marlboro stickers in their barred windows, but little else to advertise their entry into the twentieth century. Then wide, wind-swept stretches began to open up between the villages. The further we drove, the more the landscape came to resemble some frosted scene from *Doctor Zhivago*, with beech trees glazed completely white and rough brown log cabins almost buried under pillowy snowdrifts.

At last we came to the tiny farming community of Redkino. Rafal had the look of an anxious pilgrim approaching a shrine.

"There are two neighboring farms here I want to show you," he said. "One is a Nemtsov farm. The other is a tragedy."

Rafal launched into a brief history of Russian agriculture as we slid off the main road and skidded the last few snowbound miles up to the adjoining farms. Until recently, the two farms had been one midsized collective—no different from the 26,700 agricultural communes created by Stalin's brutal collectivization of the countryside in the late 1920s and early 1930s. These *kolkhozy*, as the Russians called them, broke the peasant farmers' historical bond with their land. In Poland, that bond was judged so strong that in Warsaw the Politburo abandoned attempts at collectivization, reasoning that the drive would lead to more social unrest than it was worth. But Moscow was enthralled with Marx's misconception that farmers were no different from factory workers and could be motivated by the same incentives that governed assembly-line production. As it turned out, if Soviet factories set new standards for inefficiency, the *kolkhozy* smashed every record for unbridled waste. The Soviets' industrialized farms had survived for seventy years only because they were irrigated with the rich subsidies the Politburo could afford to ladle out when the only cost of printing money was the price of the ink. Saddest of all, they produced a nation of zombie farmers who worked mindlessly at highly specialized tasks, no longer familiar with the entire cycle of plant or animal life, and wholly dependent on instructions from the farm bosses.

Mired in the old communist ways, the *kolkhozniki* had stubbornly ignored the market revolution sweeping Moscow and Russia's big urban centers and continued to plow on as if the ghost of Lenin had not yet been buried. The farms still funded schools and maintained clinics, financed roads and retirement homes, and generally provided a welfare safety net for 40 percent of the country's population. But, beginning in 1991, they did this without the benefit of subsidies, which had trickled to a stop when the government's money spout ran dry. Left to fend for themselves, 80 percent of Russia's farms were effectively bankrupt by 1997, and yields had plummeted to their lowest levels since Panzer tanks tore up the country's fields during World War II. The rural misery was largely ignored in Moscow, where shops stocked imported food and Canadian lobster sold for fifty dollars a pound.

Only Nemtsov recognized the brewing horror in the countryside and the need to revamp a hopelessly ineffective agricultural system that could no longer provision Russian cities. Alarmed, he asked the IFC to devise a plan to dismantle collective farms in his province, and turn the land over to those farmers who wanted to try their hand at private enterprise. But though ample statistical evidence showed that privately held plots out-produced the big collectives—the tiny dacha gardens citizens received from the State only made up 3 percent of the country's total arable land but produced 57 percent of all the vegetables grown in Russia—his idea was viewed as heresy.

The communists screeched like stuck pigs. The nationalists warned that foreigners would buy up the land if it was broken up. The powerful farm bosses fought the dismemberment of their fiefs every inch of the way. And getting the notoriously backward and conservative peasants to even contemplate the notion of striking out on their own proved the most daunting task of all.

When Rafal and Nemtsov's officials first floated the possibility of privatization at the Redkino collective, the majority of the farm's two hundred members recoiled in horror. "They freaked out," Rafal recalled. "Most wouldn't even hear of it. They had spent their whole life simply following the director's orders and relied on others to run every aspect of their lives. We were suddenly asking them to make decisions for themselves. It was too much."

But a small group did find the courage to go it alone. They were led by Sergei Serov, a thirty-six-year-old agricultural engineer with strawberry-blond hair whose studious expression and deep, penetrating eyes lent him the air of an academic. Serov convinced two dozen members of the collective to pool their shares and break from the mother farm. Under the IFC plan (the same model later adopted in Ukraine at the privatization where I first met Roberta), each member of the collective received a certificate entitling them to an equal slice of the farm's 22,500 acres of land, its silos, its pigs, its machinery—even the director's battered sedan. In this manner, Serov was able to cobble together 2,338 acres to start a joint-stock farming concern. Like Boris Jordan, he christened his firm with the symbolic name *Vozrozhdeniye,* or Renaissance Ltd.

Renaissance Farm had just celebrated its first anniversary in business when we pulled up to a cinder-block garage that had been converted into the company's administrative base. Serov sat in a beaver hat beneath a bare lightbulb and surveyor's wall map of the Redkino collective on which someone had drawn a red-dotted line to demarcate the Renaissance property line. Next to him, a woman in an overcoat and headscarf tapped uncertainly at a computer with fingerless mitts, an electric heater at her feet.

"We had to take lessons in town to learn how to use it," beamed Serov, patting the newly purchased computer as if the machine were a favorite household pet, "but it's essential for efficiency." Efficiency was a tired buzzword used unconvincingly a hundred times a day by pin-striped stockbrokers and equity analysts in Moscow. Yet Serov, with his felt boots and dirty dungarees, mouthed it with conviction, as if his life depended on it. I looked at him with fresh interest.

"My whole life I wondered what it would be like to work for myself, to take pride in what I do. So when he," Serov nodded at Rafal, "came and offered that opportunity I knew I had to take it."

The first thing Serov had done as a private farmer was to put up a corrugated steel fence separating his land from the Redkino collective. After only one growing season, the fields on his side were already four to five times as productive as the much larger plots next door. The reasons were simple. At the collective, theft by unpaid workers was rampant. Crops had been left to rot because the *kolkhoz* could not afford to buy fuel for its combine-harvesters, and members routinely knocked off at 5:00 P.M. during the harvest while Serov and his co-owners, like American farmers, often worked until midnight to beat the early frost.

The fence also protected Serov's cattle from an outbreak of tuberculosis that had wiped out three-quarters of the collective's herd. The *kolkhoz*'s surviving beasts were sheltered in a crumbling barn with gaping holes in the roof; Serov's were in a clean new brick structure. Not surprisingly, Serov's dairy cows outproduced Redkino's by a factor of three. In fact, the year's results were skewed in Serov's favor in every single aspect of farming production. His success had already borne fruit; he had just purchased a new tractor and was building an extension to his cowshed. Already, he said, he was casting his eye on more land.

Next door, the picture was bleak. We made our way to the office of the collective farm boss. He occupied a large building with filthy and broken windowpanes. In the courtyard, the remains of a red combine harvester sat forlornly under a dusting of snow. It had been cannibalized for spare parts sold for cash to neighboring farms.

In the director's barren and freezing waiting room, there were about a dozen gloomy peasants, reeking of vodka and unwashed socks. They sat in dirty winter overcoats beside a dead potted plant, waiting for an audience, for a chance to plead for money. No one had been paid at the Redkino collective for over four months and the despair was visibly mounting. One woman needed fifty thousand rubles for medicine. Another said her son had outgrown his boots. A thickset man cursed capitalism and eyed us malevolently, as if we carried the plague.

Director Genady Pechushkin, gray and pompadoured in a greasy brown suit, slumped at a huge oak desk decorated with a bank of ancient rotary phones and a flip-knob switchboard—the symbol of power in Soviet times. Two red banners hung in the background, flanking a lifesize plaster bust of Lenin that had been painted bright gold, but had acquired a chipped ear that gleamed gypsum white.

Pechushkin made no effort to put on a brave face. "We're not going to make it, we're not going to make it," he moaned, when Rafal asked how things were. I told him that we had just visited with Serov.

"Oh," he said, looking glum. "Well, they were lucky with the weather. The rain wiped out our potato crop." Seeing our expressions of disbelief at the notion of rain clouds that visited only one side of the fence, he cut himself short.

"They, they work differently over there," he conceded. "For us it's too late. We cannot adjust to the new ways. The government must help us, must give us money, otherwise we won't survive another winter like this."

I returned to Moscow sneezing, yet sold on Nemtsov. He had opened his province to Western influence more than any other regional politician in all of Russia. The notion that individuals could be and had to be masters of their own destiny, without recourse to State aid or the threat of government interference, was alien to most Russians and clearly Nemtsov's greatest import to Nizhny. Now that he was deputy prime minister, the hope was that he would instill the same sense of self-determination in the rest of the country.

Nemtsov brought another fresh, and equally foreign, idea to the Kremlin: that government was for the people—and not the other way around, as Russian officialdom had presumed since the days of the tsar's venal and grasping "Table of Ranks," or civil service. It was not a historical anomaly that Russia's two wealthiest financiers, Vladimir Potanin and Boris Berezovsky, had simultaneously held senior positions in the Cabinet while their corporate empires swallowed State holdings. Nor was it uncommon or considered unbecoming for provincial governors to sit on the board of companies that were headquartered in their fiefs; that was simply viewed as a just reward for a life of public service. Even the unabashed communists and nationalists in the Duma, after a long day of foreigner-bashing and fire-breathing anti-free-market speeches, drove home contentedly in their government-issue Audis and Mercedes.

Nemtsov pledged to put an end to all these cozy conflicted-interest arrangements, and he started by trimming the fat from government perks programs with a publicity stunt that saw his popularity double overnight. It smacked of arrogance, he declared, that while Russia suffered through hard times, its officials enjoyed the comfort of Western luxury cars. The Kremlin would sell them all to raise money for the budget, and instead buy everyone Russian Volgas, which by happy coincidence were made in Nemtsov's riding.

As was often the case in Russia, even the best intentions produced unintended results. The Volga factory, upon receiving the good news, promptly raised the price of its ridiculous clunkers five-fold to an astonishing $57,500 per vehicle. The auctions of the Audis and Mercedes mysteriously failed to raise the expected revenue, or even cover a fraction of the Volgas' sticker price, and in the end the government lost millions of dollars on the exchange.

As Nemtsov received his first harsh lesson in Kremlin politics, I was taking my first tottering steps as a business reporter. Now that I had traveled outside of Moscow, the market rallies struck me as more incongruous than ever. Yet the Moscow money-men were pushing into the countryside. And the appetite for Russian debt was so insatiable that Boris Jordan's Renaissance Capital had just packaged a new type of offering called agro-bonds. These bonds were high-interest loans to collective farms, underwritten by regional governments. Supposedly dentists and other self-styled savvy investors in Luxembourg had snapped up, sight unseen, $740 million worth of the notes, which—one could only suspect—would go a long way toward getting farm boss Pechushkin's bust of Lenin repaired.

Rafal had a good laugh when I told him about the agro-bonds. "Those dentists," he predicted, "have about as good a chance of ever seeing their money again as Yeltsin has of winning a marathon."

CHAPTER FIVE

Russian Roulette

It was sometime in the spring of 1997, when the city was sodden and dripping and the ice floes snapped on the Yauza Canal, that Roberta and I began succumbing to Moscow's market madness.

We had just returned from a long weekend in the Crimean resort of Sochi, where summer came early and rich Siberians sought respite from their frozen tundra. My face still smarted from the Black Sea's surprising sun, and my mind was still filled with the rustle of palm trees and the delicate scent of the eucalyptus groves that rose in great, green tangles along Sochi's pebbly coast. Sochi was unlike any resort I'd ever seen—at least its clientele was.

We had stayed at the Lazurnaya Radisson, a brand-new establishment not far from the tennis courts of Yeltsin's government retreat, built on a bluff with an elevator bored through the rock to carry beachgoers to the water below. The hotel was owned by Gazprom, and its top floors were held in reserve for company executives who needed to thaw out for a few days after long stints in the Arctic gas fields of Yamal. Designed in the Floridian style, the Lazurnaya rose like a trapezoid from its wide base toward the heavens, where the unimpeded sea view set guests back five hundred dollars a night.

We took a middling room on the seventh floor, checking in right after an aluminum-factory boss from a miserable whistle-stop on the permafrost called Krasnoyarsk. Mr. Aluminum, I could not help but notice, nonchalantly plunked an American Express Platinum Card on the marble counter of the reception desk, which could only mean he had a bulging bank account somewhere in the West—because Amex doesn't accept aluminum ingots as payment. The factory boss did not appear to be accompanied by his wife, unless the slender long-limbed creature pouting by his side was his daughter. No, she definitely wasn't his daughter. No one carries on like that with his daughter, at least not in public.

The Lazurnaya's outdoor pool was already open for the season, and a slew of pale, fleshy men sat submerged to the waist at the sunken bar, looking alarmingly like albino sea lions with gold collars. I ordered a Long Island Iced Tea and settled into one of the recliners scattered on the terra-cotta tiles around the pool. This could have been Palm Beach or Boca Raton—if you erased from memory the decay and dusty poverty revealed during the short taxi ride from the airport. I could hear the thwangs of a spirited volley on the nearby tennis courts, the aroma of suntan lotion wafted in the warm breeze, and hamburgers sizzled on the barbecue. It was hard to imagine that we were in Russia, harder still to picture the scene less than ten miles away in Abkhazia, Georgia, where one of the bloodiest civil wars since the collapse of communism had claimed thousands of lives.

I ordered a second Long Island and then a third, and pretty soon I was engrossed in the show around me. A muscular man with a club foot was seated on the lip of the pool, his broad back toward me. On it was one of the largest and most intricate tattoos I've ever come across—and I have a pretty big Polish eagle stenciled on my chest. The tattoo depicted a battle in mountainous terrain, presumably some craggy ravine in Afghanistan. Hind-attack helicopters, identifiable by their sidewinder pods, swooped from his left shoulder, shooting at a turbaned figure crouching at the base of his spine who returned fire with what looked to be a Stinger missile of the sort the CIA had supplied to the mujahidin.

"I'm gonna ask him 'bout his tattoo," I slurred in a burst of rum-propelled enthusiasm.

"Don't you dare," warned Roberta. "Those guys are mafia." Roberta, like most Russians, used the all-encompassing definition of the word. The Russian mafia had no connection with Italian or American criminal organizations with the same name. The Russian mafia was not based on blood families and did not have ranks or rituals like the Cosa Nostra.

The term mafia in Russia was used to denote both the criminal underworld and industry based profiteering cartels that used violent means to control manufacturing, raw material exports and banking sectors of the legal economy.

The tattooed warrior limped over to a shaded table where several young men fidgeted with cellular phones. Despite the heat, they were dressed from head to toe in black, the informal uniform of those occupying the middle ranks of organized crime. They sported black suede shoes with dainty little gold buckles under tapered black slacks, into which were tucked cashmere black turtlenecks that would have been more appropriate for the lingering chill in Moscow. A good deal of jewelry hung from their thick wrists and necks. They drank Johnny Walker, Black Label.

What betrayed them irrevocably as thugs, however, were the expressions they wore. They looked as aggressively secure and above the law as movie stars, or gangsta rappers on MTV.

"Don't stare," pleaded Roberta.

"Sorry," I said sheepishly.

At that moment the gangsters' girlfriends made their high-heeled entrance, and all eyes fell on them. A hush descended over the pool, and even three pot-bellied Gazprom men, who had been yammering about a deal with Germany's Ruhr Gas, fell into silent admiration.

"Jesus," sighed Roberta, "where do they find these babes?"

The four women were breathtaking, tall and well proportioned, with silky skin, honey-mustard hair, and the succulent collagen lips for which Russia's femmes fatales were celebrated. Like their thug companions, they hid behind very dark designer sunglasses. Chanel, Roberta later informed me. Very pricey and much in vogue.

The men of the black brigade barely acknowledged the arrival of their companions, though one did lower his Russian edition of *Soldier of Fortune* momentarily in a display of chivalry.

The men from Gazprom gaped slack-jawed. They looked as if they would have traded a billion cubic meters of grade A Yamal blend for just one hour with one of those apparitions. Alas, they had brought their sturdy wives along, and presently these stout ladies were throwing murderous looks in the direction of their wayward husbands.

"I bet those guys wish it was still the Soviet era," Roberta offered.

"How do you mean?"

"In the old days the *kurorts* were only for company employees," she explained, using the Russian term for the resorts each ministry or state enterprise owned. "So if husbands and wives worked for different enterprises, they vacationed separately."

"That sucks."

"Hardly. My secretary says it was done purposely so that everyone got to screw around. She says it was like a sanctioned vacation from marriage."

Russian mores had not changed greatly since Soviet times. This, coupled with inattention to the basics of safe sex, was among the chief reasons why venereal diseases like syphilis and gonorrhea were now out of control, and AIDS was seeing such epidemic growth in Moscow that the U.N.'s World Health Organization was issuing increasingly dire warnings to travelers visiting the Russian capital.

We broke for lunch soon after and made for the Kuban restaurant near the mezzanine. (The politically sensitive diner, by the way, would be advised to avoid the "Nazi Goering" pasta platter advertised in the Kuban's menu. This spicy Indonesian rice dish, more commonly spelled *nasi goreng*, is delicious, but the poor spelling can bring on a bad case of historical indigestion.) Opportunities for gawking awaited us there. Fashion was the engine that kept the show going. As with any good theater, the actors changed their costumes frequently to keep the audience riveted. Wherever they got their inspiration, it certainly wasn't Brooks Brothers; the garb they donned was strictly of the "show me the money" variety. The good folks from Norilsk or Irkutsk seemed, in fact, to get their holiday attire ideas from their local fire department: Day-Glo orange, fiery red, and lime green predominated, and most of their outfits appeared to be made of shiny, water-repellent materials.

In the evening we positioned ourselves near the mezzanine's grand fountain, past which couples in loud evening wear made for the roulette wheels and baize-covered gaming tables of the hotel's two casinos, heels clacking on the marble floor. Every society builds monuments to itself, and post-communist Russia had chosen for its Acropolis the casino. Every flea-bitten middle-sized town had its gambling establishment, and in central Moscow one was hard-pressed to walk two blocks without running into a neon invitation to roll the dice.

In the casino we recognized the thugs, now dressed in black Armani, and the Gazprom contingent, in Soviet-style gray suits. One of the toughs was fingering a pile of red chips worth five thousand dollars each, and I counted thirteen before Roberta dragged me away with another panicked admonition not to stare. "You could get killed for just looking at those guys!" she reminded me. The thug—big forehead, little hair—was toying with more than my yearly salary at the *Journal* and didn't seem to care one way or the other what became of it. Whatever line of work he was in, one thing was clear: I was in the wrong business.

Money weighed more on my mind now that I followed it professionally and used my press credentials to trespass in its rarefied circles. I had started feeling like a voyeur lusting after something that was always in front of me, yet just beyond my reach. It was odd to realize how much I had changed since my first brush with new Russian money, in 1996, also on the shores of the Black Sea.

"Churchill sat where you're sitting. Roosevelt was over there. And Stalin—" a reverential pause—"our *vozhd'* (leader) was seated here." My host indicated the chair he occupied. We were in a cool, whitewashed dining room in the recesses of Josef Stalin's terraced seaside dacha, next to the projection room where the dictator once liked to watch Charlie Chaplin films late at night.

The dining room was large and rustic, sparsely furnished with a long pale wooden table that had a roughhewn finish. A few decorative plates hung from the walls; they had been placed so that the natural light streaming in through the lace curtains hit them just so in the early afternoon, when the nocturnal *vozhd'* rose to take his breakfast. Stalin had been a man of unusual but simple tastes, or so my host insisted.

The Stalin admirer, a successful Moscow businessman by the name of Marat Sazonikov, had arranged a lavish spread for me: fruit juices, cold meats, smoked salmon, caviar, and several varieties of salads and breads. There were also two large bottles of Stolichnaya Kristall, Russia's fanciest blend of vodka.

I didn't have much of an appetite, and eyed the booze warily. The mood here was anything but festive. Sazonikov was not a nice man, and this, after all, was the very table where Europe's postwar fate had been decided, where the Big Three had congregated during a break in the proceedings at the Yalta Conference to hammer out the ignoble details of Eastern Europe's betrayal. Yalta! The mere mention of this place used to send my gentle granddad's blood pressure roiling to levels that required medication. The deal clinched here in 1944 handed over Poland and the rest of Eastern Europe to the socialist camp. In my boyhood home Yalta was known as the "great sellout"—Roosevelt's misguided abandonment of a hundred million people.

My host knew all this very well. He'd been needling me, flashing that malevolent gold-toothed grin of his, ever since his goons had picked me up. Our meeting had been arranged by Crimea's minister of tourism, a furtive man who had sought to deflect my questions about the rash of murders in the peninsula's hotel industry by suggesting I visit Stalin's retreat, the Yusupov Palace.

In the spring of 1996, the directors of Yalta's three largest hotels, including the cavernous twelve-hundred-room Gostinitsa Yalta, had been shot gangland-style. A fourth hotelier had narrowly escaped an attempt on his life and taken refuge in Germany. From what I gathered, all three victims had been skimming liberally from the State-owned hotels they managed. Ukraine had not privatized its Crimean tourist resorts, partly because the people who ran the spas and hotels opposed any transfer of ownership that would interfere with their looting. The killing spree, it was whispered, was orchestrated by a group of unknown investors who wanted the directors out of the way so that they could take over the hotels, long the Soviet Union's premier sun-and-fun spots.

My host was himself an investor in Crimea's tourism industry and had barely survived an ambush the month before that had left him jumpy and his driver riddled with bullets. A short, stocky man in his mid-fifties, he had demanded we meet on a public road, rather than at Stalin's estate. Our rendezvous took place on a dusty lane bordered by thornbushes and flat-roofed concrete homes of the sort one sees in Mediterranean villages not recommended in tourist brochures. Chickens pecked at the dirt and laundry flapped on the lines as Sazonikov's convoy arrived, led by a police car. Sazonikov himself did not get out of his sedan, an inconspicuous beige Volga. But three bodyguards did. They scanned the road and houses and approached me carefully.

"*Dokumenty,*" one demanded. He was young, fit, and wore a military brush cut. He took my passport and press card and thrust them through a narrow crack in the Volga's tinted rear window. Another guard, his neck straining out of his cheap suit, frisked me. The third rummaged through my bag.

The show of force rattled me. Who were these frightening people? What had I just gotten myself into? Noticeably nervous, I was bundled into the third car. A slight man in his mid-thirties was in the back seat.

"Forgive the precautions," he said in perfect French. "*Monsieur Sazonikov a eu des difficultés récemment.*" ("Mr. Sazonikov has had difficulties recently.")

The man's cultured demeanor reassured me. He said he was the resident historian at the Yusupov Palace, and had gone into Sazonikov's service when the businessman had rented Stalin's *dacha* as a weekend retreat for his Russian business buddies. I asked the historian what line of business his boss was in.

"He represents a syndicate of Russian business leaders with interests in rubber and oil," the historian replied vaguely.

We swept through the estate's gated entrance, sped past sentries and vine-covered walls, and came to a halt on a crushed-stone driveway that circled a large fountain outside the main compound's shaded entrance. There were surveillance cameras everywhere, and more guards patrolled the manicured grounds. They had AK-47s and rifles slung over their shoulders.

I was now sweating with anxiety, barely aware of the flowers, palm trees, sculpted gardens, and slate-lined pools around me. Sazonikov materialized. He was dressed in a cream linen suit and a stubby brown tie. I was close enough to see beads of moisture on his heavy brow. He extended a clammy hand.

"I am familiar with the writings of Zbigniew Brzezinski," he began by way of greeting. "He was well known for his anti-Soviet activities."

I tried to muster some bravado, but my backbone and vocabulary were failing me. "He fought for what he believed," I spluttered, with a little translation assistance from the kind historian. (What was he doing mixed up with this bunch?)

"Yes, we all fought for what we believed," Sazonikov countered smoothly. He was holding my passport, making little fanning motions with it. "But come," he motioned, "children should not be held accountable for the sins of their fathers."

Fuck you too, I thought. "What a beautiful place," I said.

"*Drugovo niet*," beamed Sazonikov, his gold crowns glinting in the sun. "There's no other like it."

As we entered the neo-Gothic hacienda, Sazonikov explained that the local Crimean government, short on funds for the upkeep of the favorite *dachas* of sundry Soviet leaders, had made arrangements with wealthy Russians to lease the retreats. Khrushchev's old place down the road, a sprawling mansion in the Italian Renaissance style, was now the site of weekend orgies. The main attraction, Sazonikov said with a lusty sneer, was a glass-walled swimming pool perched on the lip of a cliff where Moscow moguls could frolic with a pair of live dolphins, as well as with several "mermaids" kept on hand for the sake of aquatic diversity. At Brezhnev's lush palace, the diversions included skeet shooting. Only Gorbachev's *dacha*, the infamous Foros, which he had ordered built at a reported cost of $45 million and where he was briefly held prisoner during the 1991 coup, sat empty. The modern marble manse, like its unhappy master, had developed serious structural problems and had been abandoned.

Sazonikov was building his own hotel near Stalin's *dacha*, an eighty-five-million-dollar five-star spa. Yugoslav contractors were halfway through the project, which Sazonikov boasted was being paid for entirely in cash. "Where is the money coming from?" I inquired.

"Russia," he answered, as if that was all I needed to know. When I pressed him, he became ill-tempered again. "Why do you ask all this? It is enough that I told you the money is from Russian investors."

We sauntered up a mahogany staircase and found ourselves standing before a dark-stained wooden door, which Sazonikov opened respectfully. This was Stalin's bedroom. It had somber red wallpaper, heavy blinds, and a door that opened onto a huge claw-footed bathtub. At the center of the bedroom was a four-poster bed with an oil painting of a combine harvester hanging behind it.

"We never use this room," Sazonikov confessed. "But you may sit on the bed if you wish," he added, all charity and charm. I dutifully sat. The mattress was firm. My host was delighted.

It was later, when we repaired to the basement dining room for lunch, that the taunting resumed. It was my fault. We had started in on the cold cuts and caviar, and I had foolishly broached the topic of politics. What did he make of Crimea under Ukrainian rule? I had asked. The Russian-dominated peninsula had become part of Ukraine after the dissolution of the USSR, and the subject was a sore one for most Russians.

"*Khokhly!*" Sazonikov roared contemptuously, using a Russian pejorative term for Ukrainians that could loosely be translated as "yokels." He launched into a rant about the bumbling incompetence of Ukrainians, and how rich Russians were now favoring Cannes over the Crimea because of Kiev's utter mismanagement of the tourist industry. "Ukrainians don't know how to run anything. They're peasants who need orders from Moscow."

His griping rang somewhat true, and I encouraged him with knowing nods that were a blatant attempt to ingratiate myself. He still had my documents, and his blond, blue-eyed bodyguards, armed Slavic supermen, were hovering nearby.

Sazonikov grabbed the Stoli and upturned two shot glasses. "*Davai,*" he cackled, black caviar eggs lodged between his gold front teeth. "*Za Khokhlov!* Let's drink to the yokels!" No sooner had he slammed back his shot than he refilled our glasses. Etiquette now called for me to make a toast. "*Uspekhi s proyektami,*" I reciprocated, wishing him success with his hotel venture.

This continued more or less genially throughout the first bottle. But by the time Sazonikov opened the second Stoli, it was obvious that his mood had darkened and he had mischief on his mind. His guards must have sensed this too, for they moved closer to the table, one standing a few feet behind me. Sazonikov had returned to the topic of Ukrainian Crimea and the breakup of the Soviet Union. After half a bottle of vodka, I was in a sort of uneasy netherworld—too fuzzy to control my words but too aware of my surroundings to relax and enter into the spirit of debate. I found myself praying I wouldn't get sloppy.

"So you agree Crimea is Russian?" my host asked sweetly.

I sensed I was on thin ice, and mustering whatever diplomatic reserves I had left, said that Crimea would have been better off economically had it remained in the Russian Federation.

"Ha!" roared Sazonikov, slapping the table as if he had just scored a major victory. "Let's drink to a Russian Crimea."

The next thing I knew we were back to my uncle, and his machinations against the Soviet people. "He wanted to destroy us," Sazonikov hissed, pieces of pickled tomato flying out of his mouth. "We accomplished great things. We were a *superpower*! But the West conspired against us. Tried to ruin us. Wanted to bring us to our knees." He had worked himself into a lather, and I found myself shrinking back in my seat. Just then, he regained his composure and was quiet, almost serene, for an instant.

Finally, he hoisted his glass. "*Za Stalina*," he said, his voice barely a whisper. "To Stalin."

I stared at him, frozen and aghast. I thought of Sakharov, Solzhenitsyn, Walesa, and all the dissidents who would have spat in this man's face. But I was intimidated by the guns, the guards, and this angry man who held my documents. He watched me hesitate, a smile creasing his round face.

I raised my glass.

When we got back from Sochi, Roberta received an interesting piece of news. Perhaps enticing is the better word. A large and very successful American investment fund—well-known and respected in the inner circles of Moscow finance, but positively paranoid about attracting attention to itself—was trying to lure her away from the IFC, in the strictest confidence, naturally.

Roberta initially wrestled with the proposition. She had come to Russia to be a part of its rebirth, to lend a helping hand and have an adventure or two in the process. But she had grown frustrated because the IFC and its sister organizations at the World Bank were moving too slowly to keep pace with Russia's market transformations. Multilaterals everywhere engage in quite a bit of bureaucratic wheel-spinning. Memos and meetings beget more meetings and memos, and while the technocrats talk and convene sub-committees, life's opportunities pass by. Even before this offer fell in her lap, she had begun to question whether the IFC's post-privatization mandate in Russia, to invest in promising companies the way it had once done with the Hyundais and Daewoos and Lucky Goldstars of South Korea, could not be better accomplished by the faster-moving private sector.

Few investors moved faster than the outfit that wanted to hire her. It was known only by its initials, which I have taken the liberty of changing to VSO, for Very Secretive Organization. In the murky waters of international finance, VSO was to the IFC what a mako shark is to a blue whale. The IFC was gigantic and well-intentioned, docile and lumbering. VSO was ravenous and swift and compactly built for feeding frenzies. The two swam in entirely different leagues.

VSO had approached Roberta after a chance airborne meeting she had had with one of its senior executives on the busy Kiev-to-Moscow run. The executive had chatted with Roberta throughout the flight and concluded that she was a tough customer whose talents might not be fully appreciated in a gentle bureaucracy like the IFC. VSO quietly asked Roberta to submit to a psychological evaluation, a three-hour test that gauged the participant's decision-making abilities, level of aggressiveness, and appetite for risk. The results of the examination, apparently, showed that while Roberta was handicapped by do-gooder tendencies, she had a nice set of baby shark teeth that under the right conditions could develop quite a bite. This pleased the men on the forty-sixth floor of VSO's Fifth Avenue headquarters, who smiled at views of Central Park, the Plaza Hotel, and Tiffany's flagship store as they watched their money multiply in faraway Russia.

And multiply it did. VSO's growth was already the stuff of legend in the tightly-knit emerging-market community. In an industry where *cojones* count most, VSO had a reputation for having the biggest set. Competing fund managers used to mouth VSO's acronym wistfully, as in: "No, unfortunately I don't own any Surgutneftgaz stock, but you might try VSO. I hear they bought a big stake before the boom."

VSO's formula was simple: go where few others dare, get in early, and get in big. The fund had started humbly enough. Its founder, a young venture capitalist who had made some money in medical publishing, had scraped together $15 million in 1992 and plunged into the nascent Russian market, buying up privatization vouchers at a time when few people other than Boris Jordan recognized the potential value of these shares. In short order VSO had tripled its initial investment, and on the strength of this windfall started raising larger and larger sums of money to invest in Russia. The fund repeated its success with early forays into the stock and bond markets, returning 300 percent gains to its ecstatic investors. Word spread quickly on Wall Street that the hitherto unknown fund was paying out more than ten times the going rate of return. By the mid-1990s, people were beating down VSO's door to get them to manage their money, and VSO was being courted by pension funds, Ivy League endowments, and institutional investors who had suddenly developed a thirst for high-yield Russia risk. VSO's fortunes rode this upward wave, so that when Roberta received her offer, the fund's assets in the former Soviet Union had a market value of three and a half billion dollars and VSO was competing with George Soros for bragging rights to being the largest single foreign investor in the region. VSO's top brass were all multimillionaires, and its founder was said to be worth a cool quarter of a billion dollars.

When Roberta told me of VSO's interest in her, I must confess that dollar signs flashed before my eyes. I was familiar with VSO's Cinderella story. I had first heard of the fund while serving my time in Ukraine, nosing around for a story—any story—on foreign investors actually making money in Kiev. The expats I cornered at the Arizona Bar & Grill (run by a wily East German by the name of Falk who had never been to the United States, much less Arizona) all glumly referred to this one fund. "I don't know how they do it," one frustrated British financier had sighed into his imported onion rings.

It had taken me weeks to track down the VSO guys, and countless supplications for them to agree to see me. But I finally caught up with them in 1996, in the southern industrial city of Dnepropetrovsk. Brezhnev's home town, Dnepropetrovsk had been the site of the world's largest nuclear missile factory; you could still see the green nose cones and rocket casings of SS-18 ICBMs scattered around the plant, which now produced trolley buses under Czech license. VSO had shrewdly opted to base its Ukrainian operations in Dnepropetrovsk because the country's political elite, including the president, the prime minister, the deputy prime ministers, and the finance minister, all hailed from there. Access to decision makers was easier in Dnepropetrovsk than in the capital.

VSO's office took me by complete surprise: it looked like a heavily guarded Jewish revival center, and the young Americans who ran it were all Orthodox Jews in their early twenties. What were they doing here? Dnepropetrovsk was Cossack country, about as welcoming to Jews as Alabama had been to African-Americans during the days of the civil-rights movement.

A young man with a scraggly beard and a yarmulke greeted me. I'll call him Mordechai—not his real name, because I later learned through Roberta that he had almost been fired for talking to me. Mordechai ushered me down a long hall, which was in the advanced stages of remodeling and had cables sagging from the open ceiling. We ducked under scaffolding and into his office.

"So," he said. "Tell me about yourself."

This was not the way I usually began interviews, but for some reason I heard myself drone on about my time in Eastern Europe, my life as a student in Warsaw, and my meandering into journalism. The telephone kept interrupting my little discourse and Mordechai would snap up the receiver, listen calmly, and then issue instructions in succinct and faultless Russian. "Factory directors," he apologized. "They're not good at making decisions."

VSO owned shares in dozens of local enterprises and was in the process of consolidating its positions, which is to say of acquiring enough stock to give it controlling interest. The trick, explained Mordechai, was to buy up enough shares in a given company so that you had a big block you could sell for a large markup to what is known as a strategic investor. Strategic investors were multinational corporations such as Coca-Cola or AT&T that were interested in owning, say, sugar refineries or telecommunications-switch manufacturers but could not be bothered with the hassle of purchasing dribs and drabs of stock in those concerns. They happily paid hefty premiums to someone like VSO to accumulate the shares for them.

VSO had its fingers in many pies in Ukraine. In addition to its sundry stock holdings, the fund owned a telephone company, the notoriously horrid Lybid Hotel in Kiev (where guests were given the choice of a room with hot water or one with a television), and lots of real estate. All told, the fund had sunk four hundred million dollars into the country, a staggering sum given that total foreign direct investment in Ukraine between 1991 and 1996 barely topped one billion dollars.

"Not bad for a yeshiva boy from Miami," Mordechai laughed. He said he had to inspect an office center VSO was putting up and asked if I wanted to tag along. We piled into a Jeep, bodyguard and driver up front, and drove along Dnepropetrovsk's sad streets to a building that was remarkable not only for its modernity but for the astonishing fact that VSO had somehow managed to get the construction permits and licenses that usually tangled such projects up in red tape for years.

The local contractor, a bear of a man, was waiting at the construction site, which had a large sign out front identifying the project's promoter as a Cyprus-based firm. "We have hundreds of holding companies registered there," explained Mordechai. "For tax purposes." The contractor had just finished installing the building's heating plant, and wanted to fire it up for Mordechai. The gas furnace roared into blue life at the push of a button. The contractor beamed nastily. "Just like Auschwitz, eh?"

My jaw dropped. "Yeah, wonderful," said Mordechai, absently. When I later asked him why he let the contractor get away with Auschwitz cracks, he answered matter-of-factly: "I'm well compensated to put up with people like him. In a few years I'll be back in Miami, a rich man. He will still be living in this shithole."

Much later, when I learned a little about the family history of VSO's founder from Roberta, I understood why employees of the fund were so hardened. The philosophy behind VSO rested with its founder's father, who from his retirement condominium in Florida remained the fund's unofficial adviser and éminence grise.

The family had lived in Lvov's wealthy Jewish quarter at the outset of the war, and had managed to flee what was then eastern Poland's biggest Jewish community and buy their way into Switzerland before the SS rolled in. After the Holocaust, they went to the heart of the beast, West Berlin, and started buying bombed-out real estate with the money and gold they had managed to smuggle out of Lvov. Presumably it was sweet revenge to purchase entire blocks of Berlin property for next to nothing. In the years that followed West Germany's recovery, the once-unwanted property skyrocketed in value. The devastation in postwar Germany bore many similarities to the USSR after the collapse of communism, and the property play in Berlin served as a historical blueprint for what VSO was now trying to repeat in the former Soviet bloc.

Roberta's offer to join VSO included what is known in the fund-management industry as "upside"—a clause enabling her to receive, over and above a cushy six-figure base salary, 5 percent of the profits on any deals she worked on, an incentive that could easily push the total package well into seven figures.

Despite the millions being dangled in front of her, Roberta wavered, worried that defecting to the private sector would be selling out her ideals. After all, her entire professional career had been in aid programs. I, on the other hand, had been exposed to Moscow just long enough to pooh-pooh her qualms. Though I hadn't gone into journalism to get rich (no one does), it grated on me to see everyone in town cashing in on the boom. My job was to talk to the rich, and greed, as I was discovering, is a communicable disease. It is amazing, in fact, how little it takes for one to start building castles in the sky.

Why should Victor Paul be the only one to have a big boat, especially since the hundred million dollars of Gazprom stock VSO had bought through him would pay for a good chunk of that cruiser? I liked to sail too. Hell, I could even learn how to fish.

"Take it. Take the offer," I urged. "It's a once-in-a-lifetime opportunity."

"Well," said Roberta, looking uneasy. "I guess I'm going to have to sew on a shark fin."

CHAPTER SIX

The Eleven-Billion-Dollar Woman

On the occasion of her lucrative new employment contract, Roberta bought me an aquarium—rekindling a childhood passion of mine— and we set about stocking it with the zeal of New Russians. The tank was an imported German model with all the trimmings and had cost three times as much as it would have back home. Fish tanks were in great demand in Moscow. A tony restaurant just down the street from our office had converted its entire floor into a gigantic aquarium, and six-foot sturgeons swam beneath the glass at your feet as you dabbed sour cream on their roe. Another on Tverskaya boasted exotic saltwater species that must have cost a small fortune to import. Lukoil, Russia's biggest oil company, had dispensed aquariums to all its executives above the rank of vice president, presumably to relieve the nerve-jangling effects of falling international oil prices.

Not that the inhabitants of Russian aquaria were usually very soothing. The guy who sold us our tank said that his businessmen clients usually filled their aquariums with piranhas, pikes, and other aggressive species favored by the villains in James Bond movies.

We usually shopped for tropical fish on Saturdays, my one true day off since the *Journal* did not publish weekend editions. Saturdays were for getting out of the city; for exploring the capital's outlying regions; for picnics in the soggy battlefields of Borodino, where Napoleon battled for Moscow; for jaunts to the smoky monasteries and gilded citadels of Zagorsk, where Ivan the Terrible set out to rout the Tatars; and for excursions to open-air markets.

Moscow—like almost all cities in the former communist bloc—

was ringed by giant bazaars. Each one specialized in particular goods: used cars in rough-and-tumble Solntsevo; building materials near Star City, the creaky Mir space-control center; paintings and fine-weave Central Asian rugs in windswept Izmailovo; dried mushroom wreaths and bright red paprika strands at the spice market near Kievsky Vokzal; and pets at the Ptichy Rynok in the funky old warehouse district of Taganka.

More reminiscent of a Turkish bazaar than a Petco outlet, the Ptichy Rynok (Bird Market) was where Muscovites came to buy, sell, and trade household animals of every imaginable species and size. It was so wacky that President Reagan had asked to see it during his visit to Moscow. The Ptichy Rynok was not for the faint of heart. You had to be alert walking in the crowded paths between the its makeshift stalls; there was always some nut waving a boa constrictor in your face or a Tajik serpent poking its pug nose out of a big pickle jar. Vats of blood-red feeder larva squirmed next to gnats the size of jellybeans. A pretty girl in her late teens sold this exotic fish food, scooping them up in her stained hands and wrapping fistfuls in newspapers that buyers slipped into their pockets. Many of the traders could not afford cages, so mice, ferrets, kittens and turtles often scurried about underfoot. Sometimes someone would shriek, and there would be a commotion, which usually meant that a snake was on the loose.

True to its name, the bird market was also lined with hundreds of chicken-wire cages in which distressed fowl of every feather squawked and crapped in a permanent state of panic. Next to the bird salesmen was a row of fanatical fish breeders with miniature portable tanks and a penchant for debate. The relative merits of different aquatic species and the best methods of raising them were much discussed in this quarter of the market. The Russians call hobbyists *liubiteli*, which literally means "those in love with," and these keepers of exotic fish were as passionate about their pastime as Moscow's expats were fixated on the financial markets.

The most astonishing aspect of the Ptichy Rynok was that it was open year-round. Even in the dead of winter, when the temperature dipped to minus 20 Celsius and snow fell in great howling curtains, you could still buy fragile neon tetras, guppies, oscars, or African cichlids alfresco. The ingenious fish traders set up little gas stoves under their tanks, which steamed over the open flames and stayed as warm as the year-round outdoor swimming pools favored by Muscovites. It was a tricky business, however, keeping the temperature steady, and more than once we saw a tankful of gouramis or goldfish on the boil, bodies bloated and eyes bulging milky white. Traders of kittens and puppies (none of your finicky French poodles—the favored breeds were Rottweilers, pit bulls, and other fighting breeds adored by thugs and businessmen alike) kept them warm under their coats during the winter season, and I once saw a man open his jacket to reveal dozens of garden snakes slithering snugly inside his undershirt.

The traders themselves chased away the cold with vodka, so that by late afternoon many were in the advanced stages of inebriation. Roberta, her VSO shark fin already showing, shrewdly suggested we make our purchases just before closing, when the traders barely clung to consciousness and astounding bargains could be had. Sometimes the strategy would backfire, as with one intoxicated fish breeder who tended to grow sentimental, clutching his tank protectively. "No," he would slur. "I'm not selling to you foreigners. I don't like the look of you. You won't take care of my fish."

The frigid inconvenience Moscow's weekend pet peddlers suffered was nothing compared to the hardships I had seen Russian traders endure during the early nineties, when travel restrictions had just been lifted and Soviet citizens poured west into Poland for their first real taste of capitalism. It began in 1992, as the last Soviet troops finally withdrew from Poland. Millions of Russians streamed into the country to sell icons or caviar and buy Western consumer goods, just the way Poles, a few years earlier, had traveled to Germany to sell cheap vodka and purchase car stereos for resale at home at massive markups.

The Russians had a name for this small-time international commerce: the shuttle trade. It was big business, attracting twenty-eight million visitors to Poland in 1993 from the former Soviet Union, where it was estimated that one in five citizens participated in some form of petty trading. Shuttle traders—*chelnoki*—traveled between the two countries on decrepit trains, planes, and buses, and traded whatever they could carry, exploiting differences in exchange rates and the availability of various products to earn seed money to start businesses at home.

The Poles called this first stage of free-market development "kiosk capitalism" because goods were hawked on the street or at kiosks in makeshift outdoor markets. By late 1992 and early 1993, most Poles had already graduated from kiosk capitalism. Polish shuttle traders, who in the late 1980s plied their trade in the markets of Berlin, had now earned enough money to open their own stores in Warsaw or Krakow. Some of the more enterprising traders had even opened two or three outlets, selling Panasonic fax machines or imported women's dresses. By 1993 Warsaw had become a mecca for post-Soviet *cholniki*, in the same way that Berlin had been a magnet for entrepreneurial Poles four years earlier.

The first time I saw these petty traders was on a snowy Sunday morning in early 1992 at Warsaw's central train station. The station was an angular hangar of modern design wedged between the spooky Stalinist Palace of Culture and the new forty-five-story Marriott Hotel tower, the home away from home of the Polish government's Harvard-trained advisers. Like most big termini in train-happy Europe, the central station was a bustling place, echoing with departure and arrival announcements in five languages. The station's metal-framed mezzanine had the feel of a racetrack betting hall, with grimy glass walls, trapped pigeons flapping around, and beer and cigarette advertisements pinned to the rusty rafters. On the dark, slushy floor long lines formed in front of ticket counters, while electronic boards flashed train and platform numbers like bookies' odds.

In a dimly lit corner of the huge hall, under the shelter of a wide and dirty staircase, sat the *chelnoki*, looking as if they hadn't slept in days. There were about fifty of them, dressed in rags and sprawled on top of large parcels that seemed ready to explode from overstuffing. They were dark-skinned, with heavy five-o'clock shadows and an aura of bedraggled menace. The Gypsy children who usually begged in the station—hounding you with grasping little fingers and persistent cries of "Please, Mister, zlotys, give zlotys!"—ignored these fellow travelers. They appeared to know instinctively that there would be no profit from that quarter, only trouble if they got too close to the bulging parcels, which the traders guarded with animal ferocity.

I wondered what was in the bags, many of which had the dimensions of steamer trunks and were secured with ropes and wide tape. A few boxes were sitting out, and I could see that these contained portable stereos with Korean brand names like Lucky Goldstar.

The *chelnoki* spoke a tongue I did not recognize, but I guessed they were from Azerbaijan or somewhere else around the Caspian Sea. Whichever it was, they were far from home and apparently understood Russian, for when the train to Moscow was called (in Russian and Polish) they shouldered their great bundles and descended toward a lower platform. Out of curiosity, I followed.

The bowels of the station were filled with hundreds of other *cholniki* traders. Here Slavic faces dominated, pale and broad, bushy-browed and morosely intense. The platform was stacked with bundles and parcels of all dimensions, and though the locomotive's light had not yet appeared, people were already jostling for position. When the big Soviet train emerged through the tunnel, all green and soot-streaked and with CCCP still stamped in faded red letters on its broad side, all hell broke loose. The Russians swept up their huge bags and with astonishing strength and speed started sprinting alongside the moving wagons. They flung parcels through open windows and lunged for handrails. I saw a dozen *chelnoki* dangling from window frames, feet kicking as they tried to heave themselves in to grab the choice seats. Elbows flailed and shoving matches broke out in front of the doors, with passengers yelling and squeezing through the narrow passageways four abreast.

The *chelnoki* didn't simply board trains, they assaulted them. The blue-clad Polish policemen who patrolled the platform turned up their noses at the uncivilized display, but I knew this was as pure a representation as I would ever see of the East's scramble for the almighty buck.

The traders' Warsaw headquarters was a mammoth outdoor bazaar located in the city's biggest soccer stadium. The Dziesieciolecia stadium loomed on the left bank of the Vistula River, just above the old iron bridge that directed traffic to the posh neighborhood of Saska Kepa. Saska Kepa was an oasis of prosperity where diplomats and representatives of multinational corporations lived in splendid isolation in manicured stucco townhouses equipped with wet bars, satellite dishes, security systems, and walled gardens. Glossy chauffeured cars with cellular-phone antennas and blue diplomatic license plates glided along the flawless streets. Even the uniforms of the policemen posted in booths outside some of Saska Kepa's more elaborately overbuilt residences seemed crisper than the ones worn in the rest of the city.

A few blocks north of Saska Kepa existed a far less genteel world. It was contained by the stadium, a hundred-thousand-seat concrete monstrosity where the Rolling Stones had once played a barrier-busting concert during one of the brief thaws in the Cold War. There hadn't been a soccer match or show at Dziesieciolecia in over four years when I first visited it in the spring of 1993. Yet every single day since 1989, when the entrepreneur Bogdan Tomaszewski first leased the crumbling arena from municipal authorities, a game of economic survival had been played there with all the furious intensity of a World Cup final.

The tram stop outside the arena was connected to the main gate by a steamy underground passage covered with hundreds of banana peels. The peels rose in great mounds from overflowing garbage cans and had been trampled into a slimy brownish-yellow mush. Bananas were a novelty to Russians, unavailable in the old Soviet Union except to Party higher-ups; now gorging on bananas was a perk of the shuttle trade. I skidded through the crowded tunnel with a series of collisions and apologies that were drowned out by the pounding rhythms of techno-pop blaring from kiosks hawking audiocassettes with shoddily photocopied jacket covers. Sweden's Ace of Base seemed to be the flavor of the month, though the knock-down price of twenty-thousand zlotys ($1.25) per tape suggested that the Stockholm group wasn't likely to see any royalties from its Polish sales.

Beyond the tunnel I saw more banana peels and row upon row of kiosks, stalls, tents, and trucks with open bay doors. A quick glance at their wares revealed more unlicensed products: Mickey Mouse dolls with small, shriveled ears, "Leevis" jeans, "Phanasonic" stereos, T-shirts emblazoned with "Property of the New York Yankees Football Club," and so on. If this bazaar had been in the West, there would have been more trademark lawyers here than shoppers. As it was, everyone seemed either blissfully unaware of the fraud or a party to it.

I walked past a tent doing a brisk business selling the infamous Royal vodka. This dirt-cheap liquor, a 99-proof concoction made in underground Belarusian stills with little regard for hygiene, could be fatal. I'd read warnings in Polish newspapers to stay clear of the smuggled stuff because over fifty people had already died drinking it. Judging by the line of customers clamoring for it, somebody was getting very rich off the unsafe spirit. Oddly enough, statistics showed that Poles were drinking less and less hard liquor, especially during weekdays, now that they could actually get fired from their jobs. Still, Royal had its hard-core following.

The sheer magnitude of Warsaw's market was overwhelming. Twelve kilometers of stalls—four thousand in all, employing twenty-five thousand people—snaked their way around the stadium, which drew crowds of up to a million foreign shoppers a month. The stalls were divided into ethnic sectors. The Chinese and Vietnamese traders occupied the lower levels where consumer electronics were sold, while the Turks, one floor up, specialized in inexpensive clothing. Poles ran about half the stalls on the upper levels, where heavily guarded currency-exchange booths stood next to smoky barbecues on which grilled sausage smoldered unappetizingly. They hawked furniture, computers, toys, and all sorts of chinaware and cooking implements.

The least desirable and cheapest spots were rented to the Russians. They huddled in felt boots and padded pea jackets on the arena's windy cement crown, just above the bleacher seats, peddling everything from tarnished utensils to authentic icons, army binoculars, used sneakers, canned meats, and inflatable rafts of dubious seaworthiness. Whatever hadn't been nailed down in the former Soviet Union was available here at cut-rate prices. And what wasn't officially displayed could also be procured. "Are you looking for anything in particular?" asked some of the more shifty-looking traders, eyes darting towards suspicious bulges in their pockets. "Maybe something for protection?" they would suggest, fingering a bullet or two.

The Russians also had two mobile homes set up in the parking lot. In front of these old and dented caravans long, impatient lines had formed. A few toughs kept things orderly and collected money from clients. As I approached, it quickly became apparent what was on sale inside: ten dollars bought a shot of vodka and fifteen mechanical minutes with an exhausted young lady who typically called herself Marta or Irena.

The tension in the market was enormous. Everyone haggled hotly and angrily; in the distant and impoverished lands where most of the traders came from, even a dollar made a difference. I watched a Vietnamese seller and a Russian-speaking man fiercely hammer figures on small calculators that they thrust in each other's faces, bargaining over the price of a portable television in the common language of numbers. Almost everyone had a calculator, and more than a few stallkeepers kept large metal rods within arm's reach, in case negotiations broke down.

The shuttle trade was a magnet for criminals. Undercover Polish policemen had recently nabbed a ring of hitmen who operated out of the stadium, charging five hundred dollars for contract killings. There had also been a rash of stabbings at the market over the winter and two shootouts between rival Russian gangs. In exchange for safe passage to and from Russia, mafia groups extorted 15 percent of the value of goods transported by the post-Soviet traders. This was called a "road tax." Border guards and customs agents unofficially levied another 10 percent off the top, which they called "facilitation fees."

"Things were getting a little out of hand," confessed Bogdan Tomaszewski, the market's founder, when I went to see him after touring the stalls. "Initially, the Russian gangs only preyed on traders from the former Soviet Union. But they got greedy and started to go after Poles too. So the police assigned seventy permanent officers to the stadium, and I've hired one hundred private security guards to keep out the gangs. Now they attack the buses and trains going back to Russia, but pretty much stay away from here."

Tomaszewski, a bull of a man with a heaving belly and forearms the size of my thighs, looked like the sort of tough customer that even hardened Russian gangsters would think twice before crossing. He was also brutally frank, which I appreciated since no one at the market had agreed to talk to me—one leather-jacketed gent even becoming most unpleasant after noticing that I'd taken his picture.

"Welcome to the *dziki wschod*," Tomaszewski chuckled, using the Polish expression for the Wild East. "This place is really the world's biggest business school. I've got a million students from the former Soviet Union learning all about capitalism and profit. Most are factory workers and schoolteachers and engineers, honest people who are trying to improve their lot in life. But there are always a few troublemakers. These we strongly encourage to leave in a language they understand."

Tomaszewski had become a keen student of the former Soviet Union and said he could see the changes there through different trends at the stadium. "For instance," he explained, "there is more hard currency in Russia now than there was a year ago. Traders last year all came here to sell crap and buy dollars to bring home. Hell," Tomaszewski snorted, "they were taking so many dollars out of Poland that the Central Bank was getting worried that it would throw off monetary policy. Now the majority of Russians come with dollars to buy electronic goods and clothes. Also they're buying in bigger quantities: fifty shirts or dresses at a time, instead of three, which makes me think they're supplying stores in Moscow or Nizhny Novgorod and not peddling on the street like they used to. What we are beginning to see is the creation of more sophisticated distribution networks in Russia, like we now have in Poland."

Tomaszewski said his market, which he estimated grossed $2 billion a year in total sales and netted him $35 million in stall rentals, filled a niche that would close as Russia's economy matured and fewer people engaged in petty trading. "If Poland is an example, the shuttle trade in Russia should be over in two, maybe three years. By then, people will all have opened stores and will order directly from local wholesalers and distributors—and I'll have to think up another way to make a buck."

Tomaszewski's prophecy had come to pass. By the late 1990s, the Warsaw stadium was a shadow of its former self, Russians no longer needing to make the long trek. Not only did Muscovites own swanky shops and place orders with local distributors via computer, but now, in a complete reversal that even Tomaszewski could not have foreseen, it was Westerners who shuttled into Moscow to earn fast money.

And the trend went far beyond bankers and accountants, as I was startled to discover one evening while getting into the elevator in our apartment building.

There, standing next to me in a long dark camel-hair coat, was the actor Gabriel Byrne. Next to him, wearing brown suede pants, stood Julia Ormond, whom I had just seen play Brad Pitt's love interest in some flimsy frontier film whose plot and title have since escaped me.

"Are you—?" I started asking.

Byrne cut me off with a bored nod.

"Then you must be—"

Ormond nodded in turn, managing a weak, rehearsed smile.

I shook my head, flabbergasted.

"Four, please," said Byrne.

I dutifully pulled shut the ancient grille and pressed the floor key, all the while wondering what on earth these two were doing in my elevator, in the middle of Moscow. As it turned out, Ormond was in town filming a Russian-produced epic called *The Barber of Siberia*. In the movie, corrupt nineteenth-century American timber merchants try to deforest the tundra, pillage Russia's resources, and prey on the innocence of the good Russian people. Ormond played an American prostitute sent to Moscow (there's a fresh twist) to seduce a noble and kind Russian aristocrat opposed to Western exploitation. The film, which proved to be a hit, had a whopping $45 million budget, far and away the biggest in the history of Russian cinema, which explained why the director could afford to hire Hollywood actors to play the heavies.

All of Hollywood, in fact, seemed to be discovering the lure of easy Moscow money. Arnold Schwarzenegger and Sylvester Stallone opened a Planet Hollywood restaurant near the metropolitan zoo. Chuck Norris, the aging Texas Ranger, lent his name to a casino at the foot of a Stalin skyscraper. Michael Jackson did his gloved thing for enraptured Russian children, who remained blissfully unaware of the King of Pop's PR problems back home. Liza Minnelli had Muscovites dancing in the aisles of the Kremlin auditorium, paving the way for lucrative reunion concerts by a slew of has-been heavy-metal bands from the 1970s whose members I had thought long dead.

And then there was that blasted brooding romantic, Ralph

Fiennes, whose untimely visit to Moscow occasioned my first fight with Roberta. Fiennes was filming an independent adaptation of Aleksandr Pushkin's *Eugene Onegin,* and in between shooting had decided to do a few performances of a Chekhov play at a Moscow theater. Roberta, like much of Moscow's female population, had become most agitated at the prospect of seeing him live, and had asked me to use my press credentials to get tickets. Alas, my head was swimming with the complexities of a baffling story on syndicated loans and, preoccupied with pleasing the foreign editor in New York, I had missed the deadline for seats. A most unpleasant scene followed this omission, and on the last night of the performance I found myself haggling with a scalper outside the doors of the theater. I was on the verge of atoning for my sin, painfully counting out two hundred and fifty dollars for two tickets, when a mafia princess teetered up on six-inch spiky boots.

"How much?" she chirped to the scalper, opening her designer purse before the man even answered.

"*Prodano!*" I protested. "They're already sold!" Unfazed, the mafia moll whipped out four one-hundred-dollar bills. The scalper shot me a questioning look to see if I wanted to up the bidding, but four hundred bucks to see some scruffy guy stumble through his lines struck me as steep. Defeated, I turned away, dreading the inevitable discord. Sure enough, Roberta, standing a few paces behind, was fixing me with a wrathful gaze. As penance, I was forced to watch *The English Patient* twice in a row, a major hardship for a loather of romantic films.

Roberta's ire was compounded when she discovered that Gretchen had gotten front-row seats to the performance. Gretchen and Boris had moved to Moscow shortly after the summons from Nemtsov, and had taken up residence in a suite at the capital's most exclusive hotel, the German-run Kempinski, across the river from St. Basil's Cathedral and Red Square. This was where Bill Gates stayed when he came to town to inquire about reconfiguring old missiles to cheaply launch low-orbiting satellites for Teledesic, his "Internet in the sky."

We saw little of Boris in his early days in Moscow. The *Journal,* naturally, had become very interested in the young banker since Nemtsov appointed him to overhaul Russia's huge and hugely corrupt electricity sector. To turn the retrograde sector around, Nemtsov needed to surround himself with trusted allies, and he was noticeably short on friends in Moscow. That's where Boris came into the picture. The two natives of Nizhny went way back. Plus, Boris had some pertinent qualifications; he had studied electrical engineering in college, and as a banker was familiar with finance. What's more, his marriage to a prominent American and his knowledge of English would prove useful in dealing with international investors. To be sure, he was a tad youthful at 29, but that could be an asset in an industry dominated by Soviet dinosaurs.

As the new head of Unified Energy Systems of Russia—the mammoth electric-power producer that acted like a ministry and was the country's second largest company—Boris had entered the lofty leagues of such oligarchs as Oneximbank's Vladimir Potanin or Boris Berezovsky. Our editors had instructed us to place the young banker-cum-electricity tsar at the center of our radar screen, but I managed to disqualify myself from the assignment on the grounds of Roberta's friendship with Gretchen. VSO also owned nearly 1 percent of UES, as the energy conglomerate was generally called, and Roberta was looking at a joint VSO-UES deal in Moldova. I used this additional conflict of interest to beg off writing about electricity, which was only marginally more interesting to me than syndicated loans. I did, however, use my connections to arrange an interview for my colleague Betsy. A stipulation of that interview was that Roberta and I attend. Boris was unaccustomed to the Western media and wanted a few friendly faces around.

The four of us met in the Kempinski's sunny and well-appointed lobby bar. The place was crawling with I-bankers in leisure wear, that is to say navy blazers, monogrammed button-down shirts, penny loafers, and the weekend edition of the *Financial Times*. Some looked a little bleary-eyed, doubtless the price of a late night of number-crunching at the Metelitsa Casino. Outside, half a dozen Microsoft banners flapped in the stiff breeze, having been run up the hotel's flagpoles next to the German and Russian standards in honor of the inflated bill the Microsoft delegation was accruing.

Boris arrived punctually at one. Unlike most Russians, he was very Anglo-Saxon about such things. He ordered a freshly squeezed orange juice, leaving out the vodka, also very un-Russian. I asked for the house's best scotch, a double since this was my day off and we were on Betsy's expense account. Betsy and Boris fell into a lengthy discussion on the paradoxes of the post-Soviet electricity market, an open sore on the country's path to reform. Boris had the tough brief of cleaning up the world's largest and most corrupt electricity generator, a company where millions of dollars went missing daily. UES was a black hole sucking the life out of the economy, ground zero of Russia's money problems. Enterprises frequently didn't pay their electricity bills in Russia. As a result, everyone—factories, municipal governments, hospitals—owed money to UES, which in turn owed money to coal mines, which in turn couldn't pay their miners, who in turn beseeched Nemtsov, who in turn badgered UES in vain to settle its outstanding tax bills. Boris's job was to break this vicious circle of debt, to force deadbeat factories to pay up by cutting off their power—which was easier said than done, given that closing down the factories would wreak havoc in many one-industry towns.

When enterprises did pay their power bills, they paid in barter, claiming cash shortages. UES collected a mind-boggling 88 percent of its revenues in grain, timber, cement, sugar, spirits, tires, tractors, combine harvesters, cotton, cutlets, doors, dead-bolts, and even the occasional batch of dildos from a beleaguered former defense plant near Vladivostok. In turn, UES used the barter goods to pay its coal bills. Just imagine dumbfounded coal miners somewhere in provincial Russia puzzling over the twelve-inch oblong, rubbery objects they received instead of rubles that month.

This perverse system, said Boris, had been allowed to continue because factory managers made certain that plenty of cash changed hands at private get-togethers with UES officials in expensive restaurants all over Russia. Boris was supposed to put an end to all this nonsense, and started by turning down a million-dollar bribe in his first week on the job.

Another pricey double scotch lifted me ever so gently above the table talk of UES's antiquated transformer stations, stretched gridloads, sketchy accounting practices, soaring stock prices and prospects of issuing convertible bonds. My thoughts wandered to Gretchen and how married life was treating her. Rumor was that Boris, while doting, could be a little possessive, in the vein of many traditional

Russian men. For instance, he had provided Gretchen with a cell phone without telling her the number and left instructions for her to carry it on her person at all times so that only he could reach her. Boris also didn't approve of his wife working and so Gretchen had resigned as the chief financial officer of the paper mill in Nizhny that she had helped to privatize, and was concentrating on such wifely duties as getting pregnant. For Roberta and some of the other young expat women in Moscow who looked upon Gretchen as a feminist role model, this was all somewhat disconcerting.

In a chauvinist part of the world where companies routinely placed ads in newspapers stipulating that candidates for secretarial work should be young, pretty, and *"bez inhibitsii*—without inhibitions," bridging the gender gap was an uphill struggle for executives like Roberta and Gretchen. Roberta, in fact, had trouble getting into the Kempinski at night. On more than one occasion the establishment's doormen barred her entry, presuming that an attractive, unescorted woman arriving after dark had to be a hard-currency hooker. Only after she produced her U.S. passport and let fly with choice invective would they step aside. It was the same at some business meetings. "No, I'm not the fucking *translator,*" she was wont to growl.

So when I finally managed to invite the most successful businesswoman in the former Soviet bloc to our office for tea, nearly a year after I had started badgering her for an interview, Roberta insisted on dropping by the bureau to catch a glimpse of her. My mother happened to be in town visiting, and she too wanted a peek at the woman who was beating men at their own game.

The first thing my mother and Roberta noticed upon arriving at our office building was two huge black Mercedes limousines blocking our entrance. Milling around the giant Mercs were half a dozen alert men with walkie-talkies whom my mother later described as "East German swimming champions": blond, blue-eyed, and very impressively chiseled, like Rodin sculptures with pistol holsters. Two more supermen stood, arms folded across their rippling chests, right outside the *Journal's* office on the sixteenth floor.

"Very cold, impersonal eyes," my mother commented. "The way those bodyguards looked at us reminded me of the Gestapo in Warsaw during the Occupation, as if we weren't human."

"Yes," Roberta agreed. "But you have to admit, they're very cute."

Julia Timoshenko kept a total of twenty-two bodyguards on her payroll, all former *Spetznaz* commandos, graduates of the Red Army's most elite killing academy.

"I'm so terribly sorry about the security," Timoshenko apologized with genuine embarrassment when we shook hands, after my mother and Roberta had retreated to the *Journal*'s waiting room. "I've told them to remain outside."

She was a disarmingly beautiful woman, delicate-looking next to her commandos. There was nothing tacky or *novy russky* about Timoshenko. She wore only a hint of makeup, a dark, conservatively cut Chanel suit and unobtrusive pearls that (Roberta said) would have set me back a year's salary. Her hair was auburn, her lips crimson, and she had eyes the color of the sea.

My records indicated she was either thirty-six or thirty-four, depending on which entry one believed. The file on her was maddeningly thin, consisting of a few rumpled Ukrainian press clippings of dubious veracity and a number, underlined twice and adorned with large question marks. The number was $11,000,000,000, the gross revenue of Timoshenko's virtually unknown Ukrainian company. Only two other corporations in the former Soviet bloc, the partly privatized Gazprom and UES (if you counted all the dildos and sugar sacks it accepted as payment), could claim higher revenue. Not even Coca-Cola earned that much from its combined international sales.

How did she do it? I was still confused. Timoshenko was willing to explain, but it would take some time, she said, for me to fully comprehend how her company functioned. Unfortunately she was only in Moscow for a few hours and was already running late for her appointment with Gazprom's CEO. Could we have lunch later in the week? I quickly agreed.

"Good," she smiled. "It's all set then. I'll send the plane for you."

Plane?

"You can fly down to Dnepropetrovsk in the morning, and the jet will bring you back to Moscow by six."

I tried not to sound over-eager. "I can catch a commercial flight. I don't want to tie up your company plane."

"Don't worry," laughed Timoshenko. "I have four of them."

The VIP lounge at Moscow's Vnukovo airport was housed in a separate building, away from the jostling baggage handlers and lingering body odor that pervaded the main terminal. It was cozy and carpeted, and softly lit so that the smoke from my cigarette swirled beneath the halogen lamps over the polished bar. It was a Saturday and the only other passengers were two impatient Russian oil executives. They fidgeted over cognac and coffee and kept asking when the Lukoil jet would finish fueling.

A passport-control official came over to the bar and courteously stamped my multiple-entry Russian visa. "We are ready for you now," he said politely, pointing to a white minivan that had pulled up outside the lounge.

As we drove along the tarmac, passing a gigantic Antonov cargo plane whose hold gaped open like the mouth of a feeding whale, a sparkling apparition came into view. It was Timoshenko's jet. Its underbelly was painted gold, as was the lettering on the sleek dark-blue fuselage. The letters formed the words Unified Energy Systems of Ukraine, in English on side and in Ukrainian on the other. On the tailfin, rays of a painted sun formed a golden halo around the fiery UESU logo.

"Have a nice flight," sang the van driver, in what was rapidly becoming a day of unparalleled Slavic hospitality. I was beginning to enjoy being a Very Important Person. This was a far more pleasant way of getting to Ukraine than when I had first moved there as a stringer for the *Journal*. Then, the financial constraints of my lowly position had necessitated schlepping all my belongings on the train from Warsaw to Kiev, a hellish twenty-two-hour journey. At the border at 3:00 A.M., the train was lifted wagon by wagon and deposited with a clang on the wider Soviet gauge. Needless to say, I didn't get much sleep, especially after the entrance of Ukrainian customs officials who, on seeing my overstuffed bags, mistook me for a *chelnok* shuttle trader. To get them off my back, I ended up "donating" half my reserve of fax paper to the customs house, which apparently had run out of everything.

The flight attendant greeted me at the foot of the gangway. She was blonde and blowsy, and had obviously been instructed to be accommodating. Somewhere in the baser recesses of my mind, I wondered how far she might be prepared to go. One heard stories about what went on in Russian corporate jets, and they tended to be sala-cious. The stewardess escorted me to my seat, leading the way with her hips, and I slid gratefully into the rich leather. I noted with sat-isfaction that it swiveled in a 180-degree arc that afforded me an ex-cellent view out of the porthole and the benefit of a wide walnut dining table. Across the aisle, a sofa sprawled, and the air hostess perched seductively on its lip as she offered a choice of preflight beverages and cocktails from the jet's well-stocked galley.

The last time a Dnepropetrovsk siren had been dispatched to as-sist me, my host's motivations were unmistakably malign. It was in the fall of 1996, when I had arrived in town to interview the mayor. The night before I was to meet the city boss, his interpreter called my ho-tel room. She said her name was Olga and that she needed to see me.

"What for?" I asked.

"I want to hear you speak to see if I understand your accent. Sometimes Americans speak in accents I do not know. I have been trained in British English," she added proudly.

"You seem to understand me just fine."

"No, we must talk for practice, for me to get the way you speak before you meet the mayor. I will come to your room now."

"No, no, no," I protested, my experience with Bun and Buzz still fresh. "I'll come down to the lobby."

Olga was a busty brunette. She had doubtlessly been a head-turner during the *perestroika* days, but her radiance had faded some-what in the post-communist period. She overcompensated with copious amounts of mascara and blush.

"You are younger than I thought," she said to me in the lobby, with what I detected was a touch of disappointment—and envy.

We repaired to the little hotel restaurant. "Would you like a cof-fee?" I asked.

"*Shampanskoye*," she called out to a waiter, whose worn tuxedo jacket ended about four inches above his sleeves, revealing a pair of thick, hairy wrists. She had ordered a bottle of sweet Crimean cham-pagne—seven dollars at the current exchange rates. When it arrived and I declined the syrupy stuff, she expressed wounded astonish-ment and told the gorilla-waiter to bring a half-liter of vodka.

"You drink vodka, no?"

I confessed that I did.

"You will tell me about yourself," she said imperiously, when the vodka had arrived and the waiter had been upbraided for not bringing pickles, the traditional Russian chaser to vodka shots.

I must confess that I was starting to enjoy myself; there was something theatrical and endearingly clumsy about this faded femme fatale. But I was still suspicious. I had just published a lengthy exposé on corruption in Ukraine, and the official shaking down of American investors there, in the *Journal*. The piece had caused an uproar in the U.S. Congress, and not long afterwards the House of Representatives passed a motion threatening to cut a hundred million dollars of aid to Kiev if the investment climate did not improve. The reaction to the article had naturally infuriated the cash-strapped Ukrainian government, and President Kuchma had taken to complaining about me publicly, even suggesting that I was being paid by the Russians to drive a wedge between the United States and Ukraine. No doubt the mayor of Dnepropetrovsk had been apprised of my poisoned pen, and I wondered if Olga had been sent to uncover my intentions or, worse, compromise me—a hackneyed trick straight out of the old Soviet playbook.

Olga polished off the *shampanskoye* remarkably quickly, as if she was getting soused to ease the pain of an unpleasant task ahead. I noticed that the top two buttons of her blouse had mysteriously come undone, so that when she leaned forward I was assaulted by a veritable mountain of cleavage. Frankly, it was not an entirely unpleasant landscape, one that brought grazing to mind.

A hairy wrist ruined the picture, plunking down another bottle of champagne and a second decanter of vodka. "On the house," the gorilla declared morosely. This was a most interesting development. Hotels did not buy drinks for one-time patrons as a matter of course. But the Oktiabrskaya, where I was staying, was the former Communist Party inn, now owned not-so-coincidentally by the hospitable Dnepropetrovsk municipal government.

Olga was well into her second bottle, and appeared a little flushed for the effort. I'm not certain what my face must have been like, for another button had popped open, and she seemed to be spilling, unbridled, out onto the table and pickle jar.

"It is no good here," breathed Olga, with that husky intonation that Russian women are famed for. "Everyone is listening."

I looked around. The only other diners were a snuggling young couple in the throes of what seemed like a promising first date and a lone American pensioner whom I had met on the flight down from Kiev. He was a volunteer for the International Executive Service Corps, a sort of Peace Corps for retired executives who imparted their accumulated business knowledge in exchange for a taste of adventure in the developing world.

"We have no, how you say, private, here," complained Olga.

"Privacy."

"Yes, privacy, no. We go room. Talk there."

Olga's English was deteriorating as rapidly as my judgment. Another shot and I would be in serious trouble with Roberta, whom I had just begun dating. Some hotel rooms, I'd been told by U.S. diplomats, were wired not only for audio but video as well, and I could imagine Roberta scowling over grainy footage of my reporting trip, courtesy of the mayor's office and its bureau of interpreters. Alarm bells started ringing. Then I saw an escape.

"Let's talk to my friend over there."

The old Service Corps guy was delighted to have company. Olga fumed, her nefarious assignment foiled.

With those sobering recollections, I turned my attentions from the flight attendant and dug out my yellow legal pad. We had lifted off without incident and reached cruising altitude. While the hostess brought coffee and an ashtray, I reviewed my notes from my first brief interview with Julia Timoshenko.

The beauteous entrepreneur had explained how she first went into business in late 1990, obtaining, through her father-in-law, two videocassette recording machines. He managed the movie houses of Dnepropetrovsk for the Communist Party, and therefore had access to imported VCRs and hoarded copies of Western movies. Timoshenko set up the two machines in her living room and started copying films. The first picture she pirated was the Sylvester Stallone action drama *Rambo*. *Rambo* turned out to be a huge hit for Timoshenko; entertainment-starved Ukrainians couldn't get enough of Stallone's tough-guy act. Pretty soon she had a dozen VCRs cranking out hundreds of pirated cassettes daily.

The collapse of the Soviet Union presented far greater opportunities for the ambitious Timoshenko, and her cunning father-in-law soon saw bigger ways for the pair to make a buck. Through a Party friend, he arranged for a two-million-dollar loan from a State bank. Timoshenko used the funds to buy gasoline in Russia. At the time, an energy crisis was developing in Ukraine; the old Soviet distribution network had been completely disrupted by the creation of fifteen independent countries, each with its own currencies and customs regulations to snarl inter-republic trade. The gasoline shortage was so great that Timoshenko was able to barter fuel for finished goods on extremely favorable terms. She then shipped the goods to Siberia, where there was a shortage of everything but oil, and repeated the cycle over the next few years.

Along the way, she struck up an alliance with Dnepropetrovsk's regional governor, a wily former collective-farm boss by the name of Pavlo Lazarenko. (This was the very same Lazarenko who would end up in a San Francisco jail, charged with large-scale money laundering and receiving seventy-two million dollars directly from Timoshenko—charges both would deny). Lazarenko had quickly grasped the importance of energy in post-Soviet industry. With inflation raging in the five figures, basically rendering money useless, oil and natural gas replaced hard currency in the industrial sphere. Whoever controlled the source of energy controlled the entire production cycle, particularly since few enterprises could pay their fuel bills. Dnepropetrovsk was the country's industrial center, and thus one of Ukraine's biggest users of energy. Lazarenko granted Timoshenko the provincial energy concession, making her de facto boss of hundreds of state enterprises, which functioned or shut down operations at her whim.

Timoshenko's big break, however, came on the day of my mugging, when Lazarenko was appointed prime minister of Ukraine. One of his first moves in office was to wrest half a dozen lucrative energy concessions from several big private groups and give Timoshenko a nationwide monopoly on the import and distribution of Russian natural gas. Two days later, a bomb rocked his motorcade. Lazarenko miraculously survived the blast with only minor scratches and used the assassination attempt as a pretext to round up Timoshenko's putative rivals and put them out of business.

Thus UESU was born, and Timoshenko gained control over nearly 20 percent of Ukraine's gross national product, an enviable position that probably no other private company in the world could boast. It was not clear what Lazarenko himself gained from his creation. There was wild speculation that Timoshenko was his front, and that the prime minister was benefiting from her largesse to the tune of hundreds of millions of dollars. But when I put these rumors to him during an interview, he placed a big hand on my knee, and with wounded, misty eyes assured me he had "no commercial interests" and was motivated solely by the good of the country.

The UESU plane descended over the endless wheat fields of myriad hundred-thousand-acre collective farms, where dark blotches delineated pastures and large areas where the land had been left fallow. We passed the wide and windy Dniepr River, with its silty banks, coal barges, and rusty suspension bridges. Dnepropetrovsk's grim housing projects and factories appeared under the plane's wing, a sea of smokestacks, blast furnaces, and mile upon mile of flat tar roofs. My amiable hostess buckled up, and the jet's wheels hit the tarmac.

A convoy of expensive automobiles pulled up to the plane: two spotless Mercedes 600s bookended by a pair of burgundy Toyota Land Cruisers with muddy tires and the ubiquitous contingent of shaved-headed goons. Timonshenko's father-in-law emerged from one of the blue sedans and greeted me as effusively as a visiting head of state. He snapped his fingers, and an officer of the Ukrainian border guard jumped forward obsequiously to stamp my passport.

We piled into the Mercedes and sped off without a moment's delay. There was a little sticker in the car's bullet-proof window with the name of a German armoring company. This was comforting, given that a spectacular assassination that had recently taken place at the Donetsk airport in eastern Ukraine. A businessman in oil and alcohol distribution had just returned from a birthday party in Moscow for Yosif Kabzon, Russia's Frank Sinatra, when two police cars drove up to his private jet and opened fire, killing the tycoon, his wife, and several bodyguards. (Ukrainian prosecutors would later accuse Lazarenko of ordering the hit, a charge he would strongly deny from his jail cell in San Francisco.)

Genady Timoshenko was a wizened old guy. He had the hard face of a seafarer, grizzled and alert, and a thick, regal white mane. I guessed that he was in his late sixties, but it was clear that he hadn't lost a step yet.

"Julia has arranged for you to meet some of the factory directors we work with," he said, "so you can understand what it is we do."

Gas distribution, the elder Timoshenko explained, was only the tip of the iceberg for UESU, a springboard for more ambitious undertakings. The company had found a huge and hugely profitable vacuum created by the collapse of Gosplan—the Soviet-era organ that coordinated every move of the command economy. The demise of Gosplan left factory bosses with mountains of inventory and debt and no idea how things worked in the baffling world of capitalism. A typical Soviet enterprise had tens of thousands of employees but no marketing department, and not a single salesman on the payroll. In the past the State had simply supplied all the raw materials and taken the finished goods; there been no need for a sales force. Suddenly factory bosses not only had to find their own suppliers but also develop markets for their products. What's more, their clients and raw materials were often scattered across half a dozen countries. The factory bosses—or Red Directors, as they were sometimes called—were at a complete loss. Production plummeted, and assembly lines ground to a halt.

Enter Timoshenko and UESU. The company instituted a capitalist version of central planning, taking for itself the role of Gosplan. With its crucial control over the first link in the chain of production, the supply of energy, UESU formed an interconnected network of some two thousand companies that relied on it to coordinate the entire industrial process.

I was still trying to digest all this when our motorcade hit a dusty patch of road and we started passing hundreds of old dump trucks. About half the trucks were filled with rubble—heaps of crumbled concrete and cement slabs with twisted reinforcing bars jutting crazily in all directions. The other half had piles of furniture—mattresses, lamps, refrigerators and personal belongings—haphazardly stacked on their flatbeds.

"What happened here?" I asked.

"A tragedy," said the elder Timoshenko. "Two buildings collapsed the day before yesterday. Fifty-four people were killed."

I looked out the tinted window at two giant craters that were all that was left of a pair of fifteen-story buildings. The earth had literally opened and swallowed one up; the other had partially sunk, tilted, and snapped in two.

"They were built on sand without proper foundations." Timoshenko shook his gray head in disgust.

This was an example of the insanity of Gosplan. After the hometown hero Brezhnev ascended the Kremlin throne, Moscow had ordered the construction of dozens of new factories and apartment blocks in Dnepropetrovsk. The builders were so preoccupied with filling those sacred quotas that no one bothered to conduct geotechnical surveys to determine whether anchoring pylons needed to be driven into the soft soil. Fifty-four people had now been buried alive as a consequence, hundreds more left homeless.

We sped past the long line of trucks and arrived at a sooty, nondescript structure with an institutional feel. This was UESU corporate headquarters. The lobby was rancid and smelled of disinfectant. It was filled with dying potted plants and posters from the down-on-its-luck metallurgical institute to which the building belonged. A notice board by the bank of elevators featured a yellowed placard informing people what to do in case of a nuclear attack.

"We just moved in," apologized the elder Timoshenko. "We haven't had time to redo the entrance yet."

Commercial office space was apparently nonexistent in Dnepropetrovsk, and burgeoning companies tended to rent buildings from cash-strapped schools or the local government. (Once again VSO had shown itself to be ahead of the curve; the modern office complex Mordechai had financed in the center of town was finished now, and rented out at stratospheric monthly rates.)

We took a wobbly elevator from the dingy lobby to the fifth floor. As soon as the door rattled open, I found myself transported to another world. I stepped out onto plush carpeting and felt the refreshing chill of air conditioning. It was as if I'd magically emerged on the uppermost levels of a Manhattan skyscraper. The trappings of a prosperous and well-oiled money machine surrounded me.

A covey of four secretaries and a matching brace of bodyguards roosted outside Julia Timoshenko's office—and this was just the day shift. She employed four more secretarial assistants, who worked around the clock so that there was always someone manning the phone in case of emergencies—of which, I had the feeling, there was no shortage at UESU.

Timoshenko looked tired when she came around her massive mahogany desk to extend a dainty hand. She seemed particularly fragile in her cavernous office, a mail-order executive suite that must have arrived complete with furniture, decor, and wood paneling in a shipping container, just like the instant Irish pubs in Moscow and Kiev and Riga. To be sure, Timoshenko had added a few personal touches. A huge Gazprom map of the former Soviet Union took up one wall. It was crisscrossed by pipeline routes and dotted with little red blinking lights to denote the location of pumping stations. In a place of honor, over her high-backed chair, Timoshenko had hung a gilded photograph of that great patriot and patron, the worthy Pavlo Lazarenko.

Tea was served. We sipped from fine bone-china cups and resumed our discussion. UESU was the second largest buyer of Russian natural gas after Germany. The company imported over twenty-four billion cubic meters of the stuff, enough to heat all of France for a whole winter. What was fascinating about the transaction was the ingenious way UESU paid Gazprom for energy deliveries, through a maze of barter deals that was virtually impossible to follow. For instance, Timoshenko had just returned from a meeting with the Russian Defense Ministry, where she had struck a deal to deliver uniforms for the army. The military fatigues were sewn at a Ukrainian factory that UESU supplied with electricity. The factory paid UESU with uniforms, which UESU sent to Moscow as part of its obligations to Gazprom. Since Gazprom owed the Kremlin billions in back taxes, the gas behemoth used the uniforms to write down some of its debt to the Russian government, which grudgingly accepted the fatigues as payment because its military budget was bankrupt. The key question, of course, and one on which I was not able to get any straight answer, was how much did Gazprom charge the Kremlin in tax alleviation for each uniform? It is a safe bet to venture that UESU's uniforms were among the world's shoddiest and most expensive, and that the beleaguered Russian government came out much the worse from the deal.

"There is always opportunity in times of crisis," Timoshenko modestly commented. "Our niche is targeting the most troubled organizations, those that are desperate to work on any terms in our system. I believe this is the essence of capitalism."

The robber baroness had a point. She was simply taking advantage of the insane system that masqueraded as the post-communist economy.

Lunch was ready. Timoshenko had summoned a dozen local factory bosses for the repast, and we filed into a large conference room where little Ukrainian and American flags had been placed on the table in my honor. I did not have the heart to let on that I was actually born and raised sixty miles north of the U.S. border.

I shook hands with the assembled factory chiefs—every last one sporting a Brillo-pad pompadour of greasy gray hair, a boxy, shiny suit, and a thick gold watch—and we exchanged business cards in Japanese fashion. The calling cards ranged from gaudy (raised gilt lettering on a purple background) to ridiculous (plastic laminated with a color photograph of the bearer). Over three courses, vodka toasts, and a speech by the elder Timoshenko, I was able to glean a smattering of insights into how UESU's vaunted "system" worked for three local enterprises.

Before teaming up with Timoshenko, Alexander Stankov had nothing but headaches. The general director of the Inguletsky State Mining and Concentration Plant, an iron-ore quarry and processing facility in central Ukraine, Stankov said power brownouts were a weekly occurrence. The plant couldn't pay for the $5.5 million of electricity it used monthly because it was only getting paid for 30 percent of its sales. Production was down 60 percent from 1991 levels.

Now UESU gave the plant electricity on credit and bought its iron-concentrate powder, which it used to make cast-iron ingots, paying cash. The plant used the cash to repay UESU for the electricity. Production had increased by 25 percent since the mine hooked up with UESU. "Without Timoshenko we wouldn't survive," gushed Stankov.

UESU took Stankov's powder concentrate to the Petrovsky Metallurgical Plant, along the way supplying the energy needed for Petrovsky to smelt the powder into ingots and rolled steel. Timoshenko then shipped the steel sheets to the Novomoskovsk Pipe Production Works, where, using UESU gas, they were formed into large-diameter tubes that Timoshenko peddled to Gazprom's pipeline-construction company. "We've doubled production since we started working with UESU," cooed the Novomoskovsk boss, Anatoly Melnik.

While the factory bosses were quick to heap praise on Timoshenko, they were not so eager to discuss the financial details of their arrangements with UESU. My guess was that Timoshenko charged an absolute fortune to front the energy and inputs (raw materials) and paid little for the outputs (finished products), a usurious practice known in the industry as "tolling." In tolling, factories are run into the ground by trading companies who more often than not have no ownership stake in the enterprises they exploit. When the equipment breaks down, the traders simply move on to the next plant. The directors that I met all had Rolexes and silver Cartier pens. Trained quota-fillers, they cared only about production figures and not whether their plants were bleeding horribly because they were selling their finished goods at below the price it had cost to produce them—for UESU's benefit.

A Ukrainian parliamentary inquiry had been outraged to find that on eleven billion dollars in total sales in 1996, UESU had not paid a single kopek in taxes. Timoshenko had demurred, with a straight face, that she was nonetheless making a lasting contribution to Ukrainian welfare by personally supporting two orphanages in Dnepropetrovsk.

As I boarded yet another UESU jet for the return flight to Moscow, I was disappointed to discover that the flight attendant on duty this time was built like a linebacker.

In my absence my fish tank had begun to mirror post-Soviet society in alarming ways. Two of my swordfish and a gentle guppy had disappeared. We restocked the aquarium, checked the floor around the tank for dried-up jumpers, and put a snug lid over the aquarium. The fish kept vanishing. Those that remained hid, as if terrorized— all except for a stout pair of black-striped cichlids, which one of the fish breeders had talked us into buying. These swam about as if they owned the tank. And, we couldn't help but notice, the more depleted our aquarium became the fatter they grew.

CHAPTER SEVEN

Caviar Dreams

Wednesday was car-theft night on television. Like everyone else watching in Russia—a good many people, judging by the program's runaway ratings—I always rooted for the bad guys. The show came on at nine, and was sponsored by the makers of LoJack, a new automotive security system that used implanted homing beacons to allow the police to track stolen vehicles through transmitted radio signals. The premise was simple: The thief was given a fifteen-minute head start, and for the rest of the program, the cops tracked him down. If by the time the hour had elasped the crook had managed to elude his pursuers, he got to keep the vehicle and received a cash prize.

At the start of the show the star was introduced, to a pounding musical accompaniment, and his credentials were breathlessly enumerated—that is, the highlights from his rap sheet scrolled down the screen. A map of Moscow was next shown, detailing the location of his heist, the starting point of the competition. In map form, Moscow resembles an old oak, with a core, growth rings and an irregular bark-like perimeter. In the dense heartwood of the capital sits the *Kreml* or "fortress." Around the Kremlin's brick battlements, ring roads ripple like a series of protective moats.

The first ring is a tightly wound loop encompassing the oldest Muscovy settlements around Red and Manezh squares and Kitaigorod, or Chinatown, the district that takes its name from the Chinese traders restricted to its walled confines in the fifteenth century. Three hundred years later, Peter the Great installed his imported

German and Dutch engineers in the quarter to keep Western influences from spreading unchecked among his subjects.

A few blocks out from this historic first band runs a second, cobblestoned ring road, the stately Boulevard Ring, built over the seventeenth-century fortifications that hemmed in the aristocratic Clean Ponds neighborhood, the old Ukrainian and Armenian quarters, and the Theater district where Roberta and I lived.

Still further out, atop the earthen ramparts that once ringed the mud hovels of Earth Town, sprawls a perversely named Stalinist creation, the traffic-choked and treeless Garden Ring, an eight-lane inner beltway lined with ponderous prewar high-rises.

Closing out Moscow's orbital defenses is the massive MKAD, the new seventy-mile superhighway that circles the capital's soulless suburbs. The MKAD was the LoJack show's boundary; car thieves had to stay within its confines. That, and the time limit, were pretty much the only rules on the program. The producers apparently wanted to keep it as simple and spontaneous as possible.

A small studio audience watched the contest in a televised screening room, their gasps, whoops, and cheers punctuating the thief's every sideswipe, near miss, and traffic violation. Cameras placed inside the vehicles and in chase cars followed the high-speed action, the swerves into oncoming traffic, the red lights blown, the crunching collisions. Had the show been filmed in the United States, the lawsuits would have been the most spectacular part of the program. But thankfully this was Russia, where the court system lacked sufficient bite to interfere with our viewing pleasure.

In one of my favorite episodes, the car thief outwitted the cops, to the tremendous delight and admiration of the studio audience. The ingenious felon had driven a "stolen" Hyundai—the Korean carmaker was another of the show's sponsors—up a ramp and onto the flatbed of a dump truck. Accomplices threw a net over the Hyundai and covered it with trash. And though the police zeroed in on the beacon and repeatedly circled the truck, the audience sucking in their breath with every pass, in the end the baffled officers gave up, thinking the LoJack had malfunctioned.

Guffaws erupted from the studio audience as the pursuers, with one final curse and frustrated thump of the fist on their dashboard, drove off in defeat. Authority had been thwarted; the police, still the personification of the all-powerful State for most Russians, had come away looking hapless and human. As I had already discovered, the Moscow police were not very highly esteemed by the citizenry, due as much to the high bribes cops extracted as to the low number of crimes they solved. In fact, the police were a favored butt of jokes in Russia—in much the same way that we poor Poles used to be one-liner fodder in America.

The Moscow Police Department was also the unwitting patsy of another popular television series, *Criminal Chronicles*, which was loosely modeled on *Cops*, a perennially popular show on the Fox channel in the States. *Cops* reverently follows law-enforcement officials throughout America as they chase real suspects, arrest drug dealers, and break up domestic disputes while, in a voice-over narration, a preachy has-been actor admonishes viewers that crime never pays. The Russian version eschewed arrests in favor of gory crime scenes. Perhaps for lack of footage of Moscow's men in blue actually doing their jobs, the cameras instead focused on mangled corpses: the blown-up businessman; the machine-gunned hotelier; the garroted prostitute; the bleeding housewife, bludgeoned by her drunken lout of a husband.

Savage closeups gleefully brought the horror to life. Whether it was the rape victim's torn panties, hanging bloodily from a shrub; the white-hot pinkie ring glowing on the charred, barbecued hand hanging out of the exploded Mercedes; or the yellow stains left on the carpet by the decomposing body, no detail escaped the probing camera lens. And there was no shortage of corpses, either. With nearly eighteen hundred murders committed in the capital in 1997 (three times as many as in New York that year), the show's producers didn't want for grisly material.

Television mirrors the prevailing culture. Indeed, as I write these words America is steeped in the great Internet lottery, and the highest-rated television show rhetorically asks *Who Wants To Be A Millionaire?* In Russia during the late 1990s, outlaw culture ruled the airwaves, just as organized crime lorded it over society.

Russians seemed to have developed a morbid fascination with the violent times through which they were living, and television catered to their blood lust with astonishing enthusiasm. Newspapers also helped lead the charge. The financial daily *Kommersant*, for instance, devoted a page to contract killings. And that was just in the business section. *Pravda*, the old communist stalwart daily now owned by Greeks, chronicled the tribulations of a homicidal car-theft gang that had a most original if somewhat excessive modus operandi. The thieves responded to ads in the paper for late-model imports. Posing as buyers, they contacted the sellers and agreed on a price—pending mechanical inspection at a garage they named. Once the unwitting sellers had brought the car to the specified garage, they were strangled, their bodies buried under its cement floor. After the wife of one victim narrowly escaped, police dug up twenty-four corpses at the garage in question. What I couldn't understand was why the crooks didn't just hot-wire the cars. Why go to all that trouble?

Another case that made all the papers took place in Siberia, where a homicidal lunatic enslaved women in an underground sweatshop he had dug under the parking sheds of his apartment building. He chained his victims to sewing machines, tattooed the word "slave" on their foreheads, and ate them after they eventually succumbed to starvation. The story got so much play in Russia that even the *New York Times* sent somebody out to do a piece on "cannibal capitalism."

One reason why crime, and particularly weird crime, received so much attention in the unshackled Russian media was that it had not existed at all—at least officially—in the Soviet era. Under Marxism, there were no serial killers, rapists, or contract killers to write about. Just good communists, striving to meet quotas. So readers had a lot of catching up to do. Besides, cannibalism made better copy than the wheat harvest. Such were the privileges of freedom.

As I got to know Moscow, I hovered uncomfortably between fascination with the capital's seamy attractions and revulsion at the moral hazards those offerings posed. Fortunately Roberta's vigilant presence kept my curiosity from getting me into trouble, especially after we got engaged. The fateful day had come soon after Roberta had sat me down one evening for a rather forceful negotiating session. She was approaching thirty, and the window on her prime child-bearing years was limited. What were my intentions? My evasive answer was apparently unsatisfactory, for she then introduced a business term of art called "opportunity cost"—in this case, the foolishness of wasting time on me if I was not going to be husband material. Her argument, though somewhat wanting on the romantic front, was persuasive. The next thing I knew, we were handing over my life's savings to an old jeweler with a walleye in a dingy, State-owned workshop in Taganka. Municipal Jewelry Factory Number 142, as the workshop was uninspiringly known, was decorated in cobwebs, cigarette butts, and heavy bars. Tiffany's it was not, and I was certain that I would never see my recently acquired nest egg again. But the old jeweler had come highly recommended, and the four-carat ring he produced was sufficiently New Russian in proportions that Roberta's friends looked at me with newfound wonder. Penniless again, I was proud nonetheless; I knew I had just made the best investment of my life.

Once engaged, I was spared from wrestling with a bachelor's demons and lived vicariously through the pages of the *eXile*, Moscow's bawdy answer to New York's Zagat restaurant and nightclub guide.

The *eXile* was published in English weekly, biweekly, or monthly depending on the sobriety and finances of its two young American founders, one of whom was the enfant terrible offspring of a well-known NBC reporter, the other having enjoyed fleeting fame as a professional basketball player in Mongolia. The duo celebrated Moscow's acquired taste for decadence, devoting issue after issue to first-hand accounts of downtown debauchery, the bizarre, and the outlandishly sinful.

For its efforts, the *eXile* had developed a dedicated following among traveling executives, who prized the publication's unusual rating scale for Moscow's most notorious nightspots. These dens of iniquity were judged primarily by twin barometers known as the "flathead" and "scoring" factors. The flathead factor was rated by a little drawing of a scowling goon that looked alarmingly like my old friend Buzz. On a scale of one to five, a rating of four flatheads signified that a particular club was a serious mafia hangout and your chances of getting shot ranged from fair to excellent. You avoided dives rated five flatheads as if your life depended on it, which in fact it did.

The other determinant of a bar or disco's worthiness was the more desirable scoring factor, denoted in the *eXile*'s columns by eye-catching stick figures coupling doggy-style. Five hunched stick figures next to a club's name meant that American males needed only a pulse and a billfold to score there. Readers weighed the scoring factor against the flathead factor to calculate whether the game was worth the candle, as the French used to say before the advent of electricity.

When Roberta and I decided to sample some of Moscow's more immodest nocturnal offerings, we naturally consulted the *eXile*. Initially we set our sights on a club called Chance, a new gay and lesbian haunt that featured nude men swimming in oversized aquariums. This struck me as very nouveau Moscow, which was still a rather old-fashioned town when it came to alternative lifestyles. But some of Roberta's former World Bank colleagues mentioned that the club had been raided by the police, who made patrons lie face down in the parking lot for three hours in the dead of winter. We thus ruled Chance out on the off chance that the police would return.

Next we lit upon the idea of dinner at the Praga. The Praga was one of Moscow's most famous old restaurants. It was located at the foot of Arbat Street, the cobblestoned pedestrian boulevard where Pushkin once lived in an elegant blue townhouse and where artists now peddled *matrioshka* nesting dolls adorned with Yeltsin or Clinton's beaming features. In its heyday at the turn of the century, the Praga had been Moscow's most elegant eatery, a favored luncheon spot where aristocrats and tsarist ministers schmoozed at gilded tables under the dripping splendor of crystal chandeliers. But like St. Petersburg, this symbol of the old order had been neglected during the Soviet era.

I had dined there in 1992, under the gloom of burnt-out light bulbs and peeling wallpaper, in one of the private rooms on the second floor, which I had secured for a measly ten dollars from an ill-tempered doorman with a caveman brow. That meal had been memorable chiefly for the surliness of the staff and the astonishingly unappetizing fare. Ordering had proved a battle of attrition, as every item on the menu was declared unavailable with a peremptory *Niet* from the grubby waiter.

"Well, what *do* you have?" I had finally asked, exasperated.

"*Buterbrody*," the waiter had shot back defiantly. Sandwiches.

In the early 1990s, the Praga—despite its fancy pedigree—was no exception to the three universal communist-bloc restaurant rules; one, even if all the tables were empty you couldn't get in without a bribe; two, they were always closed during peak lunch hour on the perversely logical assumption that the staff had to eat too; and three, you were lucky if anything on the menu was actually available.

I would have not been keen on another visit to the Praga had it not just received a thirty-million-dollar facelift which, I imagined, had painstakingly restored its Old World elegance, silk wall hangings, and rococo plaster work.

Unfortunately the renovation had been a New Russian affair all the way, something out of the baroque, post-Soviet school of kitsch that inexplicably envisioned every building as a Las Vegas casino. The Praga had now been ignobly floodlit in green and pink and festooned with about a mile of hideous flashing purple neon. The neon twisted around a glittering black scorpion whose raised gold stinger was the corporate logo of the Praga's new owners, a shadowy group who traveled in the company of innumerable bodyguards. My inquiries revealed that ten thousand dollars now reserved a table in one of the Praga's private rooms, where hostesses in costumes from Catherine the Great's court had been selected from a pool of two thousand auditioning starlets, and liveried male waiters with powdered wigs and sculpted bare torsos served seven-course meals from solid silver plates.

The new Praga, alas, was a little out of our financial league. Luckily, the *eXile* touted another promising spot not far from our apartment, a place aptly named Night Flight on Tverskaya Street, near Pushkin Square. It offered the triple attraction of a low flathead factor, the full five doggy-style icons, and proximity to our apartment. Roberta and I rounded up a few colleagues and went that same Saturday.

Night Flight, as it turned out, was a house of easy virtues. We figured that out shortly after our arrival, when a flushed Japanese businessman walked into the establishment, and, without even leaving the foyer, picked three women out of the parade of lanky hopefuls, making "I'll take you, you, and you" gestures. Without so much as exchanging a word, the foursome spun on their heels and made for a limousine waiting outside.

"Hell," said a disappointed Roberta. "We didn't have to leave the apartment to see this."

A few hundred yards from our balcony, streetwalkers congregated on Tverskaya under the very arch that Stalin built in the fifties, using the Norwegian granite Hitler had commissioned in 1941, hoping to commemorate his defeat of the Soviet Union. It wasn't just one or two hookers that plied their trade beneath this historic gateway, but dozens upon dozens, standing in neat lines, watched over by vicious-looking pimps who always lurked, unshaven and predatory, behind the curtains of two minivans parked permanently under the arch. Roberta couldn't even go out at night to get cigarettes for fear of being harassed.

Every city has its red-light district, but Tverskaya Street was the equivalent of Fifth Avenue, or the Champs-Elysées. Still, the fact that the oldest profession was so brazen in Moscow, especially in the bars, hotels, and parts of town frequented by foreigners and the new rich, was not surprising. Prostitution, like the image of the *cholniki* petty traders at the Warsaw train station, was a symbol of the East's mad scramble for money during the 1990s, when everything and everybody seemed to be for sale. Pauperized aristocratic White Russian women had danced for pay in the cabarets of Shanghai and Paris in the 1920s after having fled the Bolsheviks, and this wasn't that different. People did whatever they had to in order to survive. During World War II, my grandmother and mother smuggled tobacco leaves (a crime punishable by death during the Nazi Occupation) under their skirts to make ends meet. Now, the old pensioners in Red Square sold their treasured war medals to tourists to scrape by, and the teenage girls and young women outside our building sold themselves.

While prostitution was technically illegal in Russia, it had semiofficial sanction; Night Flight, like the McDonald's down the street and the majority of Moscow's five-star hotels, was partly owned by the city of Moscow. On our corner, the police never arrested patrons. Occasionally, they dropped by to pick up one of the girls, exchanging amiable words with the pimps, and we'd see her get in the back of the police Niva and return an hour or so later after she'd made the payoff in kind.

This spectacle greeted us every night as we came home from work or dinner, until one day in June of 1997 the cops rounded up every streetwalker, homeless *bomzhi* (bum), glue-sniffing teen, and beggar from Tverskaya and dumped them outside the city limits. Moscow was about to celebrate the 850th anniversary of its founding, and its seamier citizens were suddenly less than welcome.

Yuri Luzhkov, Moscow's mayor, had seized on this unlikely date as a pretext to trumpet the city's rebirth as one of the world's great capitals. "The New York of the East," Luzhkov had pronounced his city, except that the Russian incarnation of the Big Apple was known among expats as the Big Cucumber—for the contradiction between Russia's caviar dreams and its pickle budget. Luzhkov's billion-dollar bash would showcase his own contribution to Moscow's remarkable turnaround.

Already a Stalinist-style "cult of personality" shrouded the diminutive, ambitious mayor. He had won reelection in 1996 by a 90-percent landslide that was eerily reminiscent of communism's one-candidate politics; but in this case, the voting had actually been free and fair. The mayor's photograph beamed from the walls of public schools and private businesses alike. And, in one of the oddest tributes of all, a local perfume company—an outfit that in Soviet days had produced fragrances inspired by space hero Yuri Gagarin—had just named a new line of colognes after him.

Luzhkov was an unlikely choice as a pitchman for beauty products. Short, fleshy, and hairless, he looked uncomfortably like a braised turkey after an hour in the oven. The marketing appeal of smelling like a sixty-one-year-old Russian politician escaped me, and so I called the Novaya Zarya perfume factory to inquire about their unusually homely muse.

"Mayor Luzhkov symbolizes the ideal Russian man," cooed factory spokesperson Nadezhda Petrukhina when I put the question to her. "He's responsible and a good provider—a real boss who gets things done."

Moscow was proof of that. Under Luzhkov's firm and not always benevolent hand, the capital had undergone such a transformation that its proud residents bragged that to see Russia, one had to venture outside the MKAD. Which was all fine and good, but even with all Luzhkov's civic achievements he was hardly anyone's idea of a hunk.

"Oh," chided Petrukhina playfully, when I pressed the issue. "I see you don't understand Russian women at all." In these difficult times, she explained, especially outside Moscow, where unemployment ran high and surveys showed that the biggest casualties were women's jobs, a man's appearance was the last thing women were interested in. They wanted stable and hardworking mates who put food on the table.

"The message we're selling," said Petrukhina, "is buy your man *Mer* [Mayor] cologne and maybe he'll put down the vodka and help out around the house for a change."

I decided to put her theory to the test, and on the way home one evening, dropped into a swanky perfumery around the corner from our apartment. The hour was approaching eight o'clock and the sun was low and surprisingly red. At the foot of Tverskaya, against the shadowy backdrop of the Kremlin towers, a gigantic crane hoisted a gilded two-headed eagle with the wingspan of an automobile. The tsarist emblem dangled in the pink sky like a giant Christmas ornament as welders in safety harnesses, looking tiny in the distance, tried to attach it to the tip of the Gothic spire of Moscow's Museum of History. The traditional symbol of imperial Russia was being restored to its rightful perch in time for Moscow's 850th anniversary parade, while the Stalinist star that had crowned the building since the Revolution lay defeated on the back of a flatbed truck.

A large crowd had gathered to watch the switch, and the kiosks, ice-cream vendors, and hot-dog stands that lined the bottom of Tverskaya—in front of Maxim's of Paris, where entrees started at seventy-five dollars and the doorman wore a tailcoat—were doing a brisk business. The perfume shop was a few blocks up the street, across from the Central Post Office and a busy McDonald's. Overhead, crews were stringing up garlands, paper lanterns, and large banners of the sort once used for propaganda slogans. These draped oppressively over Tverskaya, attached at intervals of a hundred yards to the freshly painted buildings on either side. They read: MENATEP

BANK CONGRATULATES MOSCOW. ONEXIMBANK WISHES MUSCOVITES A HAPPY HOLIDAY. LUKOIL CELEBRATES THE GLORIOUS FOUNDING OF THE RUSSIAN CAPITAL.

The perfume store was crowded with leggy blondes, thick-set older women with sturdy shoes, beehive hairdos, and too much blush, and a few distracted men. I found one customer who looked like he could use a dose of Mayor. He wore a black leather jacket, several days of stubble, and dark tattoos on his well-worn knuckles. Had he tried Luzhkov's cologne, I asked? Never heard of it, he grunted dismissively. "It's only been out a few weeks," a saleswoman volunteered. "Try a sample."

The man sprayed his decorated paw, which sported a large dollar sign between thumb and index finger—indicating in Russian jailhouse tattoo lingo that he had served time for hard-currency speculation in the Soviet days—and noisily inhaled a snootful. "What do you think?"

"Too fruity, " he sniffed, reaching for another brand more to his taste called Casino.

The perfumery, like virtually every other retail business in the city center, kept a red, white, and blue poster in the window celebrating the 850th. Luzhkov generously distributed tens of thousands of these posters, accepting a mere two-hundred-dollar "contribution" from every store that chose to display them. A few shops had initially balked at purchasing the signs, but after they developed sudden permit and licensing problems, all wisely jumped on the civic bandwagon.

A few blocks up the street, Trinity Motors, a successful GM dealership run by a young Persian business acquaintance of Roberta's, had donated fifty Chevy Blazers to Luzhkov's police department as an anniversary gift. The Iranian car dealer could afford such largesse in part because law-enforcement agencies in Russia did such a lousy job that Trinity enjoyed a booming trade in armored vehicles. Its flagship SUV was a modified two-hundred-fifty-thousand-dollar Suburban that not only could withstand a grenade blast but came equipped with such Bond-style options as a concealed nozzle that blew smoke and tear gas at prospective assailants through a hole in the sunroof. Q would have been proud.

Trinity Motors was not alone in helping Luzhkov prepare his

party. Western corporations went to extraordinary lengths to curry favor with the powerful mayor. Jordan's Renaissance Capital and most of the other big brokerage firms gladly ponied up for the anniversary fund. Volvo paid a million dollars to become the "official car" of the 850th. Coke bid handsomely for the privilege of calling itself Moscow's "official soft drink." Nestlé put up a children's theme park, complete with jugglers, in front of the Lubyanka KGB headquarters, whose Party bosses had orphaned more Russian children than all the twentieth century's wars combined.

The big day finally arrived, and kicked off with morning concerts and skateboarding competitions in Red Square, the military marches Russians can't seem to live without, and a procession of elaborate floats down Tverskaya. MiG fighter jets in V formations buzzed the city, trailing multicolored plumes of red, white, and blue smoke (postcommunist Russia's national colors), while a squadron of biplanes seeded clouds heading towards the city to force them to dump rain on the suburbs, not on Luzhkov's parade.

As it happened, the anniversary fell on a Saturday when neither Roberta nor I had to work. We headed for the old Intourist hotel on Tverskaya; it was still as drab and dreary as in the days of Gorbachev but afforded a bird's-eye view of the festivities. The dimly-lit lobby seemed cavernous without the ladies of the evening who usually prowled the room, smoked around the little back bar, and played the cheap slot machines that lined the establishment's greasy, faded walls. A small Mexican restaurant had opened on the top floor, staffed, like a great many of Moscow's other enchilada joints, by Cuban exchange students who had opted to remain in capitalist Russia rather than returning to Castro's Havana. It was painted bright orange and decorated with avant-garde tableaux of matadors in action. A sultry waitress in cowboy boots, cut-off jeans, and a sombrero dispensed tequila from a bandolier strung with shot glasses, a bottle of Sauza swaying from a holster around her hips.

We took a table by the window and watched the crowd congregate twenty stories beneath us. Three million people were expected, and the streets were already thick with holidaymakers and awed pilgrims from Moscow's outlying regions. The crush grew heavier as the celebrations got under way, and soon it was apparent that leaving the hotel would be impossible. Most metro stations and roads in the vicinity of the Kremlin were closed to the public so that several hundred politicians and their corporate cronies could move about unobstructed. Our own street three blocks away had been cordoned off and turned into a makeshift parking lot for Luzhkov's limousines, so we couldn't have gotten back home even if we tried. We would have to ride out the human storm in the company of the sombreroed waitress and her alcohol-bearing hips.

Luzhkov, to his credit, put on a good show. Float after float drifted down Tverskaya, turning onto Teatralnaya Way past Luzhkov's pet project, the budget-breaking Manezh Mall (completed just in time for the parade at a staggering cost of three hundred fifty million dollars), and the ornately restored Art Deco balconies of the five-star, one-hundred-twenty-million-dollar National Hotel, where television cameras had been positioned to broadcast the event live across Russia.

The procession was spiced with an exotic mix of international flavors, since various embassies and cowering former Soviet republics had been cajoled into supplying floats. Luzhkov had his sights set on the next presidential race, and this wasn't lost on the diplomatic community. The Egyptians, always eager to please their former arms suppliers, borrowed a camel from the Moscow Zoo; the beast stared around nervously as it pulled a miniature pyramid. The Chinese, whose president had attended Moscow State University (the Harvard of Russia) and whose navy was stocked with Soviet surplus submarines, sent a firecracker-breathing dragon powered by the feet of a dozen diplomats. Various African nations, long-term recipients of Soviet military generosity, were represented by loinclothed warriors, tireless dancers, and chieftains in feathered tribal garb. Not to be outdone, the British trundled out the bagpipes, the French their berets. I missed out on Canada's no doubt breathtaking contribution, but got a look at U.S. Marines and the American diplomats they protected decked out as Wild West outlaws and cowboys.

A Russian marching band trailed after the Marines. It was followed by naval ensigns in crisp dress uniforms, carrying a banner that shouted SAILORS SALUTE LUZHKOV. "They're from the Black Sea Fleet," said Roberta. Luzhkov was a big benefactor of the Fleet, hallowed symbol of Russia's bygone glory. The armada was based in historic Sevastopol, and had been founded at the height of Catherine the Great's big empire-building drive. But since the dissolution of the USSR, Sevastopol had humiliatingly become part of Ukraine, now a foreign country with what Russians regarded as uppity notions of sovereignty. Sevastopol was such a sore point for Russians that when a U.S. warship paid Ukraine a friendly visit in the spirit of NATO's Partnership for Peace program, Russian state television broadcast a manifesto by Sevastopol's patriotic Russian prostitutes, who pledged to withhold their favors from American sailors. "Let the Ukrainian officers' wives service the Americans," one of the women groused on air.

Luzhkov had made Sevastopol his cause célèbre. He railed against turning over the base to the Ukrainian *khokhly*, and put his money where his mouth was by using Moscow municipal funds to build housing in the port for Russian officers stationed there. Watching the uniformed Russian sailors march down Tverskaya brought back a flood of memories.

I had been in Sevastopol at the height of the turmoil in 1993. It had been my first taste of big-time journalism, an assignment primarily consisting of carrying expense money—ten thousand dollars strapped under my jeans in hollowed-out soccer shin guards—for a *New York Times* correspondent.

We had been told to keep our heads down and keep an eye out for military patrols. The white Toyota van bounced and rocked on the dirt path as it wound its way up a steep hill and skirted a weedy vineyard. We breathed more easily once the dusty trail disappeared under the canopy of a conifer forest.

"The Russians rarely patrol this side of the mountain," said Mustafa, our Tatar driver and guide. "Still, keep your eyes peeled." He wrestled with the gearshift as the incline grew steeper, and the van's tires bit into the pinecones and needles that carpeted the deserted road. We kicked up a small dirt storm that settled on the ferns and clumps of moss in our wake.

"Don't worry," Mustafa assured us, his broad sun-baked face creasing into a mischievous smile. "I've done this many times and have never been caught."

The van crested the mountain's ridge. Below, the Black Sea shimmered in the sun, waves crashing against chalky cliffs. Through the tall pine trees that concealed our presence, we could see windswept headlands that jutted from the arid peninsula like dorsal fins. Behind the headlands lay Sevastopol, the Soviet Union's only warm-water naval base. A brown haze hung over the harbor: exhaust from the 325 vessels of the Fleet's armada.

"When we reach the city limits," Mustafa reminded us, "keep the curtains drawn." It was 1993, and Sevastopol was still a closed military city, one of the last to keep that designation after the breakup of the Soviet empire. Outsiders, especially foreigners, would be easily spotted in the port, so we were sneaking in through the equivalent of the back door.

Jane Perlez, the *New York Times* Eastern Europe bureau chief, sat next to me in the back of the dusty van. Directly behind me, James Hill, a young freelance photographer, was polishing his camera lenses, cursing the dust that caked his Nikon. This was both James' and my first big assignment for the *Times,* and he appeared more anxious about blurred shots than roadblocks. Matinee-idol handsome, with the rich and rolling accent of England's upper crust, James wasn't supposed to be a photojournalist, playing hide and seek with Russian military police. His parents, both Lloyd's of London "names," financial guarantors of the insurance company's solvency, had intended a career in banking for their son. But after graduating from Oxford, James scorned the crunching of numbers, turned down an offer from the prestigious investment house of Lazard Frères, and announced that he was moving to Kiev to search for adventure.

We were on paved roads again. Two Russian jeeps idled on the soft shoulder a few hundred yards ahead of us. They were painted navy blue and had white canvas tops, which meant they were MPs. As we passed the jeeps, I nervously weighed what the Russians would do to us if we got caught. A few years back, it would have certainly meant jail time, maybe even espionage charges. Now, who knew?

Sevastopol was under the special jurisdiction of the Russian Ministry of Defense, since Moscow claimed the harbor for its navy. Kiev had a different view. The Crimean naval base was on Ukrainian sovereign territory, and thus Kiev had the mandate over the town's military installations. Or so said the Ukrainians. By the summer of

1993, legal arguments had given way to angry diplomatic dispatches, resolutions by Russia's parliament proclaiming Sevastopol a Russian city, mutinies on board the contested vessels, and rumblings about settling the matter the old-fashioned way. Only a month before our arrival, the United Nations had been called in to mediate, eventually ruling in favor of Kiev and suggesting that the fleet be evenly divided. It was this territorial dispute, one of the most volatile to emerge from the breakup of the USSR, that had brought us to the storied port of Sevastopol.

Sevastopol was no stranger to conflict. One of the bloodiest battles of World War II had been fought here between the Wehrmacht and the Red Army. During the Crimean War of the 1850s, Florence Nightingale had tended to the port's English wounded. At the same time, during Britain's ill-fated landing in Sevastopol, Alfred, Lord Tennyson had immortalized the city with his stirring ballad *The Charge of the Light Brigade*.

The curtains in our van were drawn tight, but occasionally I managed a peek at the town. There were sailors everywhere. Seventy thousand servicemen were stationed in Sevastopol, which had a resident population of only a hundred thousand. The seamen wore dark blue uniforms with flapping white-rimmed collar lapels. The officers sported black slacks and mustard-colored shirts that sprouted small gold-braided epaulettes. They had smart peaked caps, offering shade from the white-hot summer sun. Meanwhile, we sweated inside our van. I envied the crewmen on shore leave. They lounged under shade trees, eating vanilla ice-cream cones and sipping from large brown bottles of beer.

We passed countless war monuments and propaganda slogans in bold red letters. Every few blocks, I could see crudely painted homemade placards hung outside people's windows. These read: KRYM— ROSSIYA! (Crimea Is Russia!)

We had been given a phone number to call if we managed to get into Sevastopol undetected, and James volunteered to ring our contact, a lieutenant from the Ukrainian navy. Mustafa pulled up to a phone booth, and James, after glancing up and down the street like a purse-snatcher, scampered out of the van. He was back within seconds. "There's no dial tone," he announced. We drove to another booth: "The phone's been ripped out," said James this time. At the next phone, the rotary dial plate was missing. So we sat sweltering in the van, our paranoia rising. An hour passed before James found a pay phone in working order and arranged for a rendezvous.

Lieutenant Nikolai Savchenko poked his head into the van at three o'clock in the afternoon. He was big-boned, blond, blue-eyed and could have passed for a poster Slav in some Stalinist propaganda film. He explained that he was an ethnic Ukrainian and was risking his neck so that foreign journalists could tell the world about Russian injustice. The three hundred dollars he was pocketing for the unofficial tour, about a year's worth of his salary, apparently did not figure into his patriotic motivations.

Savchenko climbed in and directed Mustafa to the port, all the while briefing Jane on the status of the contested fleet. "The ships are rotting while the politicians squabble," he said, helping himself to a cigarette from a pack on the dashboard. "Neither side is paying for upkeep because no one knows whose ship will be whose. The docks are also crumbling. The sewers in town are bursting from disrepair and we're having outbreaks of cholera. Physically and morally, the Fleet is dilapidated. If this goes on for another few years the ships will only be good for scrap steel. This is the death of the Fleet."

Savchenko argued that Russia had no legal claim over the base, but conceded that Moscow's ties to the place ran deep. "To Russia, Sevastopol is like Pearl Harbor to you Americans. Except that to us it's a symbol of victory, not defeat," he added, looking pleased with the subtle jibe at America's biggest military setback. For a professed Ukrainian nationalist, the lieutenant at times seemed ambivalent about which country he really served.

He saluted smartly as we drove by a pair of armed sentries and entered the busy naval installation. "If anyone asks," he said, "you're journalists from Moscow."

"I don't think anyone is going to buy that," I said, remarking that we didn't look or sound the part. "Then be Polish reporters," Savchenko suggested, explaining that since Poland was an old fraternal nation, being from Warsaw would not raise too many hackles. As long as we weren't playing the part of Americans, he explained. Americans weren't very popular in Sevastopol. "The Soviet military mentality, you understand," he explained.

The pier hummed with activity. Sailors and maintenance workers in soiled coveralls unloaded large trucks and hauled tool chests into supply launches. Electric cables the size of fire hoses ran the length of the dock. At the far end of the jetty, several old men fished, though what they expected to catch in the roiling waters baffled me.

The Black Sea Fleet was anchored along the seawalls of three deep-water channels that fanned out from the harbor's protected entrance. Frigates, destroyers, missile cruisers, hospital and reconnaissance ships, and submarines wallowed in the diesel-slicked waters. The naval ships floated listlessly, as if sulking from neglect. They had rusty rudders and grimy hulls that rode high above the waterline, revealing clusters of barnacles and clumps of seaweed. The long barrels on their gun mounts pointed limply down at oily decks. Painted gray, they were moored six deep, and connected by wooden gangways. Black radar dishes mushroomed from their bridges, which bristled with communication rods.

Savchenko had arranged a motor launch at no extra charge to meet us at the pier. The two seamen aboard didn't make their views about the United States clear, but the first question they asked was whether we had any American cigarettes. I did my bit for international reconciliation and handed them each a pack of Marlboros— of which I had brought a carton for just such purposes. They smoked hungrily for the next hour as we motored around the installation.

I watched the water slide up and over the blunt, curved bow of a large supply ship putting out to sea. Its wake bounced our little launch around, making it impossible for James to steady his camera. A white and blue naval ensign fluttered from the stern of the freighter, and Savchenko explained that it was an instrument of the tug of war between Kiev and Moscow.

"That is the tsarist banner of Saint Andrew," he shouted over the din of the freighter. "Saint Andrew was the patron saint of Peter the Great's navy. The ships you see flying that ensign have declared allegiance to Russia."

As we glided by the endless metallic gray hulk of the *Moskva*, a thousand-foot-long helicopter- and jump-jet carrier, I noticed that it too had hoisted Saint Andrew's blue banner. Two sharp-prowed guided-missile destroyers flanking the carrier also flew the standard.

"The fleet is supposed to be divided equally," grumbled Savchenko as we emerged from the shadow of the carrier group. "In reality, Ukraine has a naval force that consists of four ships and an ancient submarine."

One of the Ukrainian vessels was a four-thousand-ton frigate with stubby, sloping funnels and a sleek, tapered hull. She flew a blue-on-yellow Ukrainian trident from her mast and carried three 130-millimeter guns forward of her superstructure and a battery of antisubmarine mortar launchers aft. Captain Evgeniy Lupakov, her commanding officer, waited for us at the top of the netted gangway, sporting a thick mariner's beard, bright, flashing eyes, and a wide smile. He greeted us warmly and invited us for refreshments in his cabin. On the way up, we passed two recruits peeling potatoes on deck. They looked like they'd rather be somewhere else.

The commanding officer's quarters were spartan, comprising a bunk, several built-in drawers, a desk, some chairs, and a washbasin that folded up into the bulkhead. A photograph of the captain's wife and daughter sat on the small wooden table.

"Russians can't imagine Russia without Sevastopol," Captain Lupakov said over plum juice. "It is a symbol of Russian might that harks back to Catherine the Great's conquests. The vast majority of Crimeans, not to mention sailors in the fleet, are ethnic Russian, so it's not surprising that ships are defecting in droves to the Russian side."

Indeed, the young Ukrainian armada had just suffered a crushing blow; one of its vessels, with crew, had gone over to the Russians. The reason for the defection had to do with exchange rates. The Russians paid their officers the same salary as the Ukrainians. But they paid in rubles, which were worth three times as much as the hapless Ukrainian currency, the hated karbovanets, or "coupon," as it was derisively known.

"A sailor in the Ukrainian Naval Forces earns forty thousand coupons a month, about ten dollars. But the pay for anyone serving on a ship that flies Saint Andrew's is forty thousand rubles, which are worth around thirty-five dollars. Officers are also given secret bonuses to bring over their crews. I know of more than two hundred support ships that have been bought off this way," said the captain. "Ukraine does not have the money to compete with Russia."

The For Sale sign over the entire fleet was brought closer to home as we bid Lupakov goodbye. Savchenko tugged at my sleeve and beckoned me aside. "The captain asks if he could have twenty dollars for the interview."

As late afternoon set in and the shadows grew longer over the harbor, we motored past dry docks and approached the submarine pens. The crumbling concrete piers were tangled with thick mooring lines. As a bonus to our three-hundred-dollar tour package, we would get to go inside one of the fearsome subs. Before we went aboard, though, Savchenko took off his officer's cap and slipped on another, seemingly identical, one. Noticing my quizzical look, he winked and pointed at the red Soviet star he was now wearing. The cap he had taken off bore the blue trident of the Ukrainian Naval Forces. This was the only feature of the two country's uniforms that differed, enabling the wily Savchenko to transform himself into a Russian or Ukrainian officer at the drop of a hat.

The submarines, he said, were known in NATO manuals as Kilo and Tango-class boats. They were 240-foot diesel-electric attack submarines, used primarily to patrol enemy waters because they ran silently at under five knots and were virtually undetectable by even the most sophisticated sonar array.

I recalled reading about the Kilo, which Russia was selling to all comers for three hundred million dollars a craft. The U.S. State Department was particularly annoyed that Iran and China had each bought a pair. There wasn't much chance of our gleaning any military secrets from the tub we were shown, though. It was twenty-five years old and had World War II–era pneumatic tubes, hand-cranked valves, and old-fashioned dials on instrumentation panels that looked straight off the set of the World War II movie *Das Boot*. There were pipes everywhere, and bulkheads that threatened concussions to anyone over five feet tall who forgot to stoop.

Inside, the air was stale and dead. It was stiflingly hot. The fifty-three young conscripts who crewed Boat Number 554 were all in fleet-issue undershirts, sleeveless and blue striped. They were sweating something fierce, and pretty soon I was soaked too. James handed out cigarettes and had the torpedomen pose in a group photo. They puffed out their chests and flexed their undernourished shoulders for effect.

The vessel was commanded by Captain Konstantin Vasiliev. He cut a trim, athletic figure as he sat hunched over a table thick with rolled-up nautical charts. Vasiliev held the common view on Sevastopol: "Always was and always will be a Russian city. It's nonsense to think you can divide the fleet. That's just politicians trying to save face. You can't have both Ukrainian and Russian bases in the same place." The Ukrainians, he concluded, would have to move out.

I left Jane talking with the captain and set out to explore the boat. I saw through a hatch some crew members with wrenches and spanners poking at a big bank of machinery. A young sailor told me it was the scrubbers for the air-purification system. The thought of spending weeks under water in this steel coffin terrified me. I asked the young sailor what it was like. He said he didn't know. In the six months he'd served aboard, the submarine had never ventured out of port. There was no money for fuel.

That night we stayed at a "safe house" because guests at Sevastopol's two hotels had to be registered with the military police. According to typical post-Soviet logic, we could openly tour ships, take photos of submarines, and debrief their crews, but not sleep in a hotel room. *That* posed a security risk. James and I had to share a narrow bed in the cramped apartment and traded the usual adolescent injunctions to "stay on your side of the bed!" The car that had taken us to the housing block had driven with its headlights doused—just like in a James Bond movie, except that the driver was doing it to conserve his headlight bulbs, of which, like just about everything else in Ukraine, there was a dire shortage.

We made it out of Sevastopol safely and spent the next night in the cargo hold of a freight train. It was the only ride to Kiev we could catch, the fuel shortage having grounded all domestic flights. We sat on pallets like happy hobos, sipping warm beer as the Ukrainian countryside rolled gently past the opened door of our wagon.

Russia and Ukraine eventually did settle their differences over Sevastopol in the summer of 1997, agreeing that Ukraine would lease Moscow the naval base in exchange for forgiveness on several billion dollars of natural gas debt that the Ukrainians had run up with Gazprom. For all my misgivings about Russian imperialism, the dispute had been amicably solved with economic and trade levers not so different from those the United States normally used against Canada or Mexico. It gave me hope that the Kremlin's foreign policy planners were entering the twenty-first century.

Moscow's 850th bash was certainly highly modern, particularly the multimillion-dollar laser and light show which began at dusk. The giant laser display was choreographed to music, with what had to be the world's largest stereo speakers erected on the Gothic wings of Moscow State University, high above the Sparrow Hills and the Moskva River. Since public transportation had been shut down for the "people's holiday," Roberta and I walked the four miles to the riverfront, where close to a million Muscovites had already gathered and were exhibiting very unholiday-like behavior. The hours of drinking were taking their toll. Broken bottles of vodka and beer littered the embankment. People were retching in the bushes, and every tree seemed to have been transformed into a *pissoir*. Tempers flared as partygoers jostled for the choicest viewing locations. A few fistfights settled the more intense disputes.

But the light show was spectacular, worth every penny of the five million dollars Luzhkov had paid its French producers. Lasers lit up Moscow State University, painting the sky with intricate designs to the throbbing accompaniment of Tchaikovsky and Mozart. The crowd oohed and aahed at the technological display. Well away from the mob, Luzhkov beamed like a happy potentate from his cushioned perch. His beloved Moscow was back with a bang.

It took us three hours to get home that night, the metro being reserved for Luzhkov's dignitaries. Some people spent the whole night walking home, and State television the next day showed shots of angry suburbanites who had been forced to hike for eleven hours on the "people's holiday."

CHAPTER EIGHT

Potemkin Inc.

The 850ᵗʰ anniversary passed, and a semblance of normality once more reigned in Moscow. By late August, the prostitutes and glue-sniffers had returned from exile. Construction crews had abandoned work on unfinished buildings. And the repaving of streets had come to an abrupt, shock-absorber-wrenching halt.

The show was over. Moscow had had its day in the sun, everyone had been duly impressed, and now it was back to reality. I shouldn't have been surprised at the sudden reversal. The Russians have been putting on such deceptive displays since the days of Catherine the Great's adviser (and lover) Potemkin; that canny prince caused wooden façades of villages to be created along the banks of the Dniepr River. When his royal mistress sailed by on her barge, she was convinced that Russian settlers were colonizing her new territories in southern Ukraine—and rewarded him accordingly with swaths of land that are now Dnepropetrovsk. The tradition had been adopted by Soviet provincial leaders, who went to great lengths to repave roads and splash a fresh coat of paint along any routes traveled by visiting Party higher-ups, so that they too would think everything in order in their kingdoms.

In the 1990s, capitalist Russia kept the Potemkin tradition alive, showing particular aptitude for slapping up window dressing designed to entice foreign investors. Newly privatized companies raced to produce Western-style financial statements that international lenders could peruse, their CEOs embraced American buzzwords such as "corporate governance" and "transparency," and all the big firms issued glossy English-language quarterly reports that cluttered every corner of the *Journal*'s office.

The reality could be somewhat different, as I discovered when I flew down to southern Russia to attend a shareholders' meeting that June. For all the talk about progress, boardroom maneuvers in Russia still had the uneasy feel of showdowns at the OK Corral.

Moscow's Domodedovo airport was silent when I arrived one muggy Friday evening to catch a flight to the industrial city of Lipetsk, where Russia's biggest steel mill was holding its annual general shareholders' meeting. Inside the dusty terminal, a lone pigeon flapped in the unwashed rafters, and a giant Marlboro poster exhorted travelers to smoke like cowboys. The place was deserted save for the ubiquitous taxi mafia, whose unshaven goons prowled the concourses of virtually every airport east of Berlin.

There was no sign of any of the other reporters who were supposed to fly out on the jet Boris Jordan had chartered. Nor could I see any of the lawyers and corporate types we would be traveling with. There was nothing on the Departures schedule to indicate that any flight, in fact, was due to leave for Lipetsk. The information counter, naturally, was closed.

Maybe I was at the wrong airport. No, the fax clearly stated Domodedovo. Puzzled, I sat on a radiator, and did as the Marlboro sign instructed. Twenty minutes passed and then half an hour. A neat little pile of butts was accumulating at my feet, but still no sign of life. The clock ticked off forty minutes. I asked a passing airport official if there was a chartered flight to Lipetsk. She shrugged noncommittally.

Another ten minutes crawled by. By this time I was having trouble fending off the taxi goons, who were becoming most insistent about driving me back to Moscow for fifty dollars. It was always fifty dollars, no matter what city in what country in the former Soviet Union—the airports were all controlled by gangs who guarded their turf ferociously and enforced monopoly prices. Some of the drivers were factory workers who had fallen on hard times. But many others were terrifying brutes—all knuckle tattoos and beer bellies, broken noses and black leather jackets. They crowded around you: "Feeftee dollar," they'd growl hungrily, stretching the limits of their English vocabulary, five meaty fingers splayed for emphasis.

And they could be dangerous. A colleague of Roberta's at VSO, an engineer from Missouri, had just been robbed on the way out of this very airport—driven at gunpoint to a wooded lot, stripped to his underwear, and left to the proverbial wolves. He had had to walk for hours in his skivvies until he found help.

At Sheremetyevo, Moscow's main international hub, the taxi gangs had cleaned up their image. The price was still fixed, but you could get a receipt and the German cars were a cheerful yellow, lending an air of normality to the operation. At Domodedovo, alas, reform had not yet made its civilizing mark.

I was about to give up on the flight and take my chances with the taxi mafia when a series of minibuses drew up to the concourse, disgorging a group of young men in the unmistakably well-tailored garb of investment bankers and high-powered attorneys. I was never so happy to see a bunch of pinstriped lawyers in my life.

We boarded our chartered jet, which had been sitting anonymously on the tarmac all along. It was a small Soviet-made Yak-40 of the type used by regional Party bosses and important factory directors in the communist days. We took our seats, and the lawyers stowed their briefcases for takeoff. Jordan's legal team comprised some of the best young attorneys in Russia, men (for they were all men) whose talents were wasted on the country's rent-a-judge court system. Now, en route to the shareholders' meeting of the Novolipetsk Metallurgical Kombinat—NLMK for short—they had the coiled, supercharged look of athletes preparing for a grudge match.

The fight had been brewing for months, and the Western press had been painting Jordan's forces as the good guys. That was why we'd been invited along, and each given one honorary share of NLMK stock so that we could attend. It was the first time I'd ever owned stock, and it felt pretty good to be an investor even if it was only for pretend and even if I only owned an infinitesimal piece of a faltering Russian steel mill.

In the dispute, Jordan led a coalition of half a dozen Western investors, including George Soros and the Harvard University Endowment, who had together accumulated a majority stake in NLMK. The problem was that, despite the 51-percent controlling interest held by Westerners, the Soviet-trained managers of NLMK refused to let foreigners in the factory doors, much less grant them representation on the board of directors. In other words, the majority owners of the plant had no say in how it was run, whether it paid dividends, or how it kept its books. The people who did were a shadowy group of metals traders to whom management was loyal. Even by the violent standards of the Russian metals industry, whose recent history was strewn with dead bodies, they had very nasty reputations. Not surprisingly, there was some concern on the part of the Western owners that money was flowing out the back door. And since NLMK was more than a two-billion-dollar-a-year operation, there was plenty of potential for profit skimming.

Like so many other Western investors, these owners were beginning to discover that, in their haste to cash in on the Russian bubble, they had bought a great many pieces of paper and not much more, since there was no real legal framework to uphold securities laws.

"We've got our noses pressed to the shop window," lamented one of NLMK's indignant owners, Thomas Gaffney, chairman of a Bahamas-based hedge fund called Cambridge Capital Management, which held 17.5 percent of the mill's stock. "But the Russians won't let us in. It's absurd."

Only two members of Jordan's party offered neither business cards nor elaborate greetings when the press boarded the plane. One was Jordan's security chief, a former KGB colonel with probing eyes, manicured fingers, and expensive taste in clothing. The other was the chief's minion, a well-fed guard with a blank expression and a cheap suit from which a holster bulged. It would fall to these two to make sure nothing untoward happened to us when we ventured into hostile corporate territory.

We flew into Lipetsk after dark, skirting the steel mills' towering smokestacks, whose strobe lights winked red to warn off low-flying craft. The city looked like a thousand other Soviet towns—unimaginative and unkempt. Our hotel was of pale bricks, badly laid. It was called either the Moskva or the October, Communist central planners having christened practically every dingy Intourist hotel identically. (The occasional Hotel Druzhba, or friendship, stood as testament to some odd burst of creativity.)

Checking in was hardly a friendly process. One of the Russian lawyers had only his international passport. But the bloated clerk at the check-in counter wanted his internal passport, because Russia still used the Soviet-era dual identification system. Though his documents were in good enough order to fly to London and stay at the Grosvenor, she used the pretext to deny him a room. "But where will I stay?" he pleaded. "Not in my hotel," she hissed, loud enough for the half-dozen bored prostitutes in the lobby to stir from their magazines.

It took Jordan's KGB colonel to resolve the passport problem with a few soft words and a sizable tip. He proved his usefulness again later, when we all gathered at the little black-lit bar on the top floor for a nightcap. With one call on his cell phone, he summoned the local cops in record time (for Russia) to haul away a belligerent drunk who was overturning tables and insulting our party. This showed that our new KGB friend still had his old connections, which was why he was such an important asset to an investment bank. Every bank was staffed with spooks, probably outnumbering the bankers.

The next morning we rose early to prepare for the shareholders' meeting. It was held at the Lipetsk *Dom Kultury* (House of Culture), which had been given a fresh coat of paint for the occasion. Very fresh. The paint was still sticky to the touch, and the smell of enamel hung in the air. The building itself rose unsteadily atop wide Roman-style steps and was supported by cracked plaster columns whose purpose, by the wobbly look of them, was more decorative than structural.

It was at the portico that we ran into the first sign of opposition. Inside the entrance, armed guards, some in the dull gray uniform of the local police, others hired goons in ridiculous suits, blocked our passage. I heard one whisper into a walkie-talkie "They're here." A heated discussion ensued. Our group would not be admitted, said the guards, despite the fact that Jordan's lawyers held the proxy voting rights to over half the company's stock. Rafael Akopov, lead counsel for Jordan's Sputnik Fund, waved a ream of court documents in a plant official's face. A fourth consecutive court ruling had just been handed down in favor of the foreign investors, declaring the annual meeting unlawful because the management had left off the agenda the vote for a new board of directors as required by Russian law. The problem, as Western investors were beginning to discover, was that court rulings meant little in newly capitalist Russia.

While the lawyers squabbled and the flatheads growled, I sat out on the steps and had a smoke. The city of Lipetsk spread out below, hugging the steep banks of the Don River, which flowed south into the Volga and emptied into the Caspian Sea. Directly across from me pensioners calmly played chess in a small tree-lined square, indifferent to the high-stakes game unfolding on the other side of the road.

The serenity was interrupted by the screech of tires as a convoy pulled up to the cultural center at high speed. Bodyguards spilled out of two chase cars and scanned the steps for potential trouble. The door to a white Mercedes 600 S class with jet-black windows was flung open, and from it emerged Vladimir Lisin. Lisin was the top lieutenant of the Chernoy brothers, the kingpins of Russia's metals industry. NLMK's managers answered to him. As he climbed the steps, waving airily to the masses, there was an awed silence and people scurried out of his way. He was a short, fleshy man, barely visible amid his entourage of six-foot-four bodyguards, who made no effort to conceal their sidearms.

Unlike us, Lisin had no trouble getting in. He was on the board of NLMK as the Chernoy brothers' representative. Lev and Mikhail Chernoy had been born poor but smart in rural Uzbekistan. In the crazy early days of the transition, the pair had gained a virtual stranglehold on Russia's aluminum and steel industry, so much so that a third of the metal produced in Russia went through their umbrella holding company, Trans-CIS Commodities. In 1997 they exported seven billion dollars' worth of aluminum ingots and rolled steel out of the former Soviet Union, making Trans-CIS one of the world's biggest metals traders and the Chernoys exceedingly wealthy and powerful men.

The brothers engaged in the lucrative tolling contracts that had made Julia Timoshenko a billionaire, supplying raw materials to factories in exchange for their finished products. The brothers' companies and associates had frequently drawn the attention of Russian investigators. When the director of an aluminum smelter in Krasnoyarsk, for instance, had acted against Trans-CIS' interests, he complained of receiving death threats. Placed under special police protection, he resigned soon afterward. His replacement was not so lucky. Shortly after upholding his predecessor's stance against Trans-CIS, he was shot gangland-style outside his home in 1995. Vladimir Lisin was twice questioned by police in connection with the unsolved murder, but was released without charges being filed. (A business associate of Lisin's, a former boxer by the name of Anatoly Bykov, would later be extradited from Hungary and charged with the crime.)

Soon after an American metals-trading company wooed a huge smelter in Bratsk away from its exclusive tolling contract with Trans-CIS, the head of the U.S. firm's Russian operations, Felix Lvov, was found in a ditch 67 miles outside of Moscow, his body riddled with bullets, including one to the back of the head. He had disappeared between Passport Control and the boarding gate at one of Moscow's airports. The American company, a New York–based outfit by the name of AIOC, withdrew from Russia shortly afterward. The murder was never solved.

While, according to the Russian Ministry of the Interior, the Chernoys were suspected of participating in an unsolved 1992 nationwide bank fraud that bilked the central bank out of as much as two hundred twenty-five million dollars, no charges were ever brought against the Chernoy brothers in Russia. Nonetheless, the two lived abroad, dividing their time between Monaco and Israel, where Mikhail Chernoy had survived a spectacular assassination plot. He had also been arrested and later released by Swiss police during an organized-crime crackdown in that country. The brothers maintained that Mikhail was not involved in Trans-CIS affairs, and dismissed all allegations against them as the malicious griping of jealous competitors. Both routinely declined to speak to reporters.

Since leaving Russia, the Chernoy brothers had left the shrewd Lisin in charge of day-to-day operations. Which brings us back to NLMK. The mill had an exclusive and ruinous tolling agreement with Trans-CIS that Western investors wanted ripped up. But Lisin held the voting proxy for the Chernoy brothers' 37-percent stake in NLMK, and de facto control of the board. As long as Jordan and Soros had no board representation, they had no way of stopping the tolling arrangements, which stripped the plant of profits and forced the factory to sell its steel to Trans-CIS at below production costs.

"This setup is ridiculous. We want it stopped before it bankrupts the mill," declared Akopov, Sputnik's lead counsel. Jordan's other lawyers, meanwhile, had managed to talk their way into the meeting, thanks mostly, I thought, to another hushed conversation by our KGB man, this time with the head of the plant's security. He really was earning his keep.

As a condition to our entry we would have to check our weapons at the door; this proved problematic for our hired gun, who refused to relinquish his sidearm, arguing that Lisin's bodyguards had set off all the metal detectors with theirs. "They get to keep their guns, why can't I?" he whined like a schoolboy, albeit one with a nineteen-inch neck. Jordan's KGB man finally instructed him to wait outside.

Inside, the cultural center was crammed with goons. They easily outnumbered registered voters, and followed us wherever we went, which in my case was straight to the bar. It offered cheap Crimean champagne, cognac, and gritty Turkish coffee, as well as loads of fatty cold cuts and smoked-sturgeon sandwiches. I nibbled and took in the scene. The hall had been decorated with multicolored garlands and party balloons as if for a prom. "Hotel California," the Eagles classic, played over the loudspeakers. For the first time, the line "You can check out any time you like, but you can never leave" seemed to have an air of menace. In this incongruous setting, it was hard to know whether to expect teenagers slow-dancing or a gangland-style execution.

The meeting was held in the adjoining auditorium. The directors shuffled out onto the stage, wearing Soviet suits that looked homemade and white upswept hair that sparkled against the red curtain behind them. A series of excruciatingly long speeches began. Every dubious statistic and glorious production figure was enumerated, and there was much praise for "our reliable trading partners," punctuated by obsequious nods in Lisin's direction.

Akopov seemed to be dozing. "This whole thing is a sham," he said, when I nudged him. "We're only here to prevent fraudulent voting or stock dilution." Despite their lip service to corporate governance, Russian companies had a habit of calling snap annual meetings during which they voted to issue more shares. Often Western investors were not informed of these meetings, and woke up the next day to find their stake cut in half. Akopov said that his strategy was to torpedo every proposal by the board until it agreed to hold new elections in which Western investors would get board representation proportional to their ownership. He got his opportunity moments later when the minutes of the last meeting, which had set a corporate charter, needed to be approved. Jordan's lawyers voted them down. It was clear that nothing would pass, and without a charter NLMK did not legally exist.

The directors looked at Lisin, who stood up decisively and walked off the dais. One by one, the nine board members followed, one elderly official pausing by the microphone. "Foreigners need to think about the future of the plant and about the welfare of its employees, not just about pumping profits," he spat, white with anger. "This meeting is over," he added, storming off the stage.

Thus did the 1997 shareholders' meeting of the Novo Lipetsk Metallurgical Kombinat come to an abrupt close. Akopov and Jordan's lawyers declared themselves triumphant, but it was a hollow victory. The tolling arrangements continued, and the majority owners were still denied access to the board. The old board was legally out but still in charge. Without a charter, the whole factory was now in legal limbo, easy prey for con artists because it had no rights to lawfully engage in contracts or conduct business. It was, as one frustrated Western investor put it, "a fucking mess."

Perhaps the oddest result of the NLMK annual meeting was the enthusiasm it generated in expatriate Moscow. The spin-masters, public-relations teams, and brokerage analysts—the professional optimists—touted the fiasco as progress, as a step toward real corporate governance. The market was of the same mind, for shares in NLMK rose in the aftermath of the annual meeting. Russia was strange that way. The financial boom was based on the vague, alluring promise that the so-called Red directors and oligarchs in charge of industry would one day start behaving themselves, and then the country's vast corporate entities would be worth trillions. What happened today was less important than what *might* happen tomorrow.

Progress, to be sure, was being made. Only a few years back, someone probably would have gotten shot at a bitter dispute like the one I witnessed at NLMK. Outsiders almost certainly would not have been permitted at the annual meeting. And the meeting itself, in all likelihood, would never have taken place. It was not unreasonable to hope, therefore, that if outfits like NLMK could make such strides in just a few years, Russian companies could become good corporate citizens in the not too distant future. That, at least, was the official line of the fund managers and analysts in Moscow.

Of all Russia's pitchmen, few were as charismatic and convincing as Oneximbank CEO Vladimir Potanin. Potanin was nicknamed among Moscow journalists "Russia's Great White Hope," the poster boy for the coming age of clean corporate responsibility. The most Westernized of the seven oligarchs, he frequently invited representatives of the foreign press for informal chats, and, since his bank was right around the corner from our bureau, I sometimes tagged along with my office-mate Betsy or the bureau chief when they made the rounds.

Oneximbank was a five-minute walk from our building—or ten minutes by car because of the inevitable traffic. Potanin's bank occupied an imposing edifice clad entirely in dirty white granite. It was crescent-shaped, rose twenty stories, and was flanked by identical structures that housed competing financial institutions. In spite of the Soviet-to-the-core architecture, this was the closest Russia came to Wall Street.

Inside, the Oneximbank building had an institutional feel, betraying its origins as a government office complex. It was in fact the old Soviet Ministry of Foreign Trade Relations building, where Potanin's father had been a senior apparatchik and the oligarch had gotten his start as a promising young functionary of the Communist Party's international-business arm. Some obviously new additions to the lobby, however, spoke of the building's reincarnation as a banking center. The entrance, for one, was a maze of security: metal detectors and identification-card-swipe turnstiles blocked the door. Guards sat behind Italian-made grenade-proof glass partitions, which included slide-out drawers below posted signs instructing visitors to deposit their cellular phones and sidearms.

Since Betsy and I had neither, we were quickly escorted to a private elevator that rose to Potanin's office on the upper floor. Some other journalists were already there, making idle conversation with Russia's leading banker. Potanin was talking soccer with a German reporter, something about the Moscow Spartak team's chances in the coming European championship, and how the cold would give the Russians home-field advantage, just as it had against Napoleon and Hitler.

They went on at some length, discussing the soccer playoffs, while the rest of us tried not to look bored. Potanin was a *futbol* fanatic. He owned a team, and had a regulation-sized pitch installed inside his compound, next to the private lake where he jet-skied in the summer. On most Saturday afternoons he could be found charging down his meticulously tended turf in cleats and a blue numbered jersey, leading his Oneximbank employees into battle against other banks, newspapers, or whoever could field a team. Oneximbank always won, just as it did in privatization contests and tenders to manage the Kremlin's tax receipts.

Potanin's paneled office was large; everything in it looked as if it had been lifted out of a crate and unwrapped the day before, as befitted the overnight success of its bureaucrat-turned-billionaire occupant. Like Julia Timoshenko's place in Dnepropetrovsk, the cherrywood décor seemed to have leaped straight from the pages of an Ethan Allen catalogue. The furniture conveyed an air of probity and stability. Glass cabinets lined the walls and were stacked with antique-looking leather tomes, the kind people buy for decorative purposes. More dark leather gleamed from the upholstery on couches and chairs, and light fell softly from brass lamps with green glass shades better suited to an Ivy League campus library than to the lair of a Russian *biznesmen*. The effect was one of neutrality, as if to hint that its Russian owner was Western-minded, which indeed the young oligarch professed to be.

Tea had been served and conversational formalities dispensed with, and we finally opened our notebooks. I sat between the *Financial Times* bureau chief and Betsy, opposite the soccer enthusiast from Germany's *Handelsblatt*. We had been told that Potanin had summoned us all to clear the air and to make an important announcement about a shift in Oneximbank's strategy. Now we waited for him to speak.

Russia's leading banker surveyed us silently for a moment. At thirty-six, he was only a few years older than I was, but had already served as deputy prime minister (a fringe benefit for helping Yeltsin get reelected) and had the patrician, self-confident smile of a man who directed the lives of hundreds of thousands of people. Responsibility apparently weighed heavily upon him, for Potanin had an intensity and severity about him that reminded me of my father's expression whenever I got into trouble as a kid. Potanin, for that matter, looked alarmingly like my dad and my Uncle Zbig in their youth—blond, hawk-like, steely-eyed, with strong, triangular features and a jaw like the reinforced bow of an icebreaker. He wore a well-cut navy blue suit, nice but not flamboyant. His watch was not the usual Rolex, but something inconspicuous with a brown leather strap. This billionaire of less than five years was already acting like old money—restrained, understated—and I immediately liked him.

Potanin's spectacular rise had begun in 1990, when it was becoming apparent that Marx's days were numbered, leading the more savvy functionaries of the Ministry of Foreign Trade Relations to quietly establish private companies to facilitate the export of everything from agricultural products to arms. Back in those days, when the ministry enjoyed a monopoly on all of the Soviet Union's international trade, one had to go through that all-powerful organ to get permission to sell abroad. Potanin, with the help of his well-placed father, specialized in procuring the jealously guarded export licenses. If somehow, in the confusion and chaos of the time, you managed to get your hands on a trainload of rolled steel or crude oil and wanted to ship it out for hard currency to customers in the West, you called Potanin. If you had an uncle, say, who ran an aluminum smelter, and had heard of a commodity broker in Austria willing to pay cash for cheap ingots, Potanin was your man.

The Soviet system had been all about who you knew and who they knew, and apparently Potanin knew a great many influential bureaucrats, for by 1992 his network of facilitators had grown sufficiently for him to launch a small bank in a dreary corner of the ministry building. This little bank managed the cash flow of his export-license customers, and dabbled in trade financing and currency speculation. Business was good, and eventually he inherited the entire client list of the ministry's defunct in-house bank. In this fashion Potanin became the banker to Russia's raw-materials exporters. His fortunes grew again when he landed a prized concession to manage the Kremlin's customs receipts—the duties charged on every Mercedes, pack of Marlboros, and Sony television imported into the country—so that by 1994, he had a small piece of virtually everything that came in and out of Russia.

His big break, though, came in 1995, when he pitched privatization chief Chubais and Prime Minister Chernomyrdin a bold and ingenious plan. At the time, the Russian government was in dire financial straits. Yeltsin was getting ready to run for a second term and needed funds to repay wages and pension arrears that, if left unchecked, could cost him dearly at the ballot box. Potanin proposed forming a consortium of Russia's biggest private banks to lend the Treasury the money that the Yeltsin machine required to get itself reelected. In return, the Kremlin would put up as collateral shares in Russia's biggest and best State enterprises. These shares, it was agreed, would be worth far more—as much as a hundred times more—than the value of the loans, and the Kremlin could simply turn them over to the banks instead of repaying the debt.

It was not clear what propelled the government to embark on such a ruinously one-sided arrangement. Some said Chubais wanted to create a league of home-grown superbankers to prevent foreigners from snapping up Russia's crown jewels. Others maintained that it didn't matter what the bankers paid for the State enterprises; the important thing was getting these State companies off the government's books and into more efficient private hands. In any event, the benefits of the agreement for the bankers were clear and immediate. They got billion-dollar companies for pennies on the dollar. And they used the government's own funds to do so. (Effectively, they lent the Treasury its own money, using the customs receipts the Kremlin deposited in their banks.)

When the windfall deal was done, seven men found themselves in control of nearly half of Russia's privatized economy (hence the term "oligarchs," which had up to then served mainly to denote the powerful families that ran certain Latin American nations). Of these seven superbankers, Potanin emerged as the biggest, having reaped extra reward for masterminding the scheme. By 1997, his industrial empire included the world's largest nickel mine and smelter; Russia's premier airplane-engine manufacturer; one of its biggest steel mills; its fourth largest oil exporter; its most successful investment bank; sundry media properties; and the coveted national telephone monopoly, Svyazinvest.

"My companies generate roughly one-twentieth of Russia's total Gross Domestic Product," beamed Potanin, as we scribbled that astonishing number in our notebooks. The closest analogue I could think of was John D. Rockefeller's preeminent position in America's economy at the turn of the century, which not even Bill Gates had thus far managed to replicate. But much as Potanin and the rest of the oligarchs wanted to paint themselves as modern-day Rockefellers, there was a key difference between them and America's robber barons: Rockefeller built his Standard Oil from nothing, while the oligarchs seized the assets of Soviet Russia. They had not created wealth; they had simply grabbed it.

And that was the storybook version of how they had made their fortunes. There were more detailed and gruesome accounts, mostly unsubstantiated, of the oligarchs' rapid rise. But delving too deeply in these allegations invariably begged a lawsuit—or worse, as my colleague Betsy had discovered. Before joining the *Journal*, Betsy had worked for a major American weekly in Moscow. According to her, the weekly had launched an investigative story on one of Russia's political tycoons, but had abruptly dropped it after two gunmen appeared at the weekly's Moscow office, warning that the Russian capital could be a dangerous place for nosy foreigners who were not careful. One brave journalist from the *Village Voice* went into hiding after a Russian mafia boss living in Budapest put a hundred-thousand-dollar contract out on him following an unflattering story. Given our rather modest life-insurance policies, we reporters typically contented ourselves with terms like "murky" or "mysterious" when describing the provenance of the oligarchs' wealth.

As if sensing our thoughts, Potanin launched into his sales pitch. "We are coming to the end of the first phase of Russia's capitalist transition: the accumulation of capital," he explained in the faultless English that he, like the children of many communist higher-ups, had learned at elite Soviet institutes and universities. He conceded that this had been the crude and sometimes "unfair" early stage of the market transition, when unsavory means were employed to acquire wealth and property, and newly privatized companies were often looted by their unscrupulous new owners.

"Now we are entering the second stage, where we have the holdings"—and by this he meant the steel mills and oil companies and telephone grids—"and we must make them profitable, restructure them into viable concerns, change the system."

This was music to our ears. This was what everyone in Russia had been waiting for, what every foreign stockholder had been betting on, what the IMF and the World Bank had been dishing out billions for: the day when the tycoons would have finished dividing up the Soviet Union's spoils and would start acting responsibly. We scribbled furiously, knowing that the ramifications of this transition went far beyond the realm of business.

Potanin touched on more of the West's favorite themes, lamenting that the market transformation had outpaced the legal and taxation systems and making clear that reforms in earnest were now needed. Russia's rich might have skirted laws to acquire much of their wealth, but now they wanted better laws to protect that wealth. Russian's millionaires and billionaires may have hidden their income from the tax man, but now that they were loaded, they were calling for a less prohibitive tax code, one that would permit them to display and invest their wealth more openly. What we had were early rumblings for the rule of law. That such calls came from precisely the people who had exploited Russia's chaos to enrich themselves was perhaps only natural. They had benefited most from the postcommunist chaos and now stood to gain most from stability.

"The rules are changing in Russia," said Potanin, gesturing emphatically. "What was okay two years ago"—here we knew he meant the violence and intimidation, the brazen stock swindles, the rooking of foreign joint-venture partners, the asset grabs, and so on—"is no longer acceptable." Russian business, he concluded, needed to integrate with the West, which meant becoming more like the West.

We reporters were moved nearly to the point of tears by those wise words, so badly had everyone yearned to hear such uplifting pronouncements—falling from the lips of an oligarch, no less.

Of course, Potanin could afford to play the prophet. He had already cashed in on his newfound zeal for reform and sudden love affair with the West. Banking on his growing reputation as the most progressive oligarch, he had struck a number of highly profitable alliances with Westerners. The most notable was British Petroleum, which had just snapped up a 10-percent stake in his oil company, Sidanco, for $571 million—more than a hundred times what he had paid the Kremlin for it the year before. Potanin had also merged his investment-banking arm, MFK, with Jordan's Renaissance Capital, inheriting Jordan's biggest customer, the philanthropist financier George Soros, whom he convinced to put nine hundred million dollars toward the purchase of Svyazinvest, the Soviet telephone monopoly.

The sale of Mother Russia's Ma Bell had been touted as the watershed moment in Moscow's long-awaited progression from crony capitalism to something resembling a civilized economy. Nemtsov and Chubais, to the applause of the entire foreign community, had solemnly pledged that the telephone sale would mark "a new era" in Russia, one when State assets were no longer given away to politically connected insiders, but sold at public auctions to the highest bidder.

This was a revolutionary departure for the Kremlin, and did not thrill some of the oligarchs, who had grown accustomed to easy access to any State enterprises that caught their fancy. So nonplussed were the oligarchs at the notion of a privatization that was not rigged that on the eve of the auction a group of them had flown to Cannes to quiz the vacationing Chubais. No, Chubais reportedly assured them, the clean sale was not a publicity stunt to appease the IMF. The Kremlin needed money, and the days of State giveaways were over.

Shocked, the oligarchs had returned to Moscow and held one last midnight powwow at the office of Vladimir Gusinsky, a media magnate who, under the old crony rules of collusion, should have had first dibs on Svyazinvest. There were conflicting reports as to what transpired at that session, which was mediated by Boris Berezovsky, the man who had been most instrumental in Yeltsin's reelection campaign and who held a Rasputin-like sway over the Russian leader's family. But apparently no agreement was reached because the next day, when the sealed bids were presented, Potanin had outbid Gusinsky by some two hundred million dollars.

A war began between the previously chummy oligarchs, a mud-slinging fest in which Berezovsky and Gusinsky mercilessly turned their deadliest weapons—the very television stations and newspapers they had used to put Yeltsin back in office—against Chubais, Nemtsov, and Potanin. In the so-called "new era" ushered in by the Svyazinvest sale, the oligarchs had suddenly become sworn enemies, the first victims of Russia's attempt to introduce the concepts of free and fair competition to its brand of capitalism.

"Unfortunately," Potanin sighed, as our interview wound down, "some of Russia's other business leaders are not keen for change and are using their influence to maintain the status quo."

Was Potanin Potemkin reborn? Or was Russian business entering a new and more equitable era? I was certainly hoping for the latter, since Roberta's crusade for the almighty ruble gave me an indirect financial stake in Russia's future.

CHAPTER NINE

Eastern Exposure

Autumn brought troubling news from abroad. In Asia, the so-called "tiger economies" were teetering on the verge of collapse. International demand for oil, Russia's biggest hard currency export, was dropping. And emerging markets everywhere were faltering.

Everywhere, that is, except in Moscow, where Russian share prices bucked global trends and continued to defy gravity. The business of corporate bonds was in full bloom. Bonus season was around the corner, and deals had to be closed before the checks by which brokers and bankers measured their professional self-worth were handed out at the end of the year.

On the domestic front, a very pregnant Gretchen had flown home to Kentucky to give birth. We saw little of Boris in her absence, save for his occasional appearance on television. My aquarium was coming along nicely, its inhabitants having reached an uneasy equilibrium after I purchased several large oscars that would not be intimidated by the ravenous striped cichlids—sort of like relations between the oligarchs after the Svyazinvest fracas.

Roberta's shark fin was also progressing nicely. That September she was working on the final stages of her first VSO deal, financing the construction of the largest customs terminal in Russia. With all the Western goods flowing into the country, it seemed like a sure bet. Every time she mentioned the project, I had visions of myself at the helm of a thirty-six-foot Beneteau.

At the bureau there was a merciful lull, with financial news out of Russia slowing down after the hot, acrimonious summer. Russian politics followed a predictable seasonal pattern. Spring was always hopeful, bringing the promise of major economic reforms. Summer was reserved for wrangling over the implementation of those reforms. Fall was for protests and taking stock of the damage caused by the infighting. And winter? Winter was simply about hunkering down and praying that the coal and grain reserves would last until the cycle could begin anew.

As a financial journalist who prefers the streets to the Street, I was eagerly looking forward to the prospect of Eastern European–style social unrest and its accompanying water cannons, burning tires, and riot squads. But the seasonal protests came and went with a disappointing whimper. Unpaid coal miners staged a few desultory work stoppages—though only during their lunch breaks, so as not to disrupt production. Unsurprisingly, the Kremlin didn't seem to notice or care. The passivity of the Russian laborer was mind-boggling to me, after the wild Solidarity demonstrations I'd seen in Poland and the rampages of club-wielding Romanian miners, who would tear up Bucharest at the slightest provocation. You can bet that the Polish and Romanian authorities made sure their workers were paid on time, and it was beyond me why Russian miners didn't rise up in earnest. Some hadn't been paid for over a year, and it took a special understanding of the Slavic soul to fathom why they still showed up for work.

With the dearth of adventure in Moscow, I decided to seek excitement in the provinces. Fortunately, a restructuring of responsibilities at the bureau had left the oil beat open, and Russia's oil was in satisfyingly wild and remote corners of Siberia and the Far East.

The eastward flight from Moscow had lasted nearly ten hours, about the same time it took to fly to New York. It was dawn by the time we landed in Sakhalin, off Russia's Pacific coast, and the island was shrouded in a fine mist.

Sakhalin was an old Soviet penal colony, one of the more desolate atolls of the "gulag archipelago." Its major claim to international fame was as the place where a Korean Airlines passenger liner had been shot down in 1983 after straying into the USSR's airspace. In

Russia, Sakhalin was known for two other things: king crabs, of the Alaskan variety; and oil, in Alaskan quantities.

The flight—in a wide-bodied Boeing—had been safe and pleasant enough, and I had enjoyed the company of the Canadian roughnecks and British oil executives flying out to Russia's easternmost oil province. The oilmen were a gruff bunch, refreshingly blunt after all the slick, Hermès-tied investment bankers I dealt with in Moscow. They were cynical from a life spent in Third World jungles and deserts, but there was an honest and proud quality to their banter. An easy camaraderie united them, and as the endless blackness of Siberia unfolded below us, I whiled away the hours listening to them swill booze, groan about the coming winter, and swap war stories from their previous tours of duty.

One of the tales—told by a witty Shell executive, an Englishman whose refined accent suggested attendance at all the right schools— still sticks in my mind. It was about the time he had spent working on an oil platform in the Niger Delta. The delta, he said, was a festering swamp, full of snakes and malaria-carrying mosquitoes, but soaked in crude. Crude, he remarked, always seemed to percolate in the most inhospitable places—God's way of making amends to the local residents.

In any event, Shell had towed several exploration platforms to the delta, and no sooner had they set up operations than a small flotilla of canoes and wood rafts descended on the rigs, the villagers offering to sell everything from live goats to women.

"People were shitting in the same water they butchered cow carcasses in," the Shell exec went on, "so we passed on the steaks they were offering."

Outraged, the local chieftain materialized in full tribal gear, announcing that the oilmen were trespassing on his land and would have to either purchase goods from his village, buy a few women, or pay rent. Since Shell had already paid the Nigerian government handsomely for exploration rights, they gave the chief a television and politely sent him on his way.

The canoes persisted for a few days, until it became apparent that the drillers were not going to buy their livestock or services. Then, on the fourth night, all hell broke loose. The roughnecks heard shrieks in the dark. Drums beat. Women wailed. They trained their lights on the noise and saw dozens of silhouettes brandishing spears and clubs. Panic broke out as the invaders clambered atop the rig.

"We thought we were finished," said the exec, pausing dramatically. "They turned out to be the women, wearing war paint and nothing else. And they said they were going to occupy the platform until we started servicing them, so to speak."

"So what did you do?" one of the Canadian roughnecks inquired.

"We called for volunteers," replied the Shell exec. "What else could we do?"

The roughnecks roared and slapped one another on the back, transforming the business-class cabin into a boisterous locker room. The flight attendant brought more coffee and cognac, addressing some of the men by their first names. Apparently they were regulars on this route, taking the Transaero connector flight to and from Moscow every six weeks for some much-needed R&R outside of Russia. (Oil companies take very good care of their workers.)

The island of Sakhalin was Transaero's easternmost destination, about four hundred miles past Vladivostok, across the Sea of Japan, and directly north of the Japanese island of Hokkaido. It was an untamed sliver of land on the very edge of the Pacific shelf, with vast fir forests, shifting fault lines, and dormant volcanoes. In Sakhalin, bears were said to outnumber people. The month before our arrival a Japanese wildlife photographer had been eaten by one.

We were met at the tiny airport by a blast of cold autumn air and a half-dozen mud-splattered sport utility vehicles with stickers on their windshields indicating they belonged to Shell, Exxon, and Texaco. The Seven Sisters, as the oil majors were called then, were all represented in Sakhalin; the projects here were so big and capital-intensive that even the Sisters had to pool their finances to come up with the $40 billion it was going to cost to develop the island's off-shore fields.

A fog bank had rolled in from the Pacific, and dew trickled down the terminal's steamy windows. Outside the flimsy gray building, several stray dogs shivered, tails tucked between their mangy legs. A babushka sweeping the asphalt with a twig broom shooed them away.

As we waited for our bags—a colleague from the *Times* of London cursing that he had not packed a parka—there was a sudden commotion. The regional governor was taking our flight back to Moscow, and members of his entourage were scurrying about the terminal as if the tsar himself were about to embark on his royal ship. The governors of Russia's eighty-nine regions were surprisingly autonomous, and some ran their parts of the country like personal fiefs.

Governor Igor Farkhutdinov cut a majestic figure in his tailored blue Hugo Boss suit and gold Rolex. His office was getting two hundred million dollars in concession fees from the various Western oil consortiums, and we asked what he intended to do with the windfall.

"The money has been spent wisely," he said airily, turning away, as if the question had been adequately covered. "Could you be more specific?" pressed Robin Lodge, the *Times* man. "Did you build roads, or a hospital?" Sakhalin, like the rest of the Far East, was terribly poor, with virtually no infrastructure and a reputation for gross mismanagement.

Farkhutdinov fixed us with an icy glare. His aides shifted uncomfortably. "We have used it to settle debts," the governor finally said after several seconds of silence. And then he beamed, as though he had just been struck by a novel idea. "We will use future oil income on infrastructure."

With that, the impromptu interview was over. "He's not a bad bloke," the Shell executive rationalized, as the governor and his entourage boarded the Boeing. "At least he supports foreign investment in the oil sector. Most of the other politicians in Russia these days are hellbent on keeping Westerners out."

This was true enough. Russia's parliament was blocking approval of dozens of major oil deals. Just the other week, the Kremlin had abruptly annulled a tender won by Exxon to exploit Arctic deposits, and Amoco, after spending hundreds of millions of dollars on a Siberian joint venture with oligarch-owned Yukos Oil, had been rather unceremoniously informed that it was no longer welcome. The Russians, it struck me, were only too happy to sell us their stocks and bonds, accepting hard currency in exchange for what were effectively pieces of paper. But oil was another story. Oil was real.

The only reason the Western consortia had been allowed to go ahead with the huge projects in Sakhalin was that the Russian oil companies did not yet have the resources or advanced technology required to drill far offshore, where the island's biggest deposits lay. The billions of dollars the Sisters would invest to tap hard-to-reach deposits promised to transform impoverished Sakhalin into another Alaska. Already the signs of the coming oil boom were unmistakable in the capital of Yuzhno-Sakhalinsk. At the airport, scaffolding shrouded a new terminal building. The local airline had just taken delivery of American-made planes. A casino, that monument to every gold rush, had opened, its whirling wheels-in-lights winking invitingly next to hunters' huts, mud fields, and pungent fish canneries. Smuggled-in right-hand-drive Toyotas bounced along the unpaved roads, and a new hotel materialized out of the wilderness like a mirage.

It was called the Santa. The Japanese had built it, out of prefabricated modules that had been shipped in on barges and assembled, to cater to the influx of drillers and survey crews whose Texan twangs already reverberated in the marble lobby. Much of Sakhalin's expatriate population lived permanently in the hotel, which maintained its own generators, hot-water heaters, and satellite phones, and was thus immune to the outages that routinely befell the rest of the island. If not for all the trees around it, the Santa could have been mistaken for a Tokyo Holiday Inn. The televisions in its rooms broadcast Japan's baseball playoffs. The restaurant served kelp soup for breakfast. Karaoke blared in the pub. And the minibars were stocked with *sake*.

Only the stunning chambermaids (miniskirts, high heels, and about a mile of leg in between) served as a reminder that this was indeed anything-goes Russia. One of the Canadians I met on the plane had confided that some of the girls at the Santa did a lot more than just clean your room. "They'll clean your pipe for twenty bucks," was how he put it.

The hotel, naturally, was outrageously expensive, thanks to its monopoly on civilization. It honored American Express, the first establishment in Sakhalin's history to do so. For some reason, this disappointed me. That one paid for room service with Amex on Sakhalin, flew there in business class, and drove around the tundra in GMC Suburbans took some of the romance out of Siberia. Where were the bears? The quaint trappers? The frontiersmen here all seemed to have engineering degrees from Cal Tech. I had escaped the Moscow expatriate cocoon only to enter another, equally privileged one.

This reporting trip, in fact, was starting to feel like a Club Med vacation, complete with crab feasts and island-touring itineraries. The arrangements had been made, with excruciating attention to detail, by the oil majors. When journalists visit oil fields—and this holds true throughout the world—the visit is almost always arranged by the oil company, for the simple reason that the only way to get to most drilling sites is on an oil-company bush plane or helicopter. You can't just turn up on your own, unless you fork over ten thousand dollars to charter your own plane, which most editors would frown upon, to say the least. So there is invariably a trade-off: access for freedom of movement. It is a pitfall of the profession that goes far beyond reporting on the oil industry, as any White House or Pentagon correspondent will attest.

But we reporters are a resilient lot. We suffered the temporary loss of our independence with grace, consoling ourselves with mountains of crab and gallons of free *sake*. The propensity for gorging appeared cross-cultural, for the Dutch, Japanese, British, and American reporters on the trip ate and drank the free fare with equal abandon. (One last point about newshounds while we are on the subject: we are intensely social animals, and prefer traveling in packs. Stringers, the lowly outcasts of the profession, are no exception to the rule. Travel during my own days as a minor-leaguer had been oppressively lonely—the bus rides in the Baltics; the small towns in Slovakia; the nights in torrid Crimean hotels, waiting for the water to be turned on. I would sit in my grubby room in some unpronounceable place like Jastrzebiezdroj, unwashed after two days of train travel, wondering what my friends at home were up to, feeling as if I'd fallen off the face of the earth. Traveling in groups was a lot more fun. Safer too.)

Our guided tour of Sakhalin began early the next morning. It was still dark and the dew frosty when we clambered aboard an old Antonov propeller plane and took off for the six-hundred-mile flight north to the oil fields. As the sun rose, the island's dense forests came to life in an explosion of autumn colors worthy of a *National Geographic* spread. The landscape was pristine, an uninterrupted tableau of lakes, rolling mists, and dark fast-running rivers. After a few peaceful hours, our destination came into view, a patched strip of runway and a corrugated steel shack. At the far end of the strip, several helicopters decomposed in a makeshift graveyard. They were missing rotors and landing gear. Some lay on their sides, exposing cracked ribs and shattered canopies and horribly twisted tail booms that spoke of painful landings.

"I certainly hope we're not going up in one of those," whispered Robin, the *Times* of London correspondent.

"I've flown in worse," joked another reporter. Everyone laughed nervously. A few months before, a chopper had in fact gone down in Baku, Azerbaijan, killing all eighteen oil workers on board.

The helicopter in which we would be touring the oil fields looked sturdy enough. It was a big, ungainly MI-8, originally designed as a troop carrier but modified for civilian use. MI-8s flew throughout the Russian Far North, delivering personnel and supplies to the pipelines and oil wells that crisscrossed the *taiga* (wilderness). We donned ear protectors and climbed into the noisy bird, trying not to brush against the soot and oily exhaust that caked its blue fuselage. The turbines powered up and the helicopter shuddered, kicking up a dirt storm. Within seconds, we were banking steeply and heading out towards some onshore fields operated by the local Russian oil company, SMNG.

Derricks and drilling platforms sprouted metallically through clearings in the forest. As we came in closer, we could see extraction pumps, the so-called "nodding donkeys" whose steady bowing motions brought to mind an industrial form of davening. At the foot of these pumps, huge pools of crude oil soaked the sand, running off into ditches and leaving foul black trails in the dirt where trucks had rolled through. The rivers glistened like rainbows from the slicks, and even the tips of some pine trees were drenched black from high gushers.

It made you wonder if the Russians actually managed to collect any of the oil, or if they were content just to liberate. The long, silvery pipelines that snaked around the site seemed to indicate that they were at least tapping some of the runoff. A Shell rep, a Brit by the name of Gerry Matthews, shook his head in disgust.

"They're probably pumping more mud and water out of those wells than crude," he shouted, having to repeat himself twice over the clatter of the rotor blades. Russia's oil industry was using horribly antiquated technology, one reason why the more environmentally-conscious and efficient Western majors could squeeze twice as much crude out of their wells while making half the mess.

"The Russians are about thirty years behind us," said Matthews, as we hovered over the sludge. The environmental destruction stretched in every direction. It seemed almost wanton, as if the loss of a few hundred square miles meant nothing in the limitless Far North. That same sloppiness also applied to human life, as we saw moments later, when the helicopter flew over the largest pile of rubble I'd ever seen in my life. It stretched for perhaps half a mile, and rose in some places as much as fifty feet. As the chopper set down, I realized with horror that this was the remains of a town.

This was Neftegorsk, literally Oiltown, a Soviet-era housing project for roughnecks and their families. Although it was built alongside a tectonic fault line, central planners had not bothered to pour the flexible, reinforced foundations required by building codes in earthquake zones throughout the world. Instead, they just slapped up the usual shoddy precast concrete structures. In May 1995, an earthquake measuring 8.0 on the Richter scale had erupted just as a dance was getting underway at the Neftegorsk cultural center. When the dust settled three minutes later, two thousand people were dead, and the whole place had been leveled.

Ironically, the only buildings left standing were the wooden trappers' huts on the edge of town. They stood there still, abandoned and covered in dust, with toppled telephone poles perched lazily against their roofs and electrical transmission lines draped over them. The city center was a jigsaw of concrete slabs and bent I-beams. Twisted reinforcing bars poked rustily through sand dunes that had built up over time. The top of a stop sign commemorated a buried road crossing.

Neftegorsk was what I imagined the aftermath of a nuclear holocaust would look like—nothing but wind and dust, and screaming silence.

Everyone was quiet after we took off; the disaster had had a sobering effect. We headed toward the Pacific, passing the fault line that was the cause of the earthquake. It ran along the shore, creating a six-foot-high ridge where the earth's crust had buckled. On the beach was the last derrick, the easternmost hard-currency generator on Russian soil. Beyond that point lay the shelf and the massive offshore deposits that the Russians did not have the technology or the money to tap. That would be Shell's and Exxon's turf, when they towed in their platforms and rigs.

The chopper pilot popped his head into the cabin and announced that we were running short on fuel and would be turning back to Okha, the main town in the northern part of the island, where SMNG, Sakhalin's largest oil company, was headquartered, and the earthquake's survivors resettled. Okha was possibly an even worse environmental catastrophe than the fields we had just seen. The place reeked of sulfur. Crude oil clung to weeds in the ditches, rising halfway up dead stalks that looked like bristles of a paintbrush dipped in tar. It oozed out of drainage pipes, and mixed in ugly black globs with the mud that covered absolutely everything. Pipes and ducts of all sizes ran through the town, some left exposed and rusty on the ground, others wrapped in crumbling asbestos and supported by ten-foot T brackets hammered into people's lawns. These conduits hissed and steamed and looked in desperate need of replacement.

About a quarter of Okha's buildings were uninhabitable, with collapsed roofs, missing walls, and foot-wide cracks in their charred facades. Burned-out warehouses, left unrepaired since gas mains had ruptured during the 1995 earthquake, lined the pitted main access road. People in dirty pea jackets and knee-high galoshes walked along this road carrying buckets of water. The town's water mains had also burst and gone unfixed, as had some of the electricity cables, which draped mournfully from sagging poles.

The poverty had an energizing effect on the press corps. Up to this point most of us had treated the trip as a working vacation, but now we smelled a story. Okha, after all, should have been immensely rich. Hundreds of millions, if not billions, of dollars of crude were extracted from the earth here annually, and the Russians had been drilling for oil on this spot since the late 1920s. Where was the money going? We wanted answers, and demanded in unison to see the mayor.

Mayor Naïl Yarulin greeted us in his shabby office. A small and gloomy man with soft, teary eyes, he bore no resemblance to the self-confident, resplendent governor. He wore a dusty cardigan, holes eaten through the armpits, and mittens. His office was not heated, and one of the windowpanes, I noticed, was broken and blocked with cardboard. Wherever Okha's petrodollars were flowing, it was certainly not to Mayor Yarulin's municipal coffers.

"We just don't have the money to maintain the town," he told us. "I haven't been able to pay myself for months. Some of the teachers haven't received their salaries in half a year. I have no gasoline for my ambulances. Most of them don't work anyway."

"But you're sitting on a sea of oil," one of the reporters protested. "You export millions of barrels of it. How can you not have money?"

"I just don't know," the mayor sighed. "I can't explain it. Ask SMNG (the local oil concern). Almost our entire city budget comes from them, and they haven't paid last year's taxes, let alone anything this year."

Corporate-tax deadbeats were a nationwide plague hardest felt in one-company towns like Okha. During the Soviet period, the State enterprises around which the settlements had been built had supported all schools, hospitals, and maintenance of roads and social services. These responsibilities had been shifted to the municipal government during the industrial restructuring reforms of the 1990s, with the understanding that the privatized enterprises would pay taxes to fund city budgets. All too often, however, the newly private companies ignored their tax bills, letting the towns fall apart. Virtually everyone in Russia cheated the tax man in one way or another, because paying the ruinous and always changing rates charged by the Kremlin guaranteed almost certain bankruptcy. (My own tax situation was somewhat of a mess, but I wasn't worried, since stories I had done on the tax police revealed that it was an even bigger mess.)

The Kremlin had just released figures showing that the federal government had only collected a third of projected tax revenues for 1997, leaving a gaping hole in its finances that needed to be plugged by issuing more T-bills. On the local level, where there were no bonds to bridge the shortfalls, tax evasion paralyzed entire communities. In one Western Siberian oil center, for instance, the situation grew so desperate that the mayor once held several oil executives hostage to try to force the oligarch-controlled conglomerate they worked for to make good on at least some of its back taxes. The back taxes were never paid, but two weeks after the incident the mayor's body was found in a field, riddled with bullets. His murder was never solved.

In addition to neglecting its Okha tax bill, SMNG wasn't even paying its workers on time. More than half the town's residents, said Yarulin, lived below the poverty line, hunting and fishing to put food on the table. Meanwhile, rolling blackouts were routine, and in the summer electricity was available only four hours a day. "SMNG needs the electricity to run the oil wells," Yarulin said despondently.

The contrast with the West, where roughnecks are among the best paid of all blue-collar workers, was startling. As a college student, I had done a stint in the Canadian Far North, building the huge Hydro Quebec dams that power New York City. I brought home nearly two thousand Canadian dollars a week to pay my tuition, and had known laborers up there who earned two hundred thousand dollars a year. Hydro Quebec, like the U.S. oil majors in Alaska, took great pains to coax employees to "polar bear country," building indoor pools, and flying up lobster, steak, and even a salsa-dancing troupe to boost morale. Here, people didn't even have heat.

The mayor was obviously not to blame, so we made for SMNG's offices across town. The concern occupied a freshly painted building with new PVC windows and monstrous white satellite dishes on its flat roof. A number of late-model Toyota Land Cruisers idled outside the main entrance.

SMNG local boss Sergei Bogdanchikov ushered us into a richly appointed conference room with two wide-screen Sony televisions and enough black leather furniture to reupholster a Boeing 737. "Does the sun bother you?" he asked sweetly, pointing some sort of remote-control gadget at the windows. A hidden motor whirred and the shades glided shut. He waved the gadget toward the lights, which obediently grew brighter, all the while beaming like a proud parent. He was obviously very taken with his little contraption. Bogdanchikov looked to be cut of the same cloth as the governor: young, smug, and unaccustomed to answering to anyone but his superiors in Moscow. From the look of his tailored suit, he was obviously was getting his salary on time.

"We hear that you owe significant tax arrears," we started in after the niceties had been dispensed with.

"An unavoidable circumstance," Bogdanchikov explained patronizingly. "You see, we are awaiting our transfer payments from Moscow. You must ask Moscow where our money is."

This set the tone for what became a frustratingly evasive interview. The back wages? You must ask Moscow. The funds for the clean-up? You must ask Moscow. SMNG's hard-currency earnings? You must ask Moscow.

At least I could now see where Moscow was getting its money, where the cash for the oligarchs' Mercedes and Gulfstream jets came from. The only question that remained was how many other Okhas—resource-rich but dirt-poor—were being bled dry across the Russian Far East and Siberia.

The most disturbing aspect of the looting of Okha—and here the media darling Potanin's promise that such practices were ending rang particularly hollow—was that SMNG was itself a State-controlled enterprise, a subsidiary of Rosneft, the last Russian oil giant still on the privatization block. Its sale had been delayed several times because Potanin and his archrival Boris Berezovsky were at odds over who would get it, and no one wanted another disruptive oligarch brawl after the Svyazinvest debacle. In the meantime, Rosneft's government-appointed managers were allegedly selling Okha's oil at below-market prices to private exporters. According to government regulators, this practice was systematically bankrupting Rosneft subsidiaries like SMNG. In any event, somebody was getting rich off Okha, and it certainly wasn't the people who lived there.

Since Rosneft was still State-owned, the plundering couldn't be blamed on the "sharks of capitalism." Ultimately, it was the Kremlin's fault. Moscow was surely not blind to what was going on in its distant oil provinces. Colonialism was alive and well in Russia, but with a twist—this nation was, and is, the only empire in history to treat her own citizens like slaves.

The following day, morning broke bright and clear. We were back in southern Sakhalin, lugging our bags onto the cargo bay of yet another small plane, which was to speed us across the Sea of Japan to the mainland port of Vladivostok.

I seemed to be spending half my life in the air, and worried that the law of averages would eventually catch up to me, as it had for so many unfortunate souls who had taken one Tupolev flight too many. But I was careful to keep my airborne panic attacks to myself, since my colleagues exuded enough testosterone to fuel a rugby scrum. (The one exception was the staid *Financial Times* correspondent, who stubbornly refused to relinquish his tie and business suit, even in the deepest bog and sludge.)

Everyone on the plane was in better spirits now that we were a thousand miles away from Okha, and the press passed the time napping, catching up on notes, and telling jokes and war stories. One particularly apt anecdote, given what we had witnessed in Sakhalin, went something like this: Two delegates meet at a conference of government officials from developing nations. One is from Africa, the other from Southeast Asia. They hit it off and agree to visit one another. Some months later the African official drops in on his new friend in Asia. "What a beautiful home you have," he says to the Asian bureaucrat. "How can you afford such a big house on government pay?"

"Easy," beams his host. "See that highway?" he says, pointing at a newly paved stretch of road. "I skimmed ten percent off the construction budget."

The following year the Asian official visits Africa. He calls on his old buddy, and is stunned to see him moving into an enormous villa, with swimming pools, helicopter pads, and a garage stuffed with Italian sports cars. "My God," cries the astounded Asian bureaucrat. "How can you afford all this on your government salary?"

"Simple," chuckles the African official. "See that new national superhighway?" he says, pointing to an empty, weedy field with a few surveyor's stakes. "One hundred percent of the budget."

Most of us had heard it before. Apparently so had the oilmen accompanying us, for one made the comment that postcommunist Russia was a developed nation saddled with a Third World mentality; its leaders were educated and polished, but bereft of any sense of civic responsibility. Their willingness to share the wealth would make Sakhalin as rich as Alaska—but their greed could blight it like Nigeria.

Shell, Exxon, and Texaco were no strangers to this dilemma, having seen it go either way in dozens of countries over the past fifty years. For their own survival, the Sisters had learned to be good corporate citizens; while they had no control over what the Russians did with their concession payments, they aimed to create tens of thousands of high-paying jobs and spin-off industries once their offshore sites were operational. Finally, Sakhalin would have something to show for its natural treasure. Thus far the Sakhalin projects were at the early exploration stages, the majors conducting seismic surveys to determine where to start drilling. The Shell-led consortium was furthest along, having towed a drilling platform from the Canadian Arctic to South Korea, where it was being refitted for duty in Sakhalin. Giant oil tankers were to be moored next to the platform while the construction of a connecting pipeline and a ten-billion-dollar liquid-natural-gas processing facility was finished. This would trigger the promised boom, said Frank Duffield, a tough New Zealander; he headed the Shell team, which included Marathon Oil of the United States and Japan's Mitsubishi Corporation. Already, said Duffield, the impact of the Western majors was being positively felt in the region, and contracts were being given to local companies in desperate need of business.

We were going to Vladivostok to visit one of these fortunate subcontractors, presumably so that we could see the benefits for ourselves and write nice things about Shell. Oil companies were very image conscious, and they didn't fly journalists halfway around the world for nothing. It was time to pay for all that free crab.

The Amur Shipbuilding Plant was a bumpy three-hour drive out of Vladivostok. There were no highways in this hilly region, only two-lane roads through forests, military garrisons, and the occasional dusty village clustered around the smokestack and sawdust piles of a timber mill. Our right-hand-drive Toyota minivan shared the windy road with old tractor-trailers weighed down by logs, peasants leading cows on ropes, and mud-spattered motorcycles with sidecars reminiscent of those driven by GIs in World War II movies. The shipyard took its name from the Amur River, which flowed along the heavily fortified Chinese border. The area was wild and remote, and was renowned for its dwindling population of white Siberian tigers, which had been poached to near extinction for their bones. When crushed into a fine powder, the bones were prized above all in the markets of Hong Kong, where they commanded up to five thousand dollars a pound as aphrodisiacs.

During the Soviet era, the Amur shipworks had assembled the so-called "hunter" nuclear-powered attack submarines that in Tom Clancy's thrillers chase America's big Trident-class subs in blind cat-and-mouse contests. But since the end of the Cold War, the military orders had dried up and the proud plant had fallen on hard times. Workers went unpaid for nine months at a stretch. Alcoholism was rampant; the plant's ten thousand employees had grown so desperate that anything that wasn't nailed down was stolen.

The Shell consortium placed its first order with Amur in late 1996, just as the yard was about to lay off half its personnel. Ernst Gwydir, a Marathon engineer, recalled the workers going crazy. "Fights broke out," drawled Gwydir, a big, open-faced Texan with the cowboy boots to prove it. "The welders were ready to kill each other over who would get to work for us."

The contract was to build the gigantic base on which Shell's offshore drilling platform would rest, and it paid workers up to three thousand dollars a month, a staggering sum given that most people at that plant barely made fifty dollars a month. Most of Amur's employees would have happily worked for a tenth of what the Americans were offering, which led me to believe that the generous salaries were part of a larger political game. Shell, Exxon, and the rest of the international oil majors all had Russian oil development deals languishing in the xenophobic Duma. Parliament's profane ultranationalist Vladimir Zhirinovsky was adamantly opposed to opening Russia's natural treasures to outsiders, accusing foreigners of only wanting "to screw our women and plunder our resources." The majors wanted to make a showcase of Sakhalin to convince reluctant legislators to let them in.

"The onus is on us to prove that everyone benefits if you allow foreign investment," said Gwydir, as we sidestepped a shower of sparks raining down from the nearly completed stand. The structure was to be towed out and sunk off Sakhalin in a few months. Hexagonal in shape, with the rough dimensions of a football field, it had been designed to withstand collisions with the icebergs that patrolled those icy waters. Workers were just putting the finishing touches on the massive steel stand. Blue torch flames flickered, and welders in grimy overalls and black goggles scurried up ladders. I clambered to the top of a crane to get a better view of the shipyard, hoping to catch a glimpse of one of its sleek black submarines. But all I saw were more cranes, smokestacks, empty dry docks, bubble-shaped corrugated steel hangars, and piles of metal plate—all so thoroughly rusted that it seemed as if the place had been shuttered for years. The military production was at the furthest end of the plant, where the river had been dredged and the forest cleared of potential snooping vantage points on the far bank. That part of the yard had been designated a high-security-clearance section, and foreigners were not allowed near it. Communist-era warnings to be vigilant against spies and saboteurs were still stenciled on some of the shipyard's walls. The red paint, though, had faded badly.

Conversion of military facilities to civilian uses was one of the prime objectives of U.S. policy toward Russia, and one had to wonder if Amur had really been randomly selected for this contract. More intriguing was the prospect that some of the American engineers permanently posted at the shipyard to supervise the construction of the stand might be CIA—a possibility that I was convinced had not escaped Russian counterintelligence, which probably had dispatched its own agents to the yard. Or maybe I'd just read too many spy thrillers in my youth.

Still stuck in Le Carré mode, I asked a large worker who was missing two fingers (crushed between steel plates, he explained proudly, the mark of a veteran fitter) if he enjoyed working for the Americans, who, after all, had been the enemy until recently.

"I've never actually talked to them," he said, jabbing his mangled hand in the direction of the gaggle of engineers in white hard hats standing on the edge of the dock. "But I receive my pay promptly, and I am able to buy things that my neighbors could never hope to. I am a patriot. But I also have a family to feed."

Economic necessity also trumped Soviet ideology in the yard's drab administration offices, where the corridors were lined with potted plants and dusty portraits of "Heroes of Soviet Labor," the communist equivalent of the employee-of-the-month plaques that one sees in fast-food outlets in the States. Amur's general director, Pavel Bely, looked every bit the old Cold Warhorse; his suit was dreary and Soviet, with ridiculously wide pinstripes and padded shoulders like tractor fenders. He wore his gray hair Brezhnev-style, and still addressed his subordinates as *tovarishchi* (comrades).

But Bely had a gentle, paternal air that softened his Soviet exterior. As he talked, it became apparent that he cared deeply about his plant and the welfare of its workers, and was trying desperately to preserve jobs any way he could. "Sure, building oil-rig stands is not technically challenging, compared to nuclear submarines," he said in response to a reporter's question about Amur's proud traditions. "But I wish we had more such contracts. Moscow stopped paying for military orders a long time ago," he added forthrightly, tapping cigarette ash. "Russia can no longer afford to build naval vessels, that's a sad fact of life. Our future at the factory is tied to Western oil development now."

Our last night in Vladivostok. Fog over the naval base. Ghostly freighters in the dirty harbor.

Russia's murder capital felt dark and dangerous. The few cars out on the lonely streets drove at breakneck speed. The city seemed deserted, as if its law-abiding citizens fled indoors at dusk, drawing their blinds tight against the ruffians and gangsters who trolled the waterfront. The menacing gloom reminded me of Moscow in the early 1990s, only even more frightening.

Vladivostok was five time zones ahead of the Russian capital, but a decade behind. Progress traveled slowly along the Trans-Siberian Railroad, and this place was the end of the line, about as wild as the Wild East got. Shootouts, stabbings, car bombs, rapes, kidnappings, disappearances—Vladivostok had them all on a daily basis, in greater numbers per capita than any other city in the former Soviet Union.

I had yearned for the frontier. And now that I was on it, I was scared stiff, huddled in our hotel along with most of Vladivostok's tiny expatriate community, who lived there behind a forest of security guards.

Like the Santa in Sakhalin, the Moosehead Canadian Lodge and

Inn was an oasis of civilization. The hotel was safely outside city limits, on the grounds of a leafy country estate at the ocean's edge where Nixon and Brezhnev had held détente talks in 1971. It was operated by a rugged Canadian couple, who had shipped it into the harbor in prefabricated modules, just like the Santa. The theme at the Moosehead, however, was strictly North American. Televisions pulled down the NBC affiliate in Anchorage and the CBC signal from Vancouver. The bar had Molson beer on tap, hockey on ESPN, and buffalo wings at two dollars apiece.

Like the Santa, the Lodge had its own sources of power and water. The rest of Vladivostok often went days without electricity because of corruption and mismanagement at State-owned power plants. As with SMNG, the plant managers sold power below cost to intermediary companies (run by nephews and wives of plant bosses); this ruinous practice left the plants unable to buy coal to run their generators. Gretchen's husband Boris, in his capacity as electricity tsar, had recently swung through town to fire a slew of crooked power-plant managers, but the thefts continued.

In addition to the brownouts, Vladivostok was plagued by dryouts. The city's water mains were so corroded that almost all their water drained into the soil and sea, and there was not enough pressure in the pipes for tap water to reach the top floors of buildings and housing blocks. Earlier in the day we had seen hundreds of people, pensioners and teens alike, lined up patiently with pails in front of water cisterns. The mafia, we were told, controlled water distribution, charging the poor pensioners the equivalent of about twenty-five cents a gallon.

At the Moosehead, however, Vladivostok's woes seemed a million miles away—which, of course, was the whole point of its existence. As it was our last night, our hosts from Shell and Marathon had prepared a farewell feast. The Molson had flowed in sufficient quantities that a few of us intrepid reporters worked up the courage to go into town on our own.

On the recommendation of the Lodge bartender, we hit upon the idea of checking out a casino/disco complex that he said was *klassno* (classy). Insulated by the oil companies' helicopters and plush lodges, we had hardly met any "real people" in the Russian Far East. The least we could do was schmooze with a few local players.

The establishment was on the second floor of a heavy concrete structure that had once housed the Soviet equivalent of a supermarket. At the foot of the stairs, a crumpled young woman wept, wiping her nose with a handkerchief that was stained with either blood or copious amounts of lipstick. A brutish-looking man was yelling at her. We gave them a wide berth; since for all we knew he was probably a gangster, prudence seemed the better part of chivalry.

On the second-floor landing, a large neon roulette wheel whirled over a steel door with the kind of thick glass peephole I'd seen only on U.N. armored cars on the Serbian-Macedonian border. There was a buzzer. Gerry, the Shell rep, rang it boldly. The door clicked open like a safe, and we were blasted with the throbbing beat of dance music. Four very large men—the human equivalent of Rottweilers—loomed inside. Two had AK-47 machine guns slung over their shoulders. The others wore pistols in holsters.

"What do you want?" they barked.

"Just a drink," said Robin, the cool-headed *Times* of London reporter.

The Rottweilers gave us an appraising look, and motioned us in. They passed metal detectors over us, making us raise our arms and turn full circle and, once satisfied we wore no concealed weapons, waved us on to a high-heeled hostess who inquired about our health and pleasure and collected a twenty-dollar admission fee from each of us.

The security precautions were intimidating, but apparently necessary. Two days before, a big shootout had taken place at the new Hyundai hotel, Vladivostok's only other home-away-from-home for Western businessmen. The head of one of the city's innumerable mafia groups had had his brain splattered across the lobby of the establishment, which was still scarred by bullet holes. Two gunmen had walked into the Korean joint venture and let loose with their machine guns, shredding furniture, scattering guests, and shattering mirrors. The downed crime boss's bodyguards had shot back, managing to take out the glass doors and a passerby. The fracas hadn't even made the front page of the local newspapers, so frequent were such tiffs between rival criminal gangs.

We gingerly made our way inside, trying not to look terrified. The gaming room was smoky, loud, and crowded. A group of drunken Chinese traders were enjoying a spirited game of dice, whooping and roaring at every roll while more Rottweilers looked on with disapproval. The other gamblers were Russians, and looked like petty thugs to a man. They were dressed like the Muscovites of the early nineties, in Puma tracksuits and black leather jackets, with thick gold bracelets and tattoos. Unlike the Chinese, they smoked glumly and wore expressions of intense concentration or barely controlled rage. I noticed that one had a gun in his waistband, which could only mean he was affiliated with the gang that probably ran the casino.

The ubiquitous mafia molls leaned against the bar, flicking cigarette ashes with their long black-painted fingernails. We apparently stuck out as potentially rich foreign marks, for they eyed us with commercial interest, as did the croupiers in the red vests. Several of the gamblers also gave us looks that did not seem benevolent. I was uneasily reminded of the cantina scene in *Star Wars*.

"I don't like the look of this lot," whispered Robin. "Let's have a pint in the pub."

The casino complex was divided into three separate "entertainment" centers, as was the fashion throughout the former Soviet Union, where the mob was big on economies of scale. The "English" pub had been brought prepackaged, like Potanin and Timoshenko's office suites, from some mail-order catalogue that included oak booths and tables, lamps made out of sea lanterns, and the assorted nautical knickknacks and prints that hung on the walls.

They had Japanese beer in stock and we ordered Sapporo, installing ourselves in a corner booth where we hoped we would not draw the attention of the surly and heavy-set men seated around the center table. They did not seem to be enjoying their evening, sitting with elbows hunched on the table, speaking to one another in low, conspiratorial tones. An array of beautiful women came in and out of the pub and paraded past our booth, beckoning us with inviting smiles. Robin didn't pay any attention to them. He'd been in Russia long enough to know that their enticing glances had nothing to do with our charms. I too was becoming inured to the prostitutes, who, like bodyguards, were omnipresent in the new Russia. In a place like Vladivostok, where no one was getting wages, where there wasn't even electricity or running water and opportunities for gainful employment were scant, prostitution was born out of economic necessity.

We drifted into the next room, an almost empty discothèque where about fifty working women swayed on the dance floor. Perhaps a dozen patrons, half of them Chinese, lounged on the couches watching and smoking. The strobe lights winked, illuminating gyrating bodies, as the women tried to catch a potential client's eye. Several had stripped down to their brassieres, while one did a suggestive split in front of a pair of older men. Tonight was obviously a slow night, a buyer's market, and some of the girls seemed desperate.

An attractive dark-haired woman, perhaps on the threshold of thirty, maybe a mother of two or a former schoolteacher, approached us. She leaned over to me, rubbing her breast on my shoulder. "Why aren't you dancing?" she asked, trying to sound cheerful, but mouthing the words in a slow, rehearsed sort of way. Her breath was heavy with tobacco and alcohol. Her hair spray scratched my face. The perfume she used did little to conceal the bodily effects of the water shortage. I must have recoiled, for her face instantly hardened, and she stormed off with a curse.

Jittery, depressed, feeling very much out of our depth, we decided to make our exit, the stares of these new capitalists following us back through the steel door and into the dark and dirty streets of Vladivostok. All the way back to the Moosehead I wondered about the woman who had asked me to dance—who might have had children or, at one time, a different sort of career. She had felt and been hurt by my disgust—the instinctive disgust of one of capitalism's favored children. She would remain in my thoughts as the face of the frontier I had so yearned to see.

CHAPTER TEN

The Zone

I returned from the Far East to a hostile reception from my fiancée. It seems I had neglected to call in while touring the tundra, and she had been worried sick that something might have happened to me. My excuse that the satellite phone hadn't worked properly was judged lame when it was revealed that the sober-suited *Financial Times* correspondent had managed to call his wife, twice.

I hadn't checked in with the office either, and received an equally cool welcome from the bureau chief and Betsy, who expressed their solidarity with Roberta on the matter of my irresponsibility

During my absence, business in Moscow had been surprisingly eventful. For one thing, the Central Bank had finally announced plans to redenominate the ruble. Russia's currency had performed so well in 1997 that, in a few months, on January 1, 1998, new banknotes would be introduced, stripped of the humiliating zeroes that had sprouted during the painful years of hyperinflation. Henceforth a dollar would be worth just under six rubles, rather than an uninspiring 5,860 rubles. It was a big psychological boost for the Russian economy. After all, when an imported television or microwave oven costs some ridiculous-sounding amount like three-million six-hundred-fifty thousand seven-hundred rubles, you tend to think of the local scrip as Monopoly money, and of the country that issued it as a banana republic.

Lopping off the zeroes meant the Kremlin was confident that Russia's economic recovery was almost complete. In fact the government had just projected that, for the first time in a decade, Russia's economy was expected to register growth. To be sure, the forecast called for only a tiny expansion in 1997, by less than 1 percent of Gross Domestic Product; but after years of harrowing contractions totaling a 45-percent drop in GDP, it was pretty heady stuff. (When the official figures were finally released, showing that the growth had indeed occurred, my bureau chief wrote a glowing front-page story about the recovery—a story that propelled the Russian stock exchange to a single-day gain of 9 percent and earning investors a quick billion-dollar paper profit.)

I certainly hadn't seen too much evidence of the recovery in the Russian Far East. For the neglected residents of Russia's natural-resources provinces, the postcommunist misery was perhaps hardest to swallow because they had once been the USSR's most pampered workers. During the Soviet era, central planners had lured millions of people to the inhospitable North with enticements like free, spacious housing; high wages; Black Sea vacations; and early retirement to the Soviet Union's sunnier climes. Siberia's Soviet miners and roughnecks had access to Georgian fruit in the winter, special stores, even free plane tickets to visit relatives down in the *Bolshaya Zemlya*, or Big Land, as Siberians referred to the rest of their country.

All those privileges were gone now, along with their paychecks, and because large Russian cities like Moscow still required their citizens to carry difficult-to-get residency permits, disgruntled Siberian workers couldn't simply move elsewhere. With nowhere to go, they were effectively stuck in the frostbitten wastelands, captives of the new capitalist order.

It was hard not to feel that the government had played a cruel trick on them. Yet Sakhalin's Okha was by no means the worst one-company town I ever saw in the former Soviet Union. That distinction belonged to the deceptively charming hamlet of Slavutich—the bedroom community for the engineers and technicians still working at the Chernobyl nuclear-power station.

The road was much like any country road, unhurried and unencumbered by traffic. It ran lazily past pine thickets and rolling pastures, undulated through marshes and maple groves. Sometimes a cow or a peasant on an old bicycle appeared over the horizon. The occasional combine harvester materialized in the golden wheat fields.

Suddenly a military checkpoint appeared out of nowhere: barbed wire, barking dogs, and large yellow-and-black radiation signs. Beyond this point, all semblance of normality ended. The road dipped into what was officially known as the Exclusion Zone, or more popularly as the "Dead Zone," a guarded two-thousand-square-kilometer perimeter containing the most polluted land on the planet. At the epicenter of the Zone stood Chernobyl, still operating ten years after the lethal explosion of its fourth reactor unit.

The soldiers flagged us down at the checkpoint. Our documents were examined and compared against the list of guests invited to the tenth anniversary of the 1986 catastrophe, and we were herded onto an ancient blue bus that had not left the Zone in a decade, and never would. Once inside the perimeter, vehicles were not permitted out again, lest they track radioactive dust on their tires to the outside world.

The oddest thing about the Dead Zone was that at first blush it teemed with life. The landscape resembled a national park, with lush foliage in every possible shade of green. What the eye could not detect was that the vegetation had been genetically altered by radiation. The strontium and cesium isotopes trapped in the trees and plants were sometimes released by brush fires, creating radiation spikes in the atmosphere that could be measured as far away as Finland.

The soil in the Restricted Zone was as toxic with fallout as the trees and the vines. Every spring, when the snow melted and the water table rose, streams and creeks carried the deadly runoff into the Dniepr River, from which two-thirds of Ukraine's fifty-two million citizens got their drinking water. Expatriates in Kiev, eighty miles downriver, never touched tap water. Nor did they drink locally produced milk; the cows in the region grazed on contaminated grass. Vegetables, appealing as they seemed when stacked in plump, colorful pyramids in Kiev's Bessarabia farmers' market, were also suspect; many expats subsisted on vitamin supplements or the two-dollar imported apples available at the heavily guarded Nika Swiss Superstore.

The blue bus trundled past abandoned villages whose empty buildings were being reclaimed by nature. Weathered signs with radiation symbols had been nailed to some of these weed-covered wooden structures: they read *VKHOD ZAPRESHCHON* [ENTRY IS FORBIDDEN]. The open doors and windows seemed to invite us to peer at defeat. Fear was flash-frozen in the air. The silence was unnatural. Here it seemed humanity's survival instincts had faltered.

So it was with some surprise, and a little relief, that we stumbled across people in the next village. A group of elderly women, heads swathed in black kerchiefs like old Spanish Gypsies, sat at a crumbling bus stop where the buses had long stopped running. One of them had a goat on a lead. Several leaned on canes, their chins resting casually on the cusps of their staffs, as if they had settled down to take in a show.

Apparently we were the entertainment. Word had spread that Yusuchi Akashi, second-in-command to U.N. General Secretary Boutros Boutros-Ghali, was coming to speak at the ceremony commemorating the tenth anniversary of the Chernobyl disaster that day, and the Zone elders hadn't wanted to miss seeing such a high international official.

"I thought everyone had been evacuated from here," I said to the driver.

"More than a hundred thousand people were resettled," he said, with a shake of his head. "But there are always the thick-headed ones. These pensioners came back in 1991." The driver had pulled to the side of the road because a Polish television crew wanted to interview the retirees. A camera was thrust at a wizened old woman with stained dentures and skin like sandpaper. "Why did you come back here?" the Polish reporter wanted to know.

"To live before I die," the old woman responded defiantly. "After the explosion," she went on, "they sent us to an apartment block next to a highway in Kiev. There was not a blade of grass, and all day the cars roared under our window. That is no way to live for country folk. They said we couldn't come back, that the radiation would kill us. Well, I'm not scared of radiation. We've been back for five years, and as you can see we are very much alive."

There were several hundred "returnees," as they were known, and they formed a strange, feminine community, swathed in perennial mourning veils, for virtually all their men had succumbed to cancer.

A few miles beyond this village, the vegetation thinned and a second, larger checkpoint appeared. This was the entrance to the Inner Zone, the nucleus around Chernobyl where the greatest devastation had occurred. Here too, we would change vehicles because were informed that anything that entered the Inner Zone was never allowed out again. People were the only exception to this rule. We were ushered into a large concrete building with the feel of a bomb shelter. Each person passed through a subway-station-style turnstile, with a radiation meter instead of a token box, to measure our contamination level. Past the turnstiles was a bank of shower nozzles for emergency decontamination. More specialized shower stalls awaited us in the changing rooms, where we were handed the protective suits everyone is supposed to wear inside the Inner Zone.

These so-called protective suits consisted of a hodgepodge of donated garments whose shielding qualities struck me as dubious. Egyptian Army surplus fatigues, with desert camouflage patterns and coarse, shoddy stitching, made up the bulk of the insulation. They were one-size-fits-all; my sleeves ended midway down my forearms, and my shins peeked out from the pant legs. The footwear was a gift of the Italian Red Cross: shiny burgundy-brown dancing shoes made entirely of rigid, circulation-constricting plastic. These we slipped over thin black dress socks that were the generous offering of another Western European nation. On top of this ridiculous getup—whose principal effect was to give the wearer the look of someone who might have worked in the PLO's accounting department—went white surgical gowns and headgear that looked humiliatingly like the tall paper hats the chefs wore at the Gastronom in Moscow. I imagined that this was the French contribution.

For the pièce de résistance, we were handed thick gauze face masks that stuck to stubble, leaving the men in the group picking tufts of white cotton from their chins and cheeks. We looked ridiculous, and even the dour diplomats in our party doubled over with laughter and pointed gleefully at one another like hairy participants in a fraternity cross-dressing competition.

The ribbing ceased abruptly when the bus rounded a small hill and Chernobyl's reactor blocks came into view. Against the low sky they looked like four giant tombstones. Huge transmission lines spread from the plant, forming an electrified spider web over our heads. Around us a desert of sand, earth, and rubble stretched in every direction, measured in shades of gray. This wasteland had once been the "red forest," so christened because the pine needles had all turned red and died. The entire forest had been so irradiated by the plume from the explosion of the fourth reactor unit that it had had to be buried. There was no green here. The shoots that braved Chernobyl's shadow were continually scraped away along with the irradiated topsoil, plowed into giant pits with earth-moving equipment. The bulldozers themselves would be buried in makeshift graveyards next to the hundreds of dump trucks, tractors, and giant Mi-4 helicopters that had been exposed to fatal doses of radiation during the 1986 cleanup effort.

We stopped in front of the sarcophagus, the massive cement tomb, encasing two hundred tons of uranium and plutonium, that had formed the core of Chernobyl's fourth reactor block. The ash-gray structure rose ten stories, and was capped by a slightly sloped roof next to which a rusty crane stood spookily. Fissures and cracks ran the length of the rough cement walls, and there was evidence of much patchwork on the sloppy masonry. The radiation level inside the tomb reached 2,000 REM, four times the lethal dose, enough to kill you in a single fifteen-minute exposure.

Everyone gathered a hundred feet in front of the sarcophagus, a distance that was still judged safe as long as we didn't stay too long. We took hurried turns snapping pictures of ourselves in our surgeon-cum-commando getups, as if we were on vacation, casually posing in front of the ruins of a past civilization, which in a sense was true.

"Seeing Chernobyl makes you feel strangely like a nuclear tourist," remarked Tom Kearney, a friend who worked for the World Bank in Kiev. "You've seen so many photographs of it in newspapers and on TV that it is somehow familiar, like the Pyramids or the Parthenon."

While we were strutting for the cameras, construction workers in cut-off T-shirts scrambled down from scaffolding to bum a few smokes. They weren't even wearing sunscreen, much less any of the crazy gear we had on.

"I'm not afraid of radiation," one of them, a middle-aged mason with a handlebar mustache and heavy sunburnt shoulders, bragged. "Its effects are exaggerated." He said he was being paid five hundred dollars a month to build an observation platform right at the foot of the sarcophagus, more than he earned in a year at his regular job and more money than he'd previously seen in his entire life. As he spoke, I felt as though I were staring at a ghost.

Most of the people who had built this industrial coffin were probably dead or dying, like the firefighters and young conscripts who had been frog-marched into the destroyed reactor and made to shovel debris, with only lead aprons to shield them from the exposed core a few yards away. Posthumous Heroes of Soviet Labor, some of their names were recorded on a bronze plaque and displayed to foreigners as evidence of the great devotion and sacrifice people had been willing to make for the glory of the USSR.

Now the porous sarcophagus was not only leaking but had also been declared structurally unsound. This wasn't surprising; the exposed core had been too radioactive for engineers to get near, and much of the structure had been hastily assembled using remote-controlled cranes. Ukraine was now asking the West for several billion dollars to replace it, in addition to another three billion and change to take Chernobyl's operating reactors permanently off line by the year 2000. To the great consternation of U.S. and West European leaders, two of Chernobyl's four unsafe reactor blocks were still operating at full capacity. The West was exerting tremendous pressure on Kiev to shut them down, but the Ukrainian government maintained it couldn't afford to do without the power they produced—not without serious compensation.

About half a mile downwind from Chernobyl stood the town of Pripyat, where the plant's workers had lived. It was now completely abandoned, the largest and gloomiest of the region's ghost towns. We walked down its main street, where there were still a few red banners announcing a Party Congress that had been held ten years ago, looking up at the desolate rows of fifteen-story apartment blocks and the faded Socialist Realist mosaics of atoms that adorned their prefabricated cement-slab walls. Weeds had sprouted through cracks in the sidewalk, a small tree poked through the asphalt, and

tall brown grasses swayed on the lawns. At the foot of the street, behind a squat concrete shopping plaza with broken windows, rose a
Ferris wheel that had rusted to a deep orange. Its cabins rocked and
creaked in the wind, the only noise we heard other than the sound
of our breath in the face masks.

A plant employee with a Geiger counter followed us at a distance, tagging along when we entered one of the empty high-rises.
Ten years of dirt and dust had accumulated on the landing of the
building, with a few spiderwebs for added effect. We let our eyes adjust to the stairwell's darkness—the power lines to Pripyat had long
since been disconnected—and climbed a few flights, emerging into
a long narrow corridor whose once dark-green walls were stained
with mildew. Eerily, the padded doors to most of the apartments
were open, as if the tenants had left in such a hurry that they hadn't
had time to shut them—which couldn't have been the case since the
Politburo had waited thirty-six hours before giving the order to evac-
uate Pripyat.

The apartment we entered also had open windows, and rotten
floorboards where the snow and the rain had fallen under the sills.
A layer of powdery dust covered virtually everything, and we left
footprints in the living room. A kitchen table stood under one wall,
and on it lay a badly yellowed copy of *Pravda*, dated April 23, 1986.
Alas, I neglected to record what Soviet triumph it touted.

In another room, there was a bed, but someone had made off
with the mattress. A Polish reporter from *Gazeta Wyborcza*, an old
Kiev hand, said it was probably robbers' work. There had been reports that looters dug up copper cables from the Zone and sold them
as scrap steel. More alarming were rumors that the trade included
some of the radioactive vehicles and personal belongings left behind. At the time I'd lived in Kiev for only a few months—just long
enough to believe that the stories were probably true.

The man with the Geiger counter cleared his throat. Our forag-
ing had kicked up a sufficient amount of dust to cause his radiation
meter to click several times. "I think we should go," he said. "The
ceremony is about to begin."

The catastrophe's commemoration was a simple and solemn
proceeding: Deputy U.N. Secretary-General Akashi was to plant a
row of saplings in a field next to Chernobyl. The young trees were to

symbolize life and rebirth, the first growth of a planned forest intended to carpet Chernobyl's barren courtyard.

As we made our way towards the ceremonial field, we encountered a group of women and children in civilian clothes. (We were beginning to wonder if the only people at Chernobyl who wore radiation suits were visiting foreigners and dignitaries.) The civilians bore candles, rustic picnic baskets, and sorrowful expressions. The tenth anniversary of the Chernobyl disaster happened to fall on Remembrance Sunday, a Slavic holiday on which people commemorate their dear departed by lighting candles at grave sites.

"We used to live there," explained a woman named Tatyana, pointing to an upper story of an apartment block. "My husband was a firefighter. Before he died, he lost all his hair," she said, no longer able to hold back tears. "He had such beautiful red hair."

At the ceremonial tree-planting site, the Ukrainians had erected a plaque and dug dozens of holes to receive the saplings. While the deputy secretary-general made a speech, the man with the Geiger counter thrust his meter into one of the holes. The instrument's needle shot up, showing that cesium and strontium had leached deep into the soil, where the earth-movers could not scrape it away. Akashi was just finishing his speech when the winds that had been buffeting us all day suddenly intensified. A freak whirlwind descended on the VIPs, sending dirt swirling around us and forcing us to rub particles out of our eyes.

When the vortex passed, we noticed the man with the Geiger counter scurrying away, as if he suddenly had something to hide. The Polish *Gazeta Wyborcza* reporter hurried after him. He returned moments later, pale and visibly shaken. "Shit," he said, "the Geiger's red-lining. We have to get out of here." The Ukrainian officials apparently shared his alarm, for the ceremony was cut short, and we were bundled out posthaste.

Later, at a banquet in Akashi's honor, the Ukrainians acted as if nothing had happened, but they casually stressed the curative qualities of red wine. Fermented grapes, according to local legend, help combat radiation poisoning. I don't know about that, but I did notice that, taken in sufficient quantities, the Black Sea vintage went a long way toward helping to calm frazzled nerves.

That brief visit to Chernobyl left me wondering about human

nature. Seven thousand people still worked at the condemned power plant. They trod on radioactive soil every day; risked their lives maintaining the leaky sarcophagus; raised their children in a town that had been built on a radioactive foundation at the Zone's edge. Why? I decided to find out. Some months after the ten-year anniversary, when life had returned to what passed as normal for the people who lived at Ground Zero, I returned to Chernobyl.

It was already snowing by then, and Chernobyl's one-company town, Slavutich, was bracing for winter. Slavutich was unlike any small Soviet city I'd ever seen. In a land filled with charmless settlements, Slavutich could almost have passed for the West. It had single-family dwellings with front lawns and gardens, playgrounds with swings and seesaws, outdoor basketball courts with rubber flooring, even a baseball diamond. Everything was clean, new, and well maintained.

Built by the Politburo in 1987 just outside the Zone, the construction of the town had been a national propaganda effort. Builders from every Soviet Socialist Republic had been enlisted, and they erected Slavutich's districts in the traditional architectural styles of their respective lands. No expense had been spared in this display of pan-Soviet solidarity with Ukraine. Exotic construction materials poured in from all over the empire: pink marble from quarries in the Caucasus, ceramic tiles from the kilns of Central Asia, timber framing from the Baltics, and replicas of wrought-iron lampposts from St. Petersburg.

The town had been built in less than a year. Its culturally inspired districts rose with remarkable speed. The Riga quarter, with its sharp Scandinavian pitched roofs, intricate trellis work, and manicured front yards, offered rows of coveted single-family brick dwellings—an unheard-of luxury in the USSR, except maybe among Central Committee members. The pink three-story granite housing blocks of the Yerevan quarter, complete with dentillated cornices and decorative sculptures such as one sees on Florida's coast, boasted three-bedroom apartments and kitchens loaded with hard-to-get appliances. Trees were planted; grass was sown. Schools were built with beautiful playgrounds and indoor swimming pools. An entertainment complex was added. A hospital was filled with Western medical equipment.

As the first happy residents moved into the "model city," as it was dubbed by central planners, television cameras beamed the joyous occasion across the Soviet Union. Viewers were astounded. They had never seen anything like Slavutich, so clean and new and modern. And the salaries paid there, the viewing public was further informed, were ten times higher than in the rest of the country.

"We couldn't believe our luck," recalled Svetlana Bolotnikova, a slender housewife in her late twenties, when I ran into her at the general store and asked how she came to Slavutich. "Andrei, my husband, had just finished his military service in Lithuania," she continued, as we stood in front of the well-stocked meat counter. "And we had married, thinking we'd have to live with my parents in Voronezh (a provincial Russian town). In those days you waited years, sometimes decades for an apartment. But when we saw the town on television, and they said there were apartments available right away if you took a job at Chernobyl, we knew we wanted to come here. It was so beautiful, it seemed like such a nice place to start a family."

I stared at this pretty young woman, and the little girl who clutched at the hem of her skirt, in disbelief and horror. She explained that in March 1988, Andrei applied to work at the plant, and to their great surprise landed a job monitoring Chernobyl's electricity-output control panels, despite the fact that he had no technical background or college education. In one fell swoop, the young couple, barely out of their teens and without any real prospects, received a brand-new, spacious rent-free home and a salary that was higher than all their parents' wages combined.

In this manner, Kremlin planners—who had been desperate to bring Chernobyl back on line to provide power for their military factories—enticed twenty-four thousand people to Slavutich, emphasizing the material rewards of the model city while downplaying its health risks.

"They assured us it was safe," Bolotnikova shrugged, when I pressed her on the issue. She continued to believe all was well, even after one day in 1990, at the height of Gorbachev's *glasnost,* when earth-movers came to scrape the topsoil, first from the school playground and then throughout the rest of the town.

"They said it was just a precaution," she said defensively, as if I were passing judgment on her parenting.

"You believed them?"

"I—" She hesitated, the fight leaving her. "I wanted to."

Her daughter, Larisa, was born two months after the bulldozers came. Bolotnikova claimed that, aside from recurrent headaches, the six-year-old was in perfect health. If so, Larisa was lucky. In the contaminated regions of Ukraine and Belarus, just across the border to the north, neurological, endocrinological, gastrointestinal, and urinary illnesses were fifteen times more prevalent than in the general population. The children's wards in Belarusian hospitals were heartbreaking to see: six-fingered babies, missing limbs, heads the size of basketballs. Then there were the thousands of cases of children with thyroid cancer. Larisa certainly seemed healthy, clinging shyly to her mom as they waited to pay for their sausage and cheese. The food, like the well-kept store and almost everything else in town, bore the three-letter logo of the Chernobyl Atomic Station. Even the money used at Slavutich was not the hapless *hryvnia*, as Ukraine's newly introduced currency was called, but trusted company scrip.

Even now that the potential health hazards had been documented and openly discussed, the golden chains that had first lured people to Slavutich kept them there. Slavutich was an oasis of relative prosperity in postcommunist Ukraine; Chernobyl's benefit plan offered shelter from the economic maelstrom that ravaged the rest of the country. Everyone here had free cable television, a luxury typically restricted to the new rich in Moscow or St. Petersburg. Wages were high and paid promptly. The town's streets were filled with sought-after second-hand German cars, most with the D (for Deutschland) sticker still proudly affixed to rear bumpers and windows. Brand-new Mercedes snowplows cleared the smoothly paved streets, allowing pedestrians to stroll past Danish-made kiosks that displayed all matter of imported goods.

The snowplows, like the kiosks, the medical equipment, and some of the food, had been donations from the West, though you wouldn't know it from the way Deputy Mayor Vladimir Zhigallo railed against the West.

"When the West pressured Ukraine to shut down Chernobyl by 2000," he complained, "no one seems to have given any consideration to what would happen to this town. I'll tell you what will happen: it will die."

Bolotnikova's husband was no less angry. Sipping a beer after his twelve-hour shift at the plant, he wondered where else in Ukraine he could find a four-hundred-dollar-a-month job and a free three-bedroom apartment. "Nowhere, that's where," he said gloomily. "It's stupid. Chernobyl is perfectly safe. Ukraine needs energy. They should bring more reactors on line rather than shutting them down."

"We wanted to have another child," his wife added sorrowfully. "But now with the station's future uncertain, we don't know."

Chernobyl struck me as a very good reason not to have children. Yet Slavutich boasted post-Soviet Ukraine's highest birth rate. That was the irony; people could afford to raise a family here. Svetlana Bolotnikova and the other citizens of Slavutich had chosen to mortgage their futures for a few years of peace and prosperity.

The moral and physical devastation of the provinces was so foreign to Moscow that many of the expatriates living within its privileged confines could be forgiven for not comprehending the dilemmas of Slavutich or Sakhalin. Moscow, for most of us, was the Santa Hotel or the Moosehead Lodge writ large. In our comfortable isolation, we had Jay Leno on satellite television, Sbarro's Pizza at the marbled Manezh, and the health club at the Penta—if you didn't mind paying forty-five dollars for a swim or changing next to members who had gun holsters hanging in their lockers. As further distractions, there were first-run English-language movies at the Kodak-owned multiplex, winter sales at the DKNY outlet next to the state circus, great big piña coladas at the T.G.I.F. on Tverskaya, sushi, steaks, and cell phones—everything to make us forget we were in Russia. If that weren't enough, we could pop over to Helsinki to decompress for a weekend, as the diplomats did during the Soviet era. Whatever it took to keep the deals flowing and the money coming in.

Roberta had closed her deal to build the giant customs terminal that was to process much of Moscow's imported food, and early in December we drove out to the site. It was located some twenty miles outside the MKAD beltway in the dreary, deserted town of Zelenograd.

Once, Zelenograd had been the USSR's answer to Silicon Valley, a high-technology enclave where satellites, eavesdropping equipment, telecommunication gear, and computer components were produced for the military and the KGB. As in the case of Vladivostok's Amur shipyard, the military orders had dwindled after 1991; scientists had fled to Israel, Iran or the United States, or taken lucrative employment offers from the oligarchs' private security services; and the place was falling apart.

On the way out to Zelenograd, we passed dozens of people peddling television antennas and transistor radios on the side of the slushy road. These were technicians who had been paid in kind because their factory or institute had no money. This sight was so common throughout the former Soviet Union (outside Moscow) that you could tell whenever payday came around by the crowds that converged on the nearest highway to sell the tires or sacks of sugar they had received in lieu of a paycheck. That the harsh post-Soviet reality had crept so close to the capital made the Moscow's freshly-paved MKAD seem more than just a symbolic moat.

Roberta was pleased that she was investing in a town that needed the money badly. Private equity was different from other forms of fund management; by investing directly in companies, she created jobs and tangible assets instead of speculating on stocks and bonds, transactions that tended to benefit a very small circle of already-rich investors. Still, private equity was by far the least popular form of investing in Russia because of all the red tape involved in getting anything built—not to mention the political risk of having immovable assets in a country where the court system was open to the highest bidder. Savvy investors viewed Russia as a stock-and-bond play, because you could get in and out fast, and make a killing—if you were smart.

But Roberta still had enough of the "limousine liberal" in her that she liked seeing projects rise stage by satisfying stage from the ground up, lifting all boats with the proverbial rising tide. At her customs terminal, there wasn't much to see yet—only the shell of an unfinished warehouse whose construction had been abandoned after the communist collapse in 1991, and a wintry field with a few surveyor spikes sticking out of the snow. Work wasn't slated to start until February—Q1, '98, as Roberta referred to the planned ground-breaking in the first quarter of the next fiscal year in her dispatches to her paymasters in New York. Still, she was immensely proud. "There will be a hotel for truckers there," she said, gesturing to a pile of snow. "Customs offices here," nodding in another snowy direction, "and bonded and refrigerated warehouses there," she said, motioning to a skeletal, unfinished airplane-hangar-sized building whose steel columns and girders were covered in a thick layer of ice.

The structure was known as a *nezavershenka*, literally an incomplete job. There were tens of thousands of such abandoned construction projects in the former Soviet bloc, begging for foreign investors to finish what central planners had started. Roberta had found one such bargain in a small town in eastern Ukraine: a sugar mill, 85 percent finished, with Italian-made equipment bought in 1990 still sitting in their wrappings on the factory floor. VSO could buy the plant for next to nothing if they agreed to put up the twenty-six million dollars needed to finish construction. The beauty of the deal lay in the plant's expensive Western production lines, which would allow VSO to supply high-grade sugar to Coca-Cola. Coke had built Europe's largest bottling plant in Ukraine, but was forced to import sugar from Western Europe because of the shoddy quality of the local stuff. With Coke as a customer, Roberta had done financial models showing that the finished mill would be worth between one hundred fifty and two hundred million dollars, a more than fivefold return on investment. "We'd create four hundred jobs in a town with a thirty percent unemployment rate," she said, when I asked her about it.

"Forget the jobs," I advised. "We'd get five percent of that hundred million dollars."

"Actually," said Roberta modestly, "it could be a little more."

Thirty-six feet was starting to feel a bit cramped for a sailboat. Maybe something in the range of a fifty-foot cabin cruiser was more appropriate.

It was thus with suitably high spirits, and a warm feeling of material optimism, that we prepared to usher in 1998 with a New Year's Eve party in Red Square. My bureau chief had rented a suite high atop the resplendent National Hotel, at the foot of Tverskaya Street, so we could watch the fireworks over the Kremlin from its ornate wrought-iron balconies. Lenin and his fellow revolutionaries had spoken to the crowds from these commanding heights during the October Revolution, when the Bolsheviks had commandeered the National and the now-five-hundred-dollar-a-night Metropole just down the street. Now these were our stamping grounds; this was our revolution. We spooned caviar contentedly and waited for the fireworks to start.

CHAPTER ELEVEN

"You Can't Act Like Americans in Here"

Only Askold sensed that something was wrong. On that frigid February night, the rest of us had no idea the end was near. That evening Moscow still gleamed like a polished ruby, and its streets still seemed paved with gold.

The city began its usual primping for Saturday night. The neon facades of the capital's casinos pulsed into life, flashing green, the color of money. The GAI traffic cops took up their vigils beneath billboards praising Templeton Mutual Funds and the efforts of Russia's Federal Tax Police.

By six, Pushkin Square was teeming with teenagers. Outside the Kodak KinoMir movie house, scalpers were doing a brisk trade in fifty-dollar tickets to the movie *Titanic*. Punks with mohawk hairdos promenaded in the square's central plaza, eating ice cream and sipping beer next to an ice sculpture exhibition that featured two-headed eagles and a miniature Kremlin. Across Tverskaya Street, an endless stream of hungry patrons spilled into a mammoth McDonald's, reportedly the world's most profitable Golden Arches.

Our dinner reservation was at eight. We were a large party of Russians, Americans, Brits, and Canadians, a self-styled cosmopolitan bunch, all prospectors in the great post-Soviet gold rush. Our spirits were high, for we would be rubbing elbows with the captains of Russian industry at one of Moscow's most exclusive eateries, the "White Sun of the Desert."

The restaurant was on Neglinnaya Street near the Sandunovsky Baths, where the new rich cured hangovers in private steam rooms for two hundred dollars an hour. A cream-colored Rolls-Royce, several big BMWs, and a dozen identical Mercedes 600s with tinted, bulletproof windows crowded the snowy parking lot. The limousines were bookended by the usual Toyota Land Cruisers and GMC Suburbans, in which bull-necked bodyguards played cards while their bosses gorged themselves on some of the world's most expensive food. Bringing guns or guards inside was considered bad form.

We presented ourselves before two gilded dragons standing sentinel outside the establishment's door. A surveillance camera over the entrance whirred into focus. The black steel door clicked open, and a large man filled its frame.

"We have a reservation," said our friend Chrystia before the man could say anything. "I am a member," she added in rapid-fire Russian. The doorman paused, mulling over this improbable information. Westerners, as a matter of course, were not members of this club, much less women who looked barely old enough to vote.

"Name?" he asked, squinting doubtfully.

"Freeland, Chrystia." By her tone she could have added, "Of the *Financial Times*" out of habit, as a door opener.

He was back within a few seconds, all smiles now.

"Please come in." While we passed through an airport-style metal detector (the mark of Moscow's truly exclusive restaurants) I wondered how Chrystia had finagled entry into the inner sanctum of the men who ran Russia. A Harvard graduate, Rhodes Scholar, and, at twenty-eight, the youngest and first female bureau chief in the *Financial Times'* stodgy history, she was one of those people who ruined the curve for mere mortals.

Chrystia was also one of Roberta's best friends. They had known each other in college and in Ukraine, and had briefly lived together when Roberta first moved to Moscow. Like me, Chrystia had started as a humble stringer in Kiev, but now was probably the most plugged-in foreign correspondent in Russia, certainly among the most respected. She lunched with Prime Minister Chernomyrdin, dined with IMF reps, took tea with the oligarchs in their walled estates, and always seemed to be one step ahead of the rest of the press corps.

She had just broken a big story on Potanin and the Svyazinvest sale that discredited the much-hyped auction that was to have ushered in the second, more equitable stage of the Russian market revolution. Apparently Chubais and half a dozen other senior officials at the Ministry of Privatization had each received one hundred thousand dollars from Oneximbank prior to the hotly contested sale. The money had come from one of Oneximbank's Swiss affiliates and was ostensibly the advance for a book, or books, on Russian privatization. Journalistic eyebrows, however, were raised because Oneximbank was not in the book-publishing business and none of the authors had written a single page of their alleged manuscripts.

Boris Jordan, Potanin's partner in the Syazinvest deal, also got mixed up in the scandal when the *Financial Times* revealed that the Swiss affiliate that had paid the book advances was run by an American relative of his. Both Jordan and Potanin strongly denied any wrongdoing, claiming the book contracts were legitimate and not in the least related to any expected favoritism in the telephone monopoly's privatization tender. (In fact the books were eventually written and published.) Still, it all looked pretty suspicious, and Berezovsky and Gusinsky raised such a sanctimonious fuss about the alleged impropriety in their newspapers and television stations that Yeltsin was forced to sack Privatization Minister Alfred Kokh and to demote Chubais.

So much for the end of the crony-capitalist era.

What puzzled me, however, was the trifling sum of money involved. Chubais had presided over what was probably the greatest transfer of property in recorded history. Tens, if not hundreds, of billions of dollars worth of State assets had changed ownership under his watch. The beneficiaries of his largesse had grown rich beyond their wildest dreams. And what did he receive in exchange for his patronage? A measly six-figure advance. The man truly deserved a T-shirt: I PRIVATIZED ALL OF RUSSIA AND ALL I GOT WAS A CRUMMY $100,000 "BOOK CONTRACT."

Since I toiled for a competing publication and frequently had to suffer the wrath of our editors when Chrystia scooped us, which was all too often, it was with a pang of professional jealousy that I handed over my jacket to the coat-check attendant. Only then did I notice that she was dressed like a belly dancer. That's when I took a good look around.

I was inside the tent of a desert sultan, surrounded by spiny cactus plants and sandy outcrops dotted with snakeskins and dried scorpions. Kilims, Bokharas, and other carpets from Central Asia covered the terra-cotta floor and hung from the rough whitewashed walls. Tarpaulins suspended from thick wooden tent poles gave the effect of a *yurt* (dwelling). Ornate hookahs, studded shields, and filigreed scimitars completed the illusion.

Gretchen and Boris were waiting for us at our table. Gretchen looked her usual marvelous self, movie-star thin, radiant, and none the worse for wear for having just delivered her first baby, a strapping boy christened Georgy, at age thirty-eight. One couldn't say the same for Boris, though child rearing had nothing to do with his malaise.

Roberta greeted him Russian-style with three kisses on the cheeks. "You look terrible," she growled in her smoked-oyster baritone. "Don't let them get to you."

Boris did look haggard. His Rolex hung limply as we shook hands. Dark circles shaded his eyes. Since coming to Moscow as a bright-eyed reformer a year ago, he had aged noticeably. I suppose we had all lost some of our youth and innocence, but on Boris it showed.

Boris may have still clung to the hope that Russia's electricity sector could be reformed, but like a great many Kremlin officials, he had become embroiled in intrigue and preoccupied with his own political survival. Firing corrupt power-plant bosses had made him a good many enemies within the crony-ridden energy sector. Worse, a war had broken out between two rival Kremlin factions, and Boris had landed smack in the middle. A campaign to discredit him was already in full swing, and poor Boris found himself fending off the allegations of impropriety that magically surfaced whenever officials fell out of favor.

His troubles had started with a plane ride, a very expensive flight of fancy. Boris had taken the UES corporate jumbo jet, the sister ship of Yeltsin's presidential plane, to fly to Kentucky to pick up Gretchen, his newborn son, the family Rottweiler, and a truckload of carpets for the Moscow *dacha*. The new Russian-made Ilyushin jumbo was fitted with well-appointed Swiss-designed staterooms to accommodate Russia's perennially bedridden leaders. But the FAA had not yet certified the craft to land in the United States, and Boris was in a hurry. So somewhere over southern Canada he ordered the pilot to duck below radar level and, skimming the treetops, stealthily cross into American airspace. When he landed unannounced at the Cincinnati airport, the plane was quickly surrounded by a dozen police cruisers with wailing sirens. Only the intervention of the Russian ambassador, who was rousted out of bed to make apologies for the unscheduled flight, prevented an international incident.

"I don't know what got into Boris," lamented Gretchen, dismissing her husband's childish impulse as the work of a teenager. Except that this hadn't been his dad's car he borrowed without permission: this had been Russia's equivalent of Air Force One.

Back in Moscow, Boris's enemies had gotten wind of the trip. Citing the six-figure jet-fuel bill charged to UES, they called for his head. Boris apologized on national television and reimbursed the company. Though his transgression was minor in comparison to the stunts some of his accusers routinely pulled off, he was still in deep trouble: Prime Minister Chernomyrdin had just called him to profess his continued support. This, in the Kremlin's Byzantine body language, was a sure sign that Boris's days as the head of the giant utility were numbered.

Our waitress arrived, bearing a tray of drinks and a striking resemblance to Scheherazade. While she poured vodka shots, Boris explained how "The White Sun of the Desert" came by its intriguing name. *Beloye Solntse Pustyni* is a famous Soviet spaghetti Western, in which Bolshevik cowboys conquer Central Asia, save the seven beautiful wives of a vengeful sultan, and spread the good gospel of socialism across the wind-swept steppe.

"That is the hero of the film." Boris pointed across the room to a life-size wax figure of a Russian cowboy who looked remarkably like Clint Eastwood. It stood next to an empty table that was always held in reserve for oligarch Mikhail Khodorkovsky, one of Russia's richest corporate raiders whose companies were the subject of numerous lawsuits by Western investors.

Our other dinner companions started trickling in: the *Economist*'s bureau chief, a few corporate executives, several World Bank/IFC officials, and a slick Wall Street lawyer who was in town suing Mr. Khodorkovsky's oil company, Yukos, on behalf of aggrieved American shareholders; they were accusing Yukos of Sakhalin-style asset stripping. Money was our common denominator. Some of us made piles of it. Boris made sure not too many people stole it. Others advised Russia on how not to mismanage it. We business reporters wrote about its ebb and flow in loving detail.

Only my buddy Askold, a newcomer to Moscow, had nothing to do with the machinery of commerce. And he was late as usual. By the time he finally arrived, the waitress had obligingly brought Uzbek lamb-dumpling appetizers and another round of Kristall vodka, the Stolichnaya premium brand that was now deemed too good for export.

"Did you see all the goons outside?" he asked, grabbing a chair. "This place looks like a bad day in Bosnia."

"They could be some of your old pals from Afghanistan," I volunteered. The best Russian bodyguards, the fashion accessories of the new rich, were frequently veterans of the Afghan war. Askold had covered the Soviet invasion for the *Times* of London, among other papers, and the Red Army had put a bounty on his head as a result. After the collapse of the USSR, Askold was once chatting with a taxi driver in Ukraine when the driver suddenly slammed on the brakes. "Repeat your name," he demanded. When Askold did so, the cabby burst out laughing. "I was in a unit assigned to kill you! We spent months looking for you." The two repaired to the nearest bar to reminisce and later appeared together on the German equivalent of *60 Minutes*.

At forty-one, Askold Krushelnycki was the senior member of our party. Big and burly, he had close-cropped sandy hair tinged with gray around the temples. Though he had been raised in privilege at London's finer schools, he had become the sort of person who wore a bulletproof vest to work. In addition to dodging hit squads in Afghanistan, he had reported on some of Africa's deadlier spats, the bombing of Chechnya, and most recently the conflict in Yugoslavia, where a well-aimed grenade had forced him to abandon what was left of his rented car. The folks at the rental agency's Vienna office were none too pleased to discover that Askold had surreptitiously driven their car to Sarajevo. He told them they could pick it up in Sniper Alley. The matter was currently in the capable hands of his newspaper's solicitors.

"What shall we drink to?" asked Chrystia, acting the host.

Someone suggested Yeltsin's health. That got a laugh. Yeltsin had returned to his role as absentee landlord, once again plagued by medical problems. Public sightings of the increasingly erratic president had become so infrequent that they spurred rallies on the stagnating Russian stock exchange. The exchange had shed a few points in the opening months of 1998, though the losses were nothing serious given the mayhem in Asia, where markets were crashing, currencies were devaluating, and the IMF was busy putting out financial fires. So far, Russia was weathering the Asian storm admirably well. Nonetheless, the hemorrhaging in Hong Kong, Thailand, and South Korea had made international investors jittery, and the Kremlin had sought to dispel rumors of Yeltsin's impending demise by parading him on television, just as the Politburo used to prop up ailing Soviet leaders for every May Day parade. Yeltsin was seated on a snowmobile and instructed to strike a virile pose as he drove around in circles before the cameras. The shot, aired on State television, abruptly ended as the president started tilting and falling off the Ski-Doo, stiff enough to appear to be in the advanced stages of rigor mortis. After that, many a journalist rushed to update Yeltsin's obituary. Every major news organization in Moscow kept a ready-to-print farewell piece in the event that the Russian leader should inconveniently pass away ten minutes before a filing deadline.

One of the most contentious issues among the foreign press corps was how history would treat Yeltsin and whether he was clean. His close ties to Boris Berezovsky, particularly his daughter Tatyana's cozy association with Russia's most prominent tycoon, gave some pause, since Berezovsky seemed to make his money primarily by managing the cash flow of state-controlled companies like ORT-TV or Aeroflot. The partly privatized Aeroflot, for instance, which was run by Yeltsin's son-in-law, funneled its hard-currency earnings through two Swiss-based firms, Andava and Forus, both set up by Berezovsky. (Russian and Swiss prosecutors would later investigate without success the whereabouts of six hundred million dollars that flowed into these two Aero-linked accounts. No charges would ever be laid.)

Despite the questionable ties, the consensus at our table that night was that Yeltsin was not overly interested in money. Perhaps, some ventured, he had a few foreign bank accounts with "one or two million" stashed away for a snowy day, but that this was such a small sum compared to the billions the region's other post-Soviet leaders had allegedly stolen as to render him "relatively uncorrupt."

"That is like saying you're a little bit pregnant," grumbled Askold.

The conversation shifted to typical expatriate topics: business-class travel and frequent-flyer miles; billable hours and bonuses; upside potential and points; nannies and maids. The exorbitant grocery prices at Stockmann's were reviled. The new menu at the Gastronom was praised. There was talk of which cellular-phone service was the best, and of long weekend getaways to the Greek Isles; of scandals and adulteries; payoffs and abductions. Much grumbling was devoted to traffic and the difficulty of finding good drivers. Gretchen griped about her telephone being tapped by Boris's enemies. Roberta suggested buying a special scrambler phone like the one her new Russian partners had. At seventeen thousand dollars, the unit was a steal. Boris asked the waitress to send coffee out to his shivering driver and the bodyguard who now accompanied him everywhere. Askold smoked sullenly, taking this all in.

"Bloody hell!" he said after a while. "You're starting to sound like *them*." He pointed at the restaurant's other patrons.

I paused to digest this, glancing around the room. The men wore mostly black and jewelry, the women mostly nothing and jewelry. Two pencil-thin mafia molls, skirts no wider than belts, teetered on impossibly high heels near the lush buffet. A teenage platinum blonde pouted at a table while her potbellied date yammered on a tiny cell phone. A man with tattoos on his knuckles was waving an empty bottle of Courvoisier and shouting loudly for a refill.

"Behold," said Askold, making another sweeping gesture. "Russia's elite. How many people do you have to kill to get a membership to this place?" The question hung uncomfortably in the smoky air.

The charge vexed me somewhat. Yet I had to allow Askold his high moral ground. He had earned it, uncovering mass graves and massacres in Sarajevo while I power-breakfasted with investment bankers in five-star hotels. Askold's was indeed a refreshing breeze of outrage, since my own seemed to have ebbed with the passage of time. Newcomers to Moscow were always shocked by its vulgar excess. I remembered my own bemused revulsion that first night at the Bolshoi. But what I hadn't counted on then was how much I would become inured to this atmosphere. Almost everyone did—gradually, imperceptibly at first until, inexorably, you lost your observer status and became part of the landscape.

The moral slide from citizen to lout could start innocently enough, with a simple cigarette. How many times had I seen people light up with the disclaimer "I only smoke in Russia"? How many of our friends bought furs in Russia that they left with their drivers at Sheremetyevo airport when visiting the States, lest they get pelted with paint balloons back home? Our party alone accounted for three such politically incorrect minks. The same held true for infidelity; often it began and ended at the gates of Sheremetyevo, where lissome and obliging interpreters met and sent off their expat bosses. Our table counted at least one such married culprit.

At the very bottom of the expat slope were those men who had taken up "trolling for Tanyas." Trolling for Tanyas was the practice of going out to Moscow's provincial satellite towns such as Zielonograd to pick up impressionable young women. In the boondocks there was no competition from wealthy Muscovites to cramp one's style. Women there were still impressed with Western passports and cell phones, and didn't break into a wounded pout if you balked at buying them a car. They were easy pickings, as Moscow girls had been back in 1991. Tours were even organized to the surrounding towns, where the local ladies were duly informed that a trainload of charming American executives was on its way. The organizer of one such sex tour assured the readers of the *Moscow Times* that he guaranteed customer satisfaction or a full refund. In the pages of the *eXile*, Moscow's rambunctious English-language weekly, the topic of trolling for Tanyas was the subject of much advice-giving. *If she doesn't put out, kick her out*, opined one pundit on what to do once you invited a Tanya to the big city for a weekend, where she had no money or friends and could thus be quite malleable.

The *eXile* captured the moral vacuum that Moscow seemed to create. Part of the allure of expatriate life is that you are neither subject to the local mores nor constrained by the prevailing value system of your own culture. Since you're a million miles from home, you can act like a frat boy during spring break in Tijuana and save the false sanctimony for later, when you're safely stateside.

"Something happens to guys when they get out here," Julie, a

Canadian cosmetic executive at our table that night, often lamented to Roberta and Chrystia, echoing the bitter refrain of expatriate women throughout Eastern Europe. "All of a sudden it's as if women's lib never existed, and they're acting like they'd never dare at home."

Roberta said Russian women were equally to blame. Often beautiful, and extremely well educated, they routinely prostrated themselves before Western businessmen, promising to cook, darn socks, and stay silent. "They've set women's lib back fifty years," she frequently griped.

Of course, most expat peccadilloes paled in comparison to the exploits of many Russian businessmen. Our fellow diners that evening certainly looked like a frightening bunch. But that was also part of the allure of expat life. When in the Third Rome, one was happy to rub elbows with the Romans—and if they fed a few business rivals to the lions, that was just good copy.

After all, it was hypocritical to deride a boom that had turbocharged our careers and made some of us very rich. We journalists, many of us mere stringers a few years ago, were suddenly moving in high political circles. We could move markets with a single story, and often did. We'd brag about it among ourselves, a mark of how *important* we were. Before leaving Canada and the hemorrhaging corpse of Brezco, my ill-fated construction company, I had had my credit cards and car taken away by the bank. Now the vicechairman of Citibank called me, hoping I'd quote him. When starting out as a freelance journalist in Poland, I used to send the same photocopied story to twenty Canadian newspapers and pray to all the gods that the *Edmonton Journal* or the *Winnipeg Register* would consent to publish me. Now I did live color commentary for CNBC's European Edition and complained bitterly about the inconvenience of early-morning tapings.

I don't remember how the argument had started, what we had done to so outrage the gentleman at the next table. Perhaps he had heard Askold's disparaging remarks. Perhaps it was the fact that we were interlopers speaking English in an establishment where Russians took refuge from the foreigners who overran the capital's expense-account nightspots. Or maybe it was something unflattering I said in the blush of impending alcohol poisoning.

"Shut the fuck up."

A hush descended over our corner. The speaker was bald, with a boxer's splayed nose and heavy folds of skin draping down his size-twenty neck. He was seated a few feet away at a long table jammed with dishes and half-empty bottles of vodka and red wine. Five large young men in satin shirts and six breathtaking women in spandex outfits rounded out his party. Were they bankers, brokers, or just plain bandits? That none of us could tell made Askold gleeful. He said he rested his case.

"Shot de fook," our new friend bellowed again to no one in particular.

"Oh my. Quite the linguist," drawled Gretchen, playing the dainty Southern belle. We snickered nervously.

A napkin sailed through the air, bouncing off the top of Gretchen's head. The linguist was standing now, veins bulging from his broad forehead. He rocked on his heels, his brow furrowing in drunken concentration. Then he smiled a broad smile, as if a clever rejoinder had suddenly struck him.

"Beetch! Foook," he repeated, clearly pleased with his expanding repertoire.

Now it was Askold's turn: "Oh sit down, you bloody Neanderthal!" Boris burst out laughing, obviously comforted by the nearby presence of his bodyguard. "I drink to Askold," he declared. "For my wife's honor."

We raised our glasses to chivalry while our belligerent neighbor turned his frustration on his buxom dinner companion. She had placed a restraining hand on his large forearm in an attempt to calm him and was now being showered with particles of food as he ranted through mouthfuls of shish kebab.

Meanwhile, the maitre d', costumed in the felt tunic of a turn-of-the-century Cossack, materialized. He exchanged a few words with the people at the next table, bowed obsequiously and shot us a malevolent glance.

My shot glass shook a little as I tilted it back. But Askold's hand was steady as he downed his drink. His cousin had been an enforcer for the NHL's Boston Bruins, better known for his right jab than for his puck-handling abilities. Maybe sangfroid was a family trait. Someone suggested that our new friend was probably in debt collection, or a similarly lucrative line of work that required "people skills."

"Beeeetch!" interrupted our exchange of bons mots. The linguist was back, looking angrier than ever. "I keel you alllll!" he rumbled, jumping unsteadily to his feet and sending a wine glass crashing.

The maitre d' rematerialized. This time he was flanked by two doormen with machine guns. The AK-47s' blue metallic barrels were trained at Askold and me.

"You must leave," he said firmly. "This is a Russian establishment. You can't act like Americans in here."

There are certain watershed moments in life and history on which you later look back and say *that* was the turning point.

The unfettered sale of Svyasinvest was to have been such an event for Russia. Instead it served to unmask the fraud that paraded itself as the free market, and to highlight just how deeply entrenched crony capitalism was in the former Soviet Union.

The downside of crony capitalism—and this was why entrepreneurs in the region took such great pains to stash their loot abroad—was that what the State gives, it can just as easily take away.

Julia Timoshenko was proof enough of that. In the months that had passed since I had last seen her, political infighting in Ukraine had conspired against her $11 billion company, UESU. Timoshenko's patron, Prime Minister Lazarenko, had fallen out of favor with Ukraine's president, Leonid Kuchma. Lazarenko's chokehold on the all-important energy sector in Ukraine, and his close—and, some alleged, extremely profitable—association with UESU, had emboldened him to start usurping President Kuchma's powers. In doing so, he had committed the cardinal sin of post-Soviet politics: he had started gunning openly for his boss's job. It was a mistake that the more seasoned time-server Chernomyrdin studiously avoided making in Moscow.

Kuchma, who like all postcommunist leaders tolerated all sorts of corruption from his subordinates as long as they remained unflaggingly loyal, finally sacked the uppity Lazarenko for "health reasons"—the standard Soviet pretext for dismissal.

No sooner had Lazarenko been safely packed off to an elite government hospital—for a complete blood transfusion, the doctors there said with straight faces—than a whole world of trouble rained down on Timoshenko. Some two hundred prosecutors, police officers, and investigators from the SBU (as the KGB was renamed in Ukraine) descended on UESU's headquarters in Dnepropetrovsk. The company's lucrative natural-gas distribution concession was revoked, its records were hauled away, and several of the company's officers were charged with allegedly misappropriating foreign aid. Apparently UESU had sold for profit two hundred Volkswagen minivans given to Ukraine by Germany. The company was also accused of numerous currency violations, and of illegally spiriting funds out of Ukraine. Timoshenko's husband was arrested. Timoshenko herself had been briefly detained at the airport with a suitcase full of dollars, but she was not charged with anything, perhaps because she was an a member of parliament and therefore enjoyed parliamentary immunity. (It was amazing how many entrepreneurs in the former Soviet Union felt the call of public service.)

"All nonsense," Timoshenko huffed when I called her from Moscow. "There is no basis for any of the allegations," she said. "I am the target of a political witch hunt and a smear campaign. We created jobs and kept enterprises from closing. As for the minivans, the government asked us to sell those. We did it as a favor, as charity, and took only a small commission."

Whatever the truth, Timoshenko's UESU was, for all intents and purposes, out of business. The third-largest private company to emerge from the ashes of communism had disappeared just as quickly as it had arisen.

Just as the fallout from Svyazinvest's "book contracts" disillusioned many of Russia's outside boosters, that drunken dinner at the White Sun of the Desert ripped the curtain off the life we were leading.

Askold had opened a sort of moral Pandora's box, which I could never quite close again so long as I lived in Moscow. He had made all too plain that we Westerners were beginning to accept a brand of capitalism that our own societies had cast aside as unjust a hundred years ago. It became harder for me to rationalize Russia's extremes. A Saturday, for instance, might find Roberta and me in St. Petersburg, celebrating the fortieth birthday of the local VSO rep with a party in a nineteenth-century palace hall inlaid with thirty varieties of Italian marble. The place would be lit by hundreds of beeswax candles, and a string ensemble would gently pluck at gilded harps while white-gloved caterers dispensed *blini* (crepes) and caviar from silver plates. By Monday I would be slogging through the frozen mud fields of a cattle collective, talking to toothless peasants who hadn't seen a paycheck in six months.

Of course I still wanted that yacht, and I continued to take a keen interest in Roberta's deals. The sugar mill was moving along nicely, but a Hilton hotel proposal in St. Petersburg had stalled. Construction on the customs terminal had miraculously started on schedule, and she had taken me out to view the satisfying sight of excavation trucks and cement mixers at work. Still, the project was not trouble-free. The general contractor, a shrewd Azerbaijani who carried thousands of dollars on him at all times, had been brought on as minority partner in the terminal, but that didn't stop him from trying to pad his construction bill, and Roberta was spending a good portion of her time fighting cost overruns.

Building in Russia involved a great many surprises. One of these called for VSO to provide rent-free luxurious office suites, built according to the latest European standards, to the grasping Russian Customs Bureau. This turned out to be common practice in Russia, a form of hidden tax imposed on Westerners, and only one of the many reasons why the overwhelming majority of foreigners stayed well away from foreign direct investment. F.D.I., as it was known, also required the taking on of local partners, one of the riskier aspects of investing in a part of the world with no effective court system to resolve disputes. And local partners—the types who had enough connections or cash to merit making a deal—invariably turned out to be the sort of people you did not want to cross.

Roberta's partners in the customs terminal were no exception to this rule. One was an active general in FAPSI, the electronic surveillance arm of the old KGB, and the equivalent of America's National Security Agency. The other was a retired colonel in the Interior Ministry, a former *gulag* supervisor who had spent a life patrolling the forced-labor camps and prisoner-manned diamond mines of Siberia.

In the deal, VSO funded the construction. The KGB general provided the land, which was next to a factory he ran that made snooping devices and spy-satellite components as well as the scrambler phones that retailed for $17,000. The colonel supplied the muscle and law-enforcement contacts to keep out organized crime, specifically the Chechens, who controlled that distant suburb of Moscow and extorted a 15 to 25 percent cut from every business that operated there. Without some sort of formal protection—it was called a *krysha,* or "roof" in Russian—you simply couldn't go into business in Russia.

The way a *krysha* worked was explained to me by a crazy Canadian by the name of Doug Steele. Everyone in Moscow knew Steele, partly because he ran two of the capital's wildest nightspots, the Hungry Duck and Chesterfields, and partly because he was said to have a death wish. Steele had learned about the *krysha* the hard way. His first venture in Moscow had been a popular pub known as the Moosehead Bar and Grill. He opened it in 1993, when Moscow was still a culinary wasteland. The pub's famous buffalo wings were an immediate success, drawing the attention of expats and Russian businessmen—and eventually the neighborhood Chechen gang, which demanded a stake in the Moosehead. Steele wanted no part of the Chechens, so he went looking for a *krysha.* "I interviewed several gangs," he recalled. "Some even provided references from other Western businesses they protected. It was all very professional." He settled on a local Slavic group headed by a wizened old *vor v zakone,* or thief in the law, one of the traditional mob bosses anointed in Soviet prisons by fellow inmates to adjudicate disputes between criminals. A deal was sealed with a vodka shot and the ceremonial exchange of a hundred-dollar bill, the underworld equivalent of signing a formal contract.

Everything went well until Steele's thief in the law fell victim to a sniper's bullet during the Great Mob War between the Chechens and the powerful Solntsevo Brotherhood, a loose affiliation of Slavic gangs. The next thing Steele knew, he had been kidnapped, roughed up, and forced to hand over the Moosehead to the Chechens. He licked his wounds for a while, and decided to start the Hungry Duck. The Chechens wanted a piece of that too. This time though, Steele signed a deal with the FSB (the successor to the KGB) to provide protection. "They have an official department that provides security," Steele said. The monthly fee was steep, almost 20 percent of his gross, but apparently worth it because he never heard from the Chechens again. "It's the cost of doing business in Russia," he shrugged. "You have to play by the local rules."

Naturally none of this was ever mentioned in all those optimistic investment-banking brochures that so breathlessly touted Russia's prospects. Nor was Roberta's the sort of joint venture they made case studies out of at the Harvard Business School. Nonetheless, she defended her deal. "Better the police mafia than the mafia mafia." Besides, she argued, if we did business with the Russians, they would eventually become more like us. This, in fact, was the Clinton administration's position toward Russia, as articulated by Deputy Secretary of State Strobe Talbott, an Ivy-educated Russophile like Roberta. In the lofty circles of American foreign affairs, this policy was known as "engagement," and it meant encouraging contact and cooperation with postcommunist Russian officials and business leaders and showering them with aid money in the hope that they would take to Western ways. (The opposing school of thought in Washington, led by a Polish-born former national security adviser who shall remain nameless, sought to isolate and encircle the Russians by focusing on the newly independent republics such as Ukraine and Kazakhstan.)

Perhaps for genetic reasons, the whole thing scared the hell out of me. As far as I was concerned, Roberta was mixed up with a potentially nasty bunch. While she had worked at the IFC, she had been protected by the World Bank's diplomatic cocoon. But now she was on her own. And business disputes could get ugly. For instance, an analyst Roberta had hired, a half-Russian, half-Iraqi Kurd named Miran Husni, had been kidnapped his second week on the job. Some thugs abducted him from outside Chesterfields, the expat bar, and chained him to a radiator for a week while they emptied his ATM account to settle a debt they claimed he owed.

For now Roberta was safe because the customs-terminal project was still at the disbursement stage, and her partners needed VSO's money. Everything was always okay while foreigners were putting in their millions. It was once the business was up and running that trouble started. And if I ever needed a reminder of what could happen when joint ventures went sour, all I had to do was drop by the Moscow Radisson.

The Radisson Slavyanskaya Hotel perched on the banks of the Moskva River, next to the Kiev train station and a floating casino done faux-Chinese style, with a fire-breathing dragon for a figurehead and a wooden gangway draped with neon trim and Corona beer flags. The hotel formed a long, pale, low-slung crescent. Its dark, smoky windows looked across the river at yellow billboards for Slovenian-made bouillon cubes that crowned the deluxe apartment buildings on Embankment Street.

The Radisson had been the first big American-Russian joint venture, an undertaking that had received the presidential seal of approval from both sides of the ideological divide back in 1990, when capitalism was still a dirty word in Moscow and Gorbachev was slowly loosening the leash on Soviet business. The sleek 430-room hotel had been touted as a symbol of rapprochement, a gleaming example of the dawning capitalist era. But by 1998 it had become a cautionary tale, and a place associated with murder and the darker side of Russia's market revolution.

Even so, the Radisson was a unique locale for people-watching. Roberta and I would take a table at the Mozart Café in the lobby, sit on its wrought-iron chairs under a canopy of lush plants and international flags that fluttered beneath the long skylight illuminating the lobby's polished marble floors, and take in the crowd. There were buttoned-down U.S. government officials, looking lost and stiff in their somber suits; Western tourists in hiking boots and Patagonia sweatshirts; traveling salesmen, with their pretty interpreters; Chechen mobsters, with their bodyguards and molls.

Young, arrogant toughs, the Chechens acted as if they owned the place, swaggering from table to table hugging and triple-kissing their associates on the cheeks. They were by and large big men, with barrel chests, thick black manes, and tiny cell phones. You could tell that they had an appetite for the finer things in life, with their chauffeur-driven Mercedes idling out front, their Cartier watches, their Versace slacks, and the ubiquitous dainty black suede shoes with gold tassels that sold for eight hundred dollars and wore out after a week of Moscow slush.

The hotel's staff treated them like dignitaries, scurrying at the snap of their fingers while the rest of us muttered about the lousy service. But we didn't mind too much. After all, it's not often that you can safely sit next to a table of predators and observe their habits for the cost of a soup and salad.

And it was relatively safe. Only once in St. Petersburg had two Brits been accidentally killed, when gunmen from a rival gang opened fire on the mobsters at the table next to theirs. There had been one shoot-out inside the Radisson, but that was a few years back, before the Chechens took complete control. Now, they were so numerous that any hit at their hangout would be a suicide mission.

The Chechens were the most ruthless and feared of all of Moscow's criminal gangs. There were barely a thousand Chechens in the capital, but they controlled vast swaths of both the underground and the legitimate economy, and reportedly had many politicians on their payrolls. I was secretly sympathetic to them, because these proud mountain people of the Caucasus had not asked to be part of the Russian empire, and had been brutally conquered by tsars and Soviets alike. Their capital, Grozny, had been laid waste, their people herded into refugee camps. It was hard to blame them for wanting a little payback.

At the Radisson, they kept mostly to themselves and were a cheerful lot, often roaring with laughter at some joke, sometimes so heartily that their gold necklaces danced, and startled patrons spilled their soup. Their bodyguards stood off to the side, chatting quietly among themselves or with the broad-shouldered hotel security guards while their bosses ate. Their girlfriends usually sat at separate tables, with shopping bags bearing the logos of the hotel's expensive Italian boutiques and fine jewelers tucked under their tables. They were Russian or Ukrainian women, stunning blondes and redheads, with plump mouths and faces like angels, and we could often overhear them calling their girlfriends, mothers, or nannies on their mobile phones. "Do you need anything from the store? How's father feeling? Don't worry so much, Mama, I told you I wouldn't be home last night."

Chechens congregated at the Radisson because the place was run by a young, handsome native of Grozny named Umar Dzhabrailov, known around Moscow simply as Umar. Even the local newspapers referred to him by his first name, in the time-honored fashion of a soccer superstar or the lead singer in a rock band. Umar's offices were on the seventh floor of the Radisson business center, and some weeks after our dinner at the White Sun of the Desert, around the Ides of March, I made an appointment to see him.

The elevator door opened and I slammed straight into a man who stood six foot five inches tall and must have weighed over three hundred pounds. This was one of Umar's nine bodyguards. With apologies, I explained the purpose of my visit and was curtly told to wait while the human mountain spoke into his sleeve. He had one of those earpieces with a spaghetti wire curling into his collar, like the Secret Service.

"This way," he mumbled, handing me off to another goon, who stood by a glass side door. Inside the hallway I was passed on, rather like a human baton in a relay race, to two more flatheads, who positioned themselves at my flanks as we marched in silence toward Umar's office. There, a breathtaking receptionist put me at ease with her flawless English. "Mr. Brzezinski," she greeted me, rising from her computer terminal. "Good of you to come. Make yourself comfortable." She pointed to an elegantly dimpled leather couch. "Can I get you anything? A drink? Mineral water? Umar won't be a minute. Perhaps you'd like to see his press clippings while you wait?"

I was more than a little surprised that Umar would keep, much less show visitors, his portfolio from the crime pages of the Russian tabloids. Umar had been a frequent subject of articles after the high-profile murder of his Oklahoman ex-partner, the Radisson's original promoter, Paul Tatum. The two had been involved in a bitter ownership dispute until Tatum was felled by eleven bullets to the head and neck in late 1996.

Tatum's story was well known in Moscow. He had first visited the Soviet Union in the late 1980s and been struck by the country's insatiable appetite for all things Western. He had taken particular note of the lack of decent accommodations, of how visitors were forced to stay at the drab Intourist hotels, which had creaky beds and creaky phone lines and no fax machines for executives. It was his notion to build Russia's first full-service international hotel and modern business center. A born salesman, he talked Radisson into lending its name to the venture, got the spy-ridden Intourist chain to agree to contribute some riverfront land, and contracted with Yugoslav builders to transform his dream into reality in 1990.

For a while everything went smoothly. The hotel offered an oasis of climate-controlled luxury that drew hordes of businessmen; rich Russians to its European restaurants and high-end clothing stores; and the likes of NBC News and Reuters to its fiber-optic-wired office space. U.S. Presidents Bush and Clinton stayed in its suites; Sharon Stone swam in its pool. On weekends everyone crowded into the American movie theater, Moscow's first. Tatum was the toast of the town, cruising the capital's casinos and night spots in his company Mercedes and leading a bachelor's life in a city that offered wealthy bachelors ample diversion.

But then things started to go sour. After the collapse of the Soviet Union, Russia's government started feuding over the Intourist stake. First the new Russian Federation claimed the prize hotel from the old Soviet tourist agency; then Mayor Luzhkov set his sights on it. In the end, after several years of protracted wrangling, the Moscow City Council wrested the property from the Kremlin. Tatum suddenly had a new and unwanted partner. Mayor Luzhkov appointed Umar to comanage the hotel, and Umar had his own ideas about how the complex should be run.

The appearance of Luzhkov and Umar frightened Tatum's Western bankers, who withdrew some twenty million dollars in promised financing. This forced the Oklahoman to dip into cash flow to refurbish office space and run the hotel, which enraged his new partners. They apparently had other plans for the hard currency the hotel generated, and accused Tatum of using the joint venture's money to support his own lavish lifestyle. Tatum's American backers also started to complain about irregularities, and lawsuits against him were filed in the United States.

Meanwhile a new clientele had started to appear in the lobby bars and restaurants: the men in black and their scarlet women. The new patrons soon attracted the unwanted attention of Russia's organized-crime police units, and scenes of thugs lying face down, spread-eagled on the lobby floor while masked Russian SWAT teams handcuffed them at machine-gun point, frightened off guests, who fled to other new hotels being opened in the capital.

Tatum accused his partners from the city of Moscow of skimming profits and publicly labeled their board representative, Umar, as a "Chechen mafia underboss who had gotten his start as a contract killer," allegations that he did not support with evidence and that Umar hotly denied. As the acrimony grew, Tatum hired bodyguards to protect him. On Valentine's Day 1995, one of the bodyguards was slashed across the chest in a hotel washroom and told to pass on a message to his employer: it was time to leave Moscow.

Tatum did not heed the warning. Instead he filed a thirty-five-million-dollar lawsuit against the city of Moscow with international arbitrators in Sweden, hired a dozen more bodyguards, bought a bulletproof vest and barricaded himself in his office, sustaining himself with take-out food and a collection of *Star Trek* videos.

The standoff lasted a year until a snowy Sunday in November 1996, when Tatum received a call on his cell phone from an unidentified woman who claimed she had incriminating information on his partners that would help his cause. As he rushed out to meet her, flak jacket under his trench coat and bodyguards in tow, he was felled just outside the hotel he had helped build. The shots that killed him were expertly fired at the head and neck, where his body armor offered no protection. Though suspicion fell on Umar, he was questioned by the police and cleared. The murder was never solved.

A reporter from *USA Today* happened to be staying at the hotel the day of the shooting. He began asking hard questions about the contract killing and received a knock at his door. Two men with pistols told him to leave Moscow. He wasted no time following their advice, and was escorted to the airport by a detachment of Marine guards from the American Embassy and put on the first plane out of Russia. The flight took him to Frankfurt, where he had to stay overnight at a hotel. That evening, his foreign editor later told me, he received a phone call. It was from one of the men who had threatened him in the Radisson. "Keep your mouth shut when you get back to America. We can find you anywhere," warned the voice on the other end of the line. No one other than the security personnel at the U.S. Embassy in Moscow knew the reporter was in Frankfurt, or which hotel he was staying at. A year later, *USA Today* ran the whole story. In the article, carefully clipped in Umar's scrapbook, the suave hotel manager denied any knowledge of the intimidation.

"Umar will see you now," a polite voice informed me. The receptionist led me into a dimly lit wood-paneled office with deep, dark carpeting. Umar was seated at an antique desk beneath a portrait of Napoleon, speaking softly into a cell phone. I let my eyes adjust to the darkness and drift around the room. Ceremonial daggers, like those traditionally worn by Chechen warriors, hung from the walls. They were of all sizes and varying degrees of gilt and antiquity, and they caught the thin rays of light streaming through the drawn curtains. If they were meant to intimidate, they succeeded admirably. I felt as though I'd just entered the alpha wolf's lair. At the far end of the room sat a leather couch and coffee table, both expensive and tasteful. A black Bang & Olufsen CD player, sleek as a tombstone, stood next to the couch.

My gaze fell on a lacquered credenza on which lay a solitary book. It was an autographed copy of the novel *Icon* signed by its best-selling author, Frederick Forsyth. Forsyth had visited Umar while researching his potboiler on murder and mayhem in the New Russia. In the book, a ruthless Chechen mafia boss with a taste for Italian designer clothes and interests in the hotel business comes to the aid of the protagonist. The fictional Chechen crime lord's name: Umar. Next to the book, a fire-engine-red miniature Ferrari gleamed beside the remains of an exploded artillery-shell casing.

"It landed on my house in Grozny," said Umar, who had finished his conversation and found me staring at the twisted steel memento from Russia's brutal campaign against break-away Chechnya. "I keep it so that I do not forget," he added, extending a hand. While Chechens were undeniably striking it rich in Moscow, they never forgot their centuries-old struggle for independence and what was happening to their homeland. I suppose the brutality inflicted on their people by Russia made it easier to justify their crime sprees in Moscow. Local rumor had it that the Chechen mob bosses sent a full 15 percent of their take back to their relatives in the mountains for the purchase of weapons.

Umar was a slender, handsome man, impeccably dressed in a double-breasted charcoal suit with the wide lapels that were currently all the rage in Milan and a multicolored, billowing silk tie that was equally in fashion. His shoulder-length hair was speckled with silver, but cut stylishly to preserve an air of youth and vigor. His English was perfect, as were his small, manicured fingers and expensive yet understated cufflinks.

"Call me Umar," he said. "All my friends do—even my enemies." With that he beamed a broad smile, pearly and straight and not the least bit bashful. "How about an orange juice, freshly squeezed?"

I'd met a great many interesting and quite a few frightening people in the seven years I'd spent in the Wild East, but none quite like Umar. It was the charm, the self-confidence, the hypnotic black eyes that menaced even as they soothed. No wonder Forsyth had modeled his gangster after Umar; he *was* a character right out of a book.

Gently and delicately, I steered the conversation toward Tatum. It was obvious from Umar's reaction that he had gone down that road many times before, for without hesitation he pronounced the slaying tragic.

"Terrible," he shook his head regretfully, "what happened to Paul. But in many ways I'm a victim too, because everyone pointed the finger at me." This apparently included the U.S. government, which had revoked his visa and barred him from entering the United States on the grounds that he allegedly had ties to organized crime. (The American Embassy refused to comment on the matter, either on or off the record, and a Moscow police spokesman told me Umar had no criminal record in Russia.) At the mention of the humiliating blacklist, Umar bristled. His face contorted, and his lips whitened. His fist slammed the table.

"The bureaucrat that made that decision," he hissed, "that little man in a little office, would never dare come and sit in front of me. Because he knows—" And here there was an ominous pause. "Because he knows," Umar repeated, this time more calmly, "that he is wrong."

After that outburst, I steered the conversation to the less pro-
vocative topic of real estate. Umar's property business was flourish-
ing. In addition to his running the Radisson's business center,
Luzhkov had awarded him the management contract for his prized
Manezh underground shopping center next to the Kremlin, as well
as several other big commercial developments in which the city of
Moscow had interests. Green billboards advertising Umar's management company, Gruppa Plaza, sprouted like weeds throughout town.

On the subject of Moscow, Umar was enthusiastic and passionate. He became very animated in describing his vision of the capital,
slashing the air with his hands and making sweeping gestures to denote urban sprawl. Naturally he shared his vision with his benefactor, the forward-looking mayor. Luzhkov, he explained in a hushed,
conspiratorial voice, was trying to line up financing to build the
world's tallest skyscraper, a needle-like structure that would rise one
hundred fifty stories and anchor a new financial district—the "Wall
Street of the East," as Umar exuberantly pitched it. He whipped out
a map and pointed to the location of a more modest fifty-story tower
he wanted to build next to Luzhkov's needle. He said he already had
the land.

Now that he had simmered down, I ventured a weak comment
about Moscow's dangerous business climate. To my surprise Umar
nodded solemnly. "It can be dangerous, yes," he advised, "if you are
foolish." He went on to decry the lack of a legal system and rule of
law in Russia, sounding exactly like a Western diplomat. Alas, he
said, this was why he and other businessmen felt compelled to have
so many bodyguards, though they could be a real nuisance, always
bumping into things and getting in the way. The wobbly judicial system left entrepreneurs no choice but to protect themselves, he explained. With no legal mechanisms for conflict resolution, it was
unfortunately easier to settle disputes with a gun than through the
courts. Cheaper too. Of the eighteen hundred people murdered in
Moscow in 1997, nearly a third were the victims of contract killers—
who were almost never caught.

"How do you resolve disputes?" I asked.

"You negotiate quietly, not by taking full-page ads," Umar replied
in a seeming reference to Tatum's strategy of running newspaper ads
that accused his Russian partners of all sorts of unsavory activities

in the misplaced belief that the publicity would protect him from retribution. "Say you have a fight with your partner," Umar continued more ominously, leaning forward and fixing me with a dark gaze. "And he comes to me and says, 'That Matthew is a real fucking bastard. We must do something.'" He paused, then sat back and smiled. "Then you come to me and offer to talk and show that you are a reasonable man and wanting to make, how you say, concession. So I think 'He's not a bastard.' You see, we have made human contact, and now I don't want anything to happen to you."

As I listened to him speak, my heart raced and sweat started to run down the small of my back. I knew he was probably just toying with me, yet I couldn't get over how frightening he sounded. I had even stopped scribbling notes. *"That Matthew is a real fucking bastard. We must do something"* rang in my ears. Umar, of course, was only speaking hypothetically, the way he had presumably talked to Forsyth when he had speculated about how a Russian crime syndicate could operate. I couldn't help feeling that he was hamming it up, playing a role for yet another member of the Western press who had presumed him guilty of Tatum's murder without benefit of trial solely on the basis of his Chechen ethnicity. Still, it was an effective charade: I was terrified.

I was also starting to worry in earnest about what could happen to Roberta if she ever ran afoul of her partners. Already she had been indirectly intimidated, when she refused to disburse a several-million-dollar progress payment for construction because of some legal snafu, and the ex-MVD colonel had snapped: "Who do you think you're dealing with here? We are the privatized State. What we say *is* the law."

Roberta had refused to yield. She was stubborn by nature, and tougher than I'll ever be. And while that might have been an asset in dealing with recalcitrant Ukrainian privatization officials, sticking too stubbornly to your guns in Russian business could get you killed.

CHAPTER TWELVE

The Ides of March

It was snowing outside, a bitter morning in March 1998, and we were hunkered down in the *Journal's* conference room, watching ORT-TV, Berezovsky's network. The midday news led with gory footage of fighting in Tadjikistan. Closer to home, an American had been arrested in southern Russia, accused of spying. On the financial front, the stock market was down again, increasingly volatile. Russia had caught a touch of the Asian flu; the mayhem in Hong Kong and Seoul had frightened international investors. There was a more upbeat piece on a big pipeline deal in the Caspian, and in local news, a double murder of two police officers in Moscow.

At the tail end of the broadcast there was a report that yet another Jewish cemetery had been desecrated in Siberia. The circumstances of that unfortunate act, according to the newscaster, were being investigated, and Russia's federal authorities expressed confidence that the culprit or culprits would swiftly be brought to justice, which would indeed be news.

Vandals don't move markets, so the item did not cause a great stir at our bureau, where, it being Friday, our antennas were at half-mast anyway. But I took special note, because just a few minutes before the telecast Roberta had phoned to ask if I wanted to go to temple with her that evening.

One of the unexpected consequences of Roberta's gig at VSO—aside from my sudden interest in the yacht-brokerage section of *Sail* magazine—had been to rouse her curiosity about her faith. VSO, despite its tough-guy reputation, contributed lavishly (and anonymously) to Jewish causes in the former Soviet Union. Roberta's boss had personally financed the construction of five synagogues across the old Union, so that Jews in remote places like Uzbekistan could attend services and gain strength from the knowledge that they were not alone.

Russia's Jewish revival stirred mixed emotions in Roberta. She had been raised nonobservant and was ambivalent about her heritage, more focused on looking forward than backward. On the one hand, she was apt to make self-deprecating quips about her forefathers peddling herring on the muddy streets of Bialystok. On the other, she was fiercely proud of Judaism's emphasis on education, which had helped elevate her grandfather from shoe peddler to a seat on the Superior Court of New Jersey, and set her on a path of high achievement, including early admission to Harvard and a full academic scholarship for postgraduate studies. But there was something about Eastern Europe that brought ghosts to life. And even though I had left Catholicism behind in my teens, I understood the need to search for one's roots, and encouraged Roberta to follow her heart.

Throughout Eastern Europe, religious revival was spearheaded by Western groups. In the case of Judaism, it happened that only fundamentalist sects—the Hasidim, the Lubavitchers, and other ultra-Orthodox groups—devoted the energy and funds necessary to bring religion to those who had nearly forgotten it. On the Christian front, Mormons performed the same task, sending seniors from Brigham Young University out to Warsaw, Kiev, Moscow, and points beyond. The young Mormon missionaries were often seen about town, looking uncertain, hobbled by language barriers and preaching in pairs for the sake of safety. Young, pink-scrubbed men in black suits, white shirts, dark ties, and name-tags, they invited stares on the street and were mugged so often that the State Department had taken to including their numerous misfortunes in its travel advisories.

The Roman Catholics had the fewest missionaries. Roman Catholicism had helped defeat communism in Poland, and the Church had needed no outsiders to spur religion there. The Polish Church was equally busy in some corners of the Soviet Union. Oddly, the Polish priests sent to Belarus and Ukraine had a habit of evangelizing near military bases. As a result, they kept getting accused of spying on behalf of the CIA, which had developed cordial ties to the Polish hierarchy during the struggle against communism. Moscow's Jewish community probably numbered several hundred thousand households but kept a low profile, for fear of rabble-rousers like the half-Jewish anti-Semite Vladimir Zhirinovsky. The city was now a more tolerant place than it had been during Soviet times, but it was hardly a welcoming environment for Jews. Even the Nobel-laureate dissident writer Alexander Solzhenitsyn, who had returned after decades of exile in Vermont, preached a sort of xenophobic nationalism that made it clear Jews could never be wholly accepted or trusted to be good Russians.

Two synagogues served Moscow's Jewish community. Both were Orthodox, and were headed by Americans. In the 1990s, most of the rabbis of Eastern Europe's few restored and well-funded synagogues hailed from Brooklyn, New York—traditionally one of America's largest Jewish centers.

Roberta and I presented ourselves at the Choral Synagogue in Moscow's old Armenian district shortly after dusk. The prayer house was discreetly tucked behind a worn brownstone façade that blended in with the gloomy, unrenovated neighboring buildings. Two guards paced the glassy sidewalk outside the door. The temple's benefactors had instituted round-the-clock security ever since a third synagogue in Moscow had been lost to a 1994 fire; investigators suspected it was the work of arsonists.

There were no spare yarmulkes, so I was given a Chicago Bulls cap to cover my head. I felt a little ridiculous, and sat self-consciously in a back pew while Roberta was led to an upper gallery by a wiry woman in her late forties who said she had only discovered her faith after the collapse of communism. The two fell deep into conversation and I was left alone to my thoughts. Memories of my friend Genady, and our visit to Warsaw's historic Nozyk Synagogue in early 1992, came in a flood.

Genady had been nervous, pacing outside in the drizzle, afraid to go inside. I should have been more patient, realized that this was a big step on his journey of self-discovery, but instead I was short-tempered. "Stop stalling," I said. "It's freezing. Let's go in."

"Just one more minute," pleaded Genady. "I'm sorry."

We circled the synagogue one more time, in silence, observing its fine pilasters and listening to the rain run eerily off its copper eaves. The building was stout and square, one of many built with care and elegance in the previous century, when a third of Warsaw's population spoke Yiddish and every second block boasted a great rabbinical scholar. Now it was unique for its very existence. As the lone Jewish prayer house to survive both the Holocaust and communism's repression, the Nozyk Synagogue formed a tenuous and solitary link between Poland's vibrant Jewish past and its faint and ghostly present.

Genady wiped the mist off his glasses and looked up at the building. We could see the fresh putty around the opaque, shatterproof windows that had been installed after a recent attack by skinheads. Paint blotches besmirched the synagogue's thick walls, and the faint geometric outlines of spray-painted swastikas bled through the new coat of whitewash. Ghena (his nickname) shivered and shook the rain from his curly mop of red hair.

"Do you want to go home?"

"No," he said. "I have to go in."

Ghena—Dr. Genady Mishuris—was a Russian professor of applied mathematics and a guest lecturer at the University of Warsaw, a kind and complicated man. He was also, as he had been reminded all his life, a Jew. It said so in his red CCCP passport; it was clear from his surname, which did not end in any of the traditional Slavic suffixes; and it was written all over his round and freckled intellectual face and frizzy red beard.

Ghena was my best friend in Poland. We had met at the Belvederska student hotel, a former Communist Party dorm for students from the so-called fraternal nations of the socialist camp. I lived there partly because the fifty-dollar monthly rent was all I could afford during my earliest days as an aspiring stringer, but mostly because there I had interesting neighbors: Vietnamese, Iraqis, Angolans, Palestinians, Syrians, and a few Libyans. Lieutenant-Colonel Muammar Qaddafi had been the Belvederska's most famous resident when he studied at the University of Warsaw in the 1960s.

Ghena and I met one day in the fall of 1991 in the Belvederska's

TV room while watching coverage of the dissolution of the USSR. I had difficulty following the Russian newscaster and had asked Ghena to translate. We quickly became friends, often staying up late to talk about events in Russia. A few months later he asked me to accompany him to the Nozyk Synagogue. "For moral support," he had said in a tremulous voice.

Ghena had never been to synagogue. He had never, in his thirty-four years in the Soviet Union, seen Jews being openly Jewish. He knew only one thing about being a Jew; it meant always looking over your shoulder. And though he had never picked up a torah, and couldn't speak a word of Hebrew, he said that to many of his Russian neighbors and colleagues in his hometown of Vologda, he might as well have been the Chief Rabbi of Israel, hatching diabolical plans for global Zionist domination.

An attendant, hunched behind a protective grille, scrutinized us as we walked up the slippery steps to the synagogue's main entrance. "Yes?" he inquired in a voice distorted by a crackling intercom.

"We're here for the Sabbath service," I answered in Polish. There was a pause and we could feel the attendant's probing gaze. Then the lock buzzed and as I grappled with the knob, I saw Genady take a deep, frightened breath.

The door opened onto a large and well-lit hall lined with balconies and marbled columns. Pale wooden pews ran the length of the open chamber, at the center of which stood a polished granite dais where a rabbi swayed, his long snowy beard tickling the yellowed parchment of the large ornamental scrolls he read from. Around him two dozen old men rocked in individual prayer, their murmurs soaring and drifting in the vaulted room.

"Cohen or Levi?" a tall gaunt man asked us.

"I beg your pardon?" I asked, startled. Ghena seemed too intimidated to talk.

"Cohen or Levi?" repeated the stranger.

"I think you have us mistaken for someone else."

He paused, confused that I did not understand the traditional question about ancestry. To be a Cohen signified that one's forebears had been priests; Levis had been priests' helpers. "Are you Jewish?" he asked, suddenly suspicious.

"No," I said, feeling uneasy. "But my friend is."

Ghena's gaze was firmly fixed on his shoes and he had still not uttered a word, which was highly out of character. Usually I couldn't get him to shut up. "He's from Russia," I explained, to fill the awkward silence.

"Ah," nodded the stranger, looking at Ghena with sudden sympathy and understanding. "A first-timer, eh? We get a lot of those these days." The stranger's name was Alexander Zajdeman and he introduced himself as the synagogue's caretaker. We exchanged handshakes, and Ghena mumbled his apologies in heavily Russian-accented Polish. Something, I think, about being sorry for not knowing what to do in synagogue.

Zajdeman seemed unperturbed. "Put these on and follow me," he said, handing us each a white, silky skullcap, which he fished out of a bag that hung by the door. Donning the yarmulke, I noticed the name of a Brooklyn congregation stamped on the lining.

"This is the only functioning synagogue in Warsaw," Zajdeman announced with a proud air, assuming the role of our tour guide. "It is in the neo-Romanesque style and was built in the nineteenth century by the Nozyk family. They were merchants," he added. "Very successful." He led us up a narrow creaking staircase to the second-floor gallery, where it is customary for women to attend the services separately. There were no women present on that Saturday morning, and as we looked down on the rows of vacant benches, we saw only a few frail backs draped in fringed prayer shawls. The Nozyk Synagogue had been designed to accommodate six hundred faithful, Zajdeman went on, and in its day was always overflowing. But that had been before the war, when more than three hundred thousand Jews lived in Warsaw. Now there were less than three thousand, and the chamber was hauntingly empty, like the stadium of a losing team.

"We get young people sometimes," said Zajdeman, as if sensing my thoughts. "Mostly American tourists on pilgrimages to the death camps and a few Israeli tour groups. The regulars are about fifty pensioners. It's sad. We haven't had a bar mitzvah or a wedding here since the war. We do say Kaddish [the prayer for the dead] often. When the last survivors pass away, I fear this place will close again."

The Nozyk Synagogue had been shuttered for fifteen years following the Polish Communist Party's anti-Semitic purges of 1968. Ostensibly closed for renovations, it was allowed to reopen by the

Polish government in 1983, and then only on the condition that no rabbi hold worship services there. By then there were no rabbis left in Poland anyway, and few Jews dared to be openly observant for fear of reprisals.

"Only I stayed with the synagogue throughout those years," Zajdeman told us gravely. "I had nowhere else to go."

As a cantor sang and the old men in their patchy cardigan sweaters shuffled about below, Zajdeman told us his life's story. His father had owned a small flour mill east of Warsaw before the war. Not a big mill, he insisted, but one big enough so that the family had a piano and a motorcar, rare in those days. In 1939, Zajdeman had lied about his age, joined the army, and been sent to the front to fight the Germans. His infantry unit was captured after only a few weeks of battle and, like my maternal grandfather, he had spent the next five years as a POW in Germany.

Maybe it was Zajdeman's baby-blue eyes, but no one in the prisoner-of-war camp had suspected he was Jewish, a secret he had kept to himself because he did not want to be teased. He in turn had no idea that the Nazis were exterminating Jews until after his release. "There was nobody left. My brothers, sisters, cousins; everybody was dead. So I came to Warsaw in 1945 and wandered around the rubble for months until I found the Nozyk Synagogue. It was the only building in the Jewish ghetto still standing."

He walked in and found manure scattered on the walls and floor and hay strewn everywhere. The Gestapo had converted the building into stables for its officer's parade horses, the only reason the synagogue had not been destroyed like all the others in town. "I found a shovel and started cleaning," Zajdeman recalled. "And I've been here ever since."

Ghena sat transfixed by the tale and stared intensely at the elderly rabbi below. "Do you want to meet him?" I asked. "No, no," he said softly. "Maybe we could just sit here for a few more minutes."

"That is the Chief Rabbi of Poland," Zajdeman volunteered. Rabbi Pinchas Menachem Joskowicz was, in fact, the *only* rabbi in Poland. (A rabbi from Brooklyn would arrive the following year.) Brittle yet forbidding in his severe black suit, he had a wizened face, penetrating eyes and a thick, silvery mane of a beard that was cut squarely at the ends. Ghena whispered that Rabbi Joskowicz looked like something out of an old painting. "He is how I imagined rabbis looked like in *shtetls* before the revolution," he said.

Rabbi Joskowicz was born in Lodz, an industrial city that before the war was known for its sprawling red-brick textile mills and flamboyant merchant princes who inlaid their palace floors with gold coins. A survivor of the Lodz ghetto, Joskowicz spent the final years of the war in the Bergen-Belsen extermination camp. After being liberated by the British, he emigrated to Palestine, where he fought in Israel's War of Independence. Joskowicz then spent seventeen years as an army chaplain in the Israeli Defense Force before turning his attention to establishing a pharmaceutical business in Tel Aviv and raising a family.

In 1989, when the communist edifice collapsed in Poland, he returned to attend to the spiritual needs of Warsaw's remaining Jews. A few months before our visit to the Nozyk Synagogue, the rabbi had been hospitalized with head injuries from an attack by a group of Polish skinheads. Zajdeman told us that Joskowicz had been advised to go back to Tel Aviv, but the rabbi had sworn that he would not return to Israel until a successor had been found to care for the spiritual needs of Polish Jews.

Zajdeman was looking at Ghena, who was still overwhelmed at seeing his first Sabbath service. "Is it difficult for Jews in the part of Russia where you come from?" Zajdeman inquired. Ghena's face clouded and he managed to nod his head.

It had stopped raining, but the morning sky was still heavy and dark when we left the Nozyk Synagogue. In the distance, we could see storm clouds and the sinister spire of Warsaw's Palace of Culture outlined against the city's squat skyline. The Gothic eyesore, an unsolicited gift from Stalin to celebrate the grafting of Poland onto the Soviet Empire, rose like a grimy shotgun-wedding cake, its needle-nosed radio mast piercing the dense fog. We walked in silence for a while, past a series of badly listing brick buildings propped up by large wooden beams that had been wedged at forty-five-degree angles into the fissured sidewalk. As we waited for the tram at the foot of a glistening new skyscraper that stood on the foundation of what before the war had been Europe's biggest synagogue, Genady became very solemn.

"I'm getting my family out of Russia," he pledged, eyes moist with emotion. "I don't want my son to grow up hiding like me. We are going to emigrate, leave Vologda for good."

Vologda was a timber town on Russia's northern frontier, a wild and windswept place where snowdrifts buried buildings in winter and voracious mosquitoes ruled the short, muggy summer. The tsars at one time banished revolutionaries to Vologda, and the Soviets later populated it with the outcasts of their Revolution. Lenin had reportedly spent a chilly season of internal exile in Vologda at the turn of the century. The little log cabin where he was said to have wintered was still lovingly preserved when I visited Genady in July of 1992, some six months after our visit to the Nozyk Synagogue.

I had taken the overnight train from Moscow and arrived stiff and cranky from a sleepless night of bumps and clanks on the inhospitable Russian rail system. Ghena, bubbling with excitement, met me at the planked rail platform and insisted on dragging me straight from the railway station to the Great Leader's old abode.

We piled into an ancient and overcrowded trolleybus that creaked and rattled even more than the train. After five blocks, the trolley collapsed from exhaustion and everyone spilled out: stooped war veterans with medals on their lapels, wispy girls in knee-high boots, and plump babushkas who wore sweat-stained kerchiefs in the deadening heat.

"Another bus will be by in a half-hour," Ghena informed me with the resigned calm of someone who had been putting up with this sort of breakdown all his life. The other passengers made themselves comfortable, flopping down in the weedy ditch to wait. The guy next to me decided to make a picnic of the impromptu stop and unwrapped a dry and scaly fish, which he picked apart with blackened fingertips. We sat. We perspired. We swatted the flies.

Half an hour passed, and still no bus. After forty-five minutes a truck rumbled past, trailing a foul mix of diesel and dust that matched my mood.

"Screw this," I said, spitting out the taste of diesel fumes. "Let's hail a cab."

"But that will cost two hundred rubles," protested Ghena. At the prevailing rate of exchange, that came to seventy-five cents, hardly a princely sum, even on my meager salary.

"I'll splurge."

The "taxi" turned out to be a passing Volga sedan driven by an ornery Armenian who chain-smoked filterless cigarettes and who doubled the fare as soon as he heard us speaking Polish. It was easy to see why Russians in the provinces would have thought Poles were better off. Most of Vologda looked like a flash-frozen eighteenth-century village. We drove by rows of unpainted timber-framed homes with plank-covered wells and pitched picket fences that were missing slats. The ragged huts lurched drunkenly, their transoms, doors, and cracked windows all askew. Nothing appeared plumb in Vologda, least of all the thinly-paved roads, which undulated crazily from frost heave and were pocked with axle-swallowing craters.

One building caught my eye; it was large, straight, and true, with long narrow tinted-glass windows and a fine off-white polished-marble finish. The post-modernist structure looked identical to the Soviet Embassy Chancery in Washington, right up to the pearly, dentillated capping that ran the perimeter of the flat roof. "*Raikom*," said Ghena, using the Russian abbreviation for the Regional Communist Party Headquarters. "Cost hundreds of millions of rubles. And that was back in the late eighties when the ruble was at par with the dollar."

"Who's using it now?" I asked, noticing a half-dozen black, too-clean-not-to-be-official Volgas parked outside.

Ghena seemed surprised at the naiveté of my question. "The regional government, of course. It's the same people. Only now they like to be called democrats."

We entered the center of Vologda, and I was amazed at how similar the old parts of the city were to pictures I'd seen of Main Street in American frontier towns. Every building was two-storied and wrapped in weathered clapboard. Balconies with uneven balustrades ran the length of the top floors, casting shadows on storefront displays in which dusty pyramids of canned goods with faded labels rose unappetizingly. I half expected to see signs saying Saloon or Sheriff.

Lenin's house, much to my chagrin, was indeed our first destination. Desperate for sleep after the train ride, I reluctantly got out of the car to pay my respects to the Father of All Soviets. The house, a dark single-story structure with quaint trellises and rough-hewn log walls, was positively spartan. It suggested hardiness and mental fortitude, just the sort of traits you'd expect from a revolutionary hero. I peered inside, but couldn't make out much. The cabin's windows were of old glass, thick and out of focus, with tiny air bubbles trapped in the crude panes. Fresh-cut flowers had been placed on the sill, where they crowded wilted offerings and red plastic tulips brought by previous pilgrims. The heavy planked door, mercifully, was locked, so I was spared a lengthy room-by-room tour and a mind-numbing lecture on Lenin's quill, oil lamps, and bedsheets. I couldn't help thinking that the world would have been a better place if Tsar Nicholas II had simply executed the troublemaker instead of sending him upriver for a year.

Ghena was distressed. "I don't know where the museum attendant is," he fretted. "No one goes to work anymore. We'll come back tomorrow."

I assured Ghena it would not be necessary. The fierce pride he derived from sharing a postal code with Vladimir Ilyich puzzled me. After all, Ghena was no fan of communism. His disillusionment had come long ago, shortly after he had joined Komsomol, the Young Communist League. That had been during his freshman year studying mathematics at the University of Leningrad, when he still bought into all that nonsense about building an equal society. By the time he finished university, Ghena had taken a crash course in just how unequal the Soviet Union was. Though he graduated at the top of his class, earning the Soviet equivalent of a *summa cum laude* from Yale or Oxford, and easily defended his Ph.D. thesis, the central planners had sent him to teach applied math at a third-rate junior college in the backwater of Vologda. The prestigious institutes of Moscow where he had longed to work were off limits to Jews.

Ghena lived on Shetinia Street, in one of the newer neighborhoods on the eastern outskirts of town. Shetinia Street started as a wide asphalt throughway, metamorphosed into a gravel road, and finished as a deeply-rutted, baked-mud lane for the last few hundred yards before Ghena's apartment block.

"The town ran out of money," he apologized as we bounced from rut to rut, the taxi driver cursing. A dirt path cut through tall grasses to the entrance of Ghena's building. I knew from our conversations in Warsaw that this was one of the least prestigious addresses in Vologda. Ghena had been assigned quarters here by the dean of the mathematics faculty. An unabashed admirer of Zhirinovsky, the dean spent his spare time printing and distributing rabble-rousing leaflets on campus. He took particular pleasure in presenting his compositions to the Jewish members of the faculty. Ghena showed me one of these manifestos, topped with an attention-grabbing Star of David and filled with a diatribe about hook-nosed Hebrew cabals conspiring to undermine the glory of Mother Russia. There was something about birth rates too, which implied that Jews were multiplying and overrunning the nation.

The buildings in this section of town had suffered from the same mysterious budget shortfalls that had waylaid the road. The funds for construction tended to dry up midway through projects, leaving concrete hulks with completed bottom halves and exposed cement columns and steel girders on the top floors. At night, when the cold winds whistled down from the Arctic Circle, the unfinished portions of the housing blocks howled. But people eagerly moved into the bottom floors anyway, anxious for a place of their own after many years on waiting lists.

Genady had long given up on the idea of getting a better apartment. His dean had made it clear that he would forever rot in the dorm-style quarters he had been temporarily assigned when he and his wife first arrived in Vologda in the late 1980s. The corridors in his building seemed modeled after a correctional facility: unpainted concrete and heavy steel doors, lit by exposed fluorescent tubes that flickered weakly from the low cement ceilings. The rules required announcing my arrival to the building administrator. She squinted at me self-importantly from behind a plexiglass divider near the entrance. "*Dokumenty!*" she snapped, by way of greeting.

I didn't think my documents were any concern of hers, but Ghena tugged at my elbow and beseeched me not to make a fuss. "It's just for her records," he pleaded. "I can't bring you up unless she takes down your passport number."

"Communism ended a year ago. Remember? This is no longer a

police state." I was irritated and sleepy. And this snoop with her bee-hive hair and prying eyes was keeping me up.

"Maciej"—Ghena called me by my Polish name—"it's like I told you before. Nothing has changed in Vologda except the prices. Please just give her your passport and don't make trouble."

She snatched it greedily and I watched her plump fingers leaf through all the pages, visas and entry stamps. "*Kanadets* [Canadian]," she said approvingly, and imperiously waved us through.

Lena, Ghena's wife, greeted us at the door. She was dark and sultry, with large brooding eyes and ink-black bangs. "You're late," she said, by way of welcome. Ghena explained our trolleybus troubles. Something in the way he was spluttering told me Lena was firmly in charge of the Mishuris household. They had met at university in St. Petersburg and Ghena had wooed her for an entire semester before she reluctantly agreed to go out with him. The two married just before he defended his thesis.

Lena had a master's degree in mathematics and taught calculus to the "hooligans" at a local high school. Between them, the Mishurises earned around thirty dollars a month, about the average household income in Vologda, which counted a sprawling optics plant as its main employer. The factory made targeting systems for tanks, canopies for fighter jets, and lenses for consumer cameras. Business was slow, and people all over Vologda were selling cameras they had received as part of their pay. Two new cameras served as bookends on Ghena's shelves.

The apartment made my dorm at the Belvederska student hotel seem palatial. Ghena's living room was also the master bedroom, with an old pull-out couch serving double duty. The floor was covered with an orange rubbery coating of the sort you find in weight rooms. A curtain led into the kitchen, where a dodgy-looking stove sat next to a toilet bowl. Glancing from the blue plastic toilet seat to the greasy frying pan only a few feet away, I suggested we go out for lunch.

Ghena started making his usual noises about the cost, but Lena cut him off with a few sharp words, which I assumed ran something like, "If the rich foreigner wants to spend his money, let him."

We lunched in a Roman Catholic church that the Soviets had

converted into a restaurant. It was a red brick structure, built in the Gothic style with peaked arches, ornate lead windows, and a broad, airy nave that served as the dining room. Most of the meat entrees had been crossed off the menu, indicating the short supply of beef and pork in Vologda. We were the only diners, another indicator of the tough times that had befallen Russia in its first year of post-Soviet existence. The restaurant, Ghena explained, was a cooperative, which meant that it was owned and run for profit by its workers' collective. However, the waiter-owner didn't strike me as overly concerned with whether his customers were satisfied. He seemed much more interested in watching the *Dynasty*-style Mexican soap opera *The Rich Also Cry,* which was blaring from the portable black-and-white television over the bar.

The bill came to just under three thousand rubles, and the waiter was only too happy to accept an American ten-dollar bill. Ghena suggested we have dessert at Vologda's lone synagogue, which under communism had suffered the same gustatory fate as the town's Catholic church.

"The Russian Orthodox churches were turned into warehouses," said Lena. "I think they were afraid to make them into cafés because citizens would have protested." Russians always talked about *they* and *us*. *They* denoted the powers that be and *us* referred to everyone else. You got the impression that *they* were forever screwing *us*.

On the way to the synagogue-cum-ice-cream-parlor, as we walked along a leafy street, a motorcade of two Volgas and a shiny white Volvo (the only Western car I had seen in Vologda) zoomed by at high speed. Ghena lowered his voice and murmured "Mafia." He said it the way people in movies whispered "KGB" or "Gestapo"— with fear and awe. The crime syndicate in Vologda controlled, among many things, the distribution of vodka. You could not buy booze in State stores. Instead long lines formed in front of trucks parked next to the shops. Naturally, each bottle sold out of the back of the lorries cost twice the going rate, but as long as the mafia enforced its monopoly, customers had little choice but to pay the premium. Two bullnecked bodybuilders usually rode shotgun in the mobile liquor stores to make sure all went smoothly.

The synagogue had been painted pale blue. A Soviet star was taped over a stained-glass Star of David and ringed with multicolored Christmas lights. The parlor served Pepsi in those old smoked-glass bottles and had a stack of Snickers bars neatly arranged on the counter. Snickers symbolized capitalism in the early 1990s, the low-cost candy bars being among the first Western goods to penetrate the Iron Curtain. We ordered vanilla ice cream, the only flavor available, and it arrived in pink plastic champagne glasses covered with greasy fingerprint smudges. The price of a serving, Lena grumbled, had risen sixfold in the past six months. "When will this inflation stop?" she lamented. "Every week I buy less and less with our pay."

The reason the price of ice cream, and just about everything else, was skyrocketing was that central planners, during Soviet times, had decreed that factories could charge only a fraction of the real production cost of their products. In 1992 Russia, like Poland before it, launched its own version of the so-called shock therapy program. The reforms were implemented by Yegor Gaidar, a protégé of Poland's finance minister. A portly academic, Gaidar had been appointed acting prime minister by President Yeltsin. His mandate was at once simple and daunting: to design the blueprint for capitalism's entry into Russia. His first move was to free prices, which under communism had been kept ridiculously low without any consideration of the vagaries of supply and demand. Price liberalization was the dreaded first stage in the market transition, in which the cost of goods rose far faster than wages, which had also been kept artificially low.

But capitalism was far more alien to Russia than to pro-Western Poland. During communism, millions of Poles had been allowed to spend time in the West, working off the books in places like Chicago and London and Hamburg. (I had employed a dozen such cheap Polish workers in my construction business in Montreal.) These tourist-laborers returned home with hard-currency savings and invaluable first-hand experience in how a pizza parlor or a building company was properly run (or badly run, in the case of my Brezco). What's more, Poland had permitted some private small-business activity during the communist era, had never collectivized agriculture, and had had a free-market economy within living memory. Russia, on the other hand, had gone Red in 1917, shut itself off from the outside world, and locked up its precious few entrepreneurs as black marketers and enemies of the state. So in a place like Vologda, about the only thing people knew about capitalism was that they had heard bad things about it their entire lives, but now it was supposedly okay, whatever it was.

To clear up some of the confusion, Vologda's town fathers decided to educate the next generation about the dos and don'ts of commerce. Vologda's Young Pioneers camp was chosen to teach capitalism to its adolescent charges. The Young Pioneers were part of a national communist summer-camp system that had been inculcating Leninist ideology along with swimming and soccer for sixty years, so this was a bit of a departure from the usual fare. Ghena's twelve-year-old son had taken part in the experiment. When I heard how the ill-fated exercise had turned out, I decided to visit the camp director.

It took several days for Ghena to secure permission for me to visit the Krupskaya Young Pioneers Camp—one still needed permission for everything in 1992. We whiled away the time by boating to a sixteenth-century monastery that the Russian Orthodox Church had just reclaimed from the State. It was situated a few miles upriver from Vologda, nestled on a bank of tall grasses that tickled the bellies of the grazing cows from a nearby cattle collective. The monastery's whitewashed battlement walls and onion domes were reflected in the river as we sailed past colonies of beavers and moored our launch to a listing wharf. Voices echoed clearly over the water. Looking up, we could see that they belonged to brown-clad figures scurrying along the fortifications. These turned out to be young novices, their beards still scraggly. They wore coarse frocks tied trimly at the waist with thick rope, and their work-boots dug into the soft soil as they pushed large wheelbarrows filled with the mortar mix and rough-cut beams that would help rebuild the Russian Orthodox faith after seventy years of atheism.

Inside, the monastery was crumbling; the roof had collapsed, snapping girders; belfries had shifted and toppled; and holes gaped where priceless iconostases had been ripped from walls by communist axes. I found a sliver of an icon, splintered and thrown onto a junk heap of rusted spikes and iron hinges. "It's probably three hundred years old," said Ghena, dusting off the darkly lacquered painting. It depicted a saint, or rather half of one, the vandal's hatchet having cut down the center of his amber-colored halo. "You'd better leave it," Ghena advised. "You can get into trouble with customs at the border. They check for foreigners smuggling icons."

When we returned to Vologda that night, there was a message to call the Pioneer camp. It had been left with Ghena's haughty building administrator, who relayed it along with an admonition that she was not his personal answering service. Since she had the only telephone in his building, we had to wait in line the next morning at the crowded post office to put in a return call to the camp director.

After a long wait, Ghena finally got through and was told, "You may bring the *inostranets*." The word *inostranets* means "foreigner," but in Vologda it was pronounced it as though it meant "bringer of discord and unwanted ways."

The Pioneer Camp administrator arranged for us to hitch a ride with a supply van delivering vegetables to the campers. We bounced along a logging road, overtaking tractor-trailers weighed down with fir and pine trunks, and passed through large swaths of clear-cut land where oozing stumps dotted the underbrush. After about an hour, a ranch-style gate of welded steel announced the entrance to the Krupskaya Pioneer Camp. "The camp is named after Lenin's wife," said Ghena, fidgeting with a bag of sweets we were bringing for his son.

The driver down-shifted, gears grinding, and we powered up a steep, wooded hill that opened on to a patchy soccer field with an obstacle course in one of the end zones. The main camp appeared ahead of us: white military-style barracks and a large central cement compound that housed the administration building, recreation room, and mess hall. We drove by several life-size plaster-cast statues of children wearing oversized red Pioneer scarves, shorts, and Stalinist merit badges. The plaster monuments saluted us the Young Pioneer way: flat-palmed with elbows extended. Near the central parade ground, which was outlined by neat rows of round, white painted rocks and two tall flagpoles, appeared a massive mural of an uncharacteristically jovial-looking Lenin. He earnestly addressed a throng of fit and enraptured teens, and instead of waving his trademark worker's cap, clutched a bouquet of flowers. The mural was a mosaic of tiny multicolored ceramic tiles. Over Lenin's preaching face was painted the Pioneers' motto. It pronounced the children of the Revolution *Vsegda gotov*—Always ready. Ready to serve the Party, to denounce their parents if need be.

The idea for Pioneer camps had been Felix Dzerzhinsky's. Dzerzhinsky was the Polish-born founder of the Soviet Union's secret police. He set up the first Pioneer *Lager*, as the camps were known in Russian, outside Moscow in 1925. By the late 1930s, when the Nazis adopted their own version of Pioneer camps, the Hitler Youth program, there were over seven million children between the ages of ten and fourteen attending summer indoctrination *Lagers* across the Soviet empire. They learned how to swim and march and snoop on one another, and were taught the tenets of Marxist ideology. The Pioneers were the first rungs of the Party hierarchy, and the aptest among them graduated from Pioneer to Komsomol (the Young Communist League, which supplied many of the oligarchs and government ministers in the late 1990s) and eventually to the exalted ranks of the CPSU itself.

Zhanna Nikolaevna, the camp administrator, greeted us at the door of the main building. She wore a white surgeon's coat and a matronly expression beneath her silvery curls, and extended a beefy red hand for us to shake. I was the first Westerner she'd ever met, she explained with a gold-crowned and slightly sheepish grin. I had heard this before in my travels off the beaten path. It always made me a little uncomfortable to play Western ambassador—as though I would single-handedly soil the reputation of the world's leading industrialized nations if I didn't behave well.

Nikolaevna had run the Krupskaya Camp since 1969. "The year *you* sent a man to the moon," she remarked, as if I had personally designed the Apollo space module. She was a former Pioneer, Komsomol member, and card-carrying Communist. I asked her if it had been difficult to see her life's work jettisoned almost overnight. "Change comes very slowly to a place like Vologda," she answered, after a thoughtful pause. "It remains to be seen if capitalism takes hold in Russia. We are a very *peculiar* people."

Despite her obvious misgivings about the new order, Nikolaevna was an indoctrinator by profession and said it was now her duty to prepare children for the coming times. "We have to teach the young what a free-market system is," she said, adding with a wry smile, "Actually, not only the young."

When it came to devising a method of introducing her campers to the mysterious principles of a free-market economy, Zhanna Nikolaevna had turned to one of the few people she knew who even vaguely grasped the concept, Andrei Kamin, a former Vologda Pioneer and current fourth-year economics student at Moscow State University. Together they came up with an "Economic Game." In this remote region, they recreated the prevailing market conditions of any big Western city.

"Just like in New York. If you didn't work you didn't eat," explained Nikolaevna with the cynicism of someone who was less than convinced that capitalism was her country's salvation.

For five days, the camp's Red Square parade ground was transformed into a capitalist labor exchange where the 413 campers bid on work assignments. The children were paid in the camp's own currency, the Maastricht-inspired ECU, redeemable at the cafeteria, confectionery, and entertainment center. Nikolaevna played mayor while Andrei put his economics training to use as head of the central bank. The remainder of the staff and counselors ran the labor exchange, the "Disneyland" entertainment center, and the sweets shop. The oldest campers were appointed police officers. If all went according to plan, children would be paid to wash dishes or mow grass. They'd use their pay to buy food and see movies, and the camp would have the trappings of a capitalist society.

But all did not go as planned.

On the second day of the exercise, Andrei noticed that there was more money in circulation than had originally been printed. After some inquiry, he discovered that a few of the kids had taken it upon themselves to set up their own little printing press and crank out ecus to satisfy their sweet tooth. The camp police were dispatched to apprehend the culprits, but the kids bought off the lawmen with a case of chocolate bars and continued to operate with impunity. Some other policemen, lured by the promise of Pepsi and chewing gum, threw in their lot with the counterfeiters. This prepubescent mafia began to bully other campers and exacted payments for such offenses as profanity—either fifty ecus or two waffles.

Taking one counselor's words ("there is no higher law than

money") to heart, a group of overly enthusiastic kid-capitalists stormed Andrei's office (the central bank), and in the ensuing melee made off with the labor exchange's payroll. Andrei was forced to print extra money, which caused the campers to increase the price of chocolates and services. Just as in the real post-Soviet world, hyperinflation was born.

Meanwhile some children, through ingenuity and hard work, were becoming accomplished entrepreneurs. Ghena's son Vitia (for Viktor), a miniature replica of his red-headed father, got his start bidding on the repair of a little bridge that spanned a creek on the outskirts of camp. He hired four pals and hastily fixed the structure in three hours. (It had collapsed again by the time I showed up.) With the ecus he received for the construction contract, he purchased all the tokens for the camp's most popular video game. "I could charge whatever I wanted for the tokens because no one else had any," he said, beaming. "But I didn't like the ecu, it was just paper. So I accepted only chocolates for my tokens."

Vitya paid off the bullies with some of his bartered chocolate profits, but they became too greedy, so he hired two friends to protect his stash. There was a fistfight between one of his guards and a goon, and Andrei had to intervene and threaten to call both boys' parents.

On the third day of the Economic Game, the Krupskaya camp suffered a spectacular bankruptcy. A would-be Donald Trump had bought the rights to the dormitory and demanded rent from all the campers. Unfortunately, the kids started sneaking in through the back window to sleep, and the budding landlord ended up owing more ecus to the labor exchange for rental rights than he was receiving from the campers. He abandoned his property deal and joined the police-force-cum-mafia.

By the afternoon of the fourth day, chaos reigned. Zhanna Nikolaevna, in her role as mayor, called a general meeting to restore order. When she proposed firing the corrupt police force and replacing it with a newly formed "national guard" composed of camp counselors, the police staged a coup d'état and threatened to hold her for ransom. The coup d'état proved to be the coup de grace. The game was called off.

That was good news to Seriozha, a shy thirteen-year-old with sunken blue eyes and delicate features. Sitting in the mess hall after a lunch of kasha and beans, he complained that the economic game had brought out the worst in everyone. "My friends became aggressive and the bigger boys started taking what they wanted. It was not fair," he confided.

Zhanna Nikolaevna nodded as she stirred her tea. "If this is how people act in capitalism," she said softly, "then I fear for the future of Russia."

CHAPTER THIRTEEN

Bear Market

When the trouble began, as I knew it inevitably would—because it had been foretold by the children of Vologda—I was aboard a helicopter, just below the Arctic Circle. It was late May, and the Siberian bog was finally defrosting. The sound of ice snapping rolled across the northern rivers like thunder. Huge, jagged sheets, three feet thick and a football field long, rose and fell in heaving motions. Here and there the thaw had uncovered patches of taiga, and the coarse mauve mosses poked through the snow cover like islands in a brilliant white sea.

I had felt a little guilty about taking this last trip, for we were short-staffed, and my colleague Betsy was alone in the office. As it happened, my timing was especially bad because a different sort of meltdown was under way in Moscow. I didn't know that anything was afoot until a few days later, when I borrowed the satellite phone at a remote oil field to check in with the office.

Betsy answered on the first ring, sounding harried. "You'd better get back here," she said.

"What's happened?"

"The market just crashed."

The mood at the office was glum when I returned two days later. Nonna, the office manager, was on the line, speaking in a low, urgent tone. She shot me a reproachful look.

"They've suspended trading again," she said, covering the mouthpiece for an instant.

That meant the stock market had fallen over 10 percent in morning trading, the maximum daily decline allowed before an automatic circuit-breaker kicked in and the regulators pulled the plug. This was the second day that trading had been halted to slow the stock-market slide, which had already eaten away a quarter of the RTS index's value in under a week.

Betsy was rushed, and not her usual chipper self. "New York wants four takes for tomorrow," she said. "I was in until one in the morning last night," she added. *Covering for you*, she meant. We sat down to our computers and started chipping away at the takes. A take was journalese for three hundred words, which meant we had twelve hundred words to describe the air hissing out of inflated stockbroker egos.

I started flipping through my Rolodex, searching for people to call. The business cards of my Russia experts mostly had telephone numbers that started with 212 or 171, the area codes of New York and London. With the time difference, most of my so-called Moscow contacts were still asleep in their townhouses on New York's Upper East Side.

The Salomon Brothers guy wouldn't talk. Nor would Bill Browder, the high flyer who wore gold dollar-sign cufflinks and whose Hermitage Russia Fund advertised itself as the world's best-performing emerging-market fund. The Credit Suisse First Boston rep in Moscow was "in conference," freaking out, I imagined— CSFB had huge exposure in Russia. Trying to reach brokers and bankers was a little like hailing a taxi—they were always there when you didn't need them (and when they had some stock or bond to peddle) but never around when you could really use one.

I managed to get through to a young Swedish analyst at Brunswick Warburg, one of the more respectable local houses. "How are you holding up?" I asked.

"Not so good," he said.

"What's happening?"

"Fear," he answered, speaking in a hoarse tone. "Fear is completely ruling the market. I have never seen anything like it. Investors are selling at any price. There's a stampede to get out of Russia."

What on earth could have triggered such a flight? I worked the phones in search of answers and sound bites. "There's been a sea change in the way investors look at Russia," said Morgan Stanley's man in London. By this he meant that the investment community had opened its eyes, had finally chosen to see the corruption and chaos that passed for capitalism in Russia.

"When the going was good, no one asked any pointed questions about Russia," explained yet another London analyst, this time from the illustrious house of Donaldson, Lufkin & Jenrette. "Anyway," he continued, "the answers would have scared the hell out of everyone."

Still, it was a strange sort of crisis, this brewing financial collapse, with shoppers calmly ambling along the streets of Moscow while terror swept the foreign-trading desks of the world's major investment houses. This just showed how detached the world of high finance we wrote about was from Russian reality. Average Russians didn't go near anything resembling a stock, bond, or warrant. It was a question of trust. Too many people had been burned by the pyramid schemes of the early 1990s. The get-rich-quick scams had cost millions of citizens their life savings and soured a whole generation of Russians on the idea of stocks. That 99.9 percent of the Russian populace owned no stocks, and that only wealthy Westerners were getting burned by the downturn, took some of the urgency out of reporting a "Russian crisis" that did not seem to affect the average Russian citizen.

Unfortunately, about the only contact I had with "the average Russian citizen" was waking up in the mornings to find Lev plunked on our couch, his cane propped up on the coffee table, a beer in one hand, the television remote in the other, and a cigarette burning in the ashtray. Lev was our cleaning lady Larisa's husband, and a definite blight on our domestic life. He had been the deputy director of an electronics defense plant in Gorbachev's day, but had suffered a stroke in his forties that left him with a speech impediment, partial paralysis in one leg, and an official disability ranking of *invaled vtorova klassa* (invalid of the second class).

Lev gurgled incomprehensibly when he spoke, and labored under the misconception that he could make himself understood by raising his voice. I would often roll out of bed to be greeted on the way to the shower by a shouting Lev, already installed in front of the television, working on his second beer. The living room would be heavy with the stench of black Russian tobacco, and Lev's morning snack of *salo*, three-inch-thick slabs of milky-white pig fat, would be displayed unappetizingly next to his ration of beer—the breakfast of choice for Russians with clogged arteries.

I wanted him out, and complained to Roberta, especially after he took it upon himself to redecorate my precious aquarium. (Lev fancied himself an expert on the keeping of tropical fish and was aggressively vocal on the topic, always jabbing the tank with nicotine-stained fingers and waving his cane at the glass.) Roberta, alas, felt sorry for him and let him stay, even though he leered at her in her bathrobe. Lev tagged along with Larisa to all her jobs cleaning house for foreigners, because he couldn't stand being cooped up with his argumentative mother-in-law in the one-room apartment the three shared in a soulless Moscow suburb.

In the old days, the State would have provided for Lev. But in the Yeltsin era, the safety net had been yanked and he had been left to subsist on thirty dollars' disability compensation a month, watching helplessly while his wife, a university-educated former municipal government official, went to work scrubbing the toilets of arrogant American colonizers. The stock-market crisis was not exactly at the top of Lev's list of priorities.

Nor did it seem to affect most other Muscovites. On the streets of the capital, it was business as usual. Traffic snarled at its habitual dust-gathering pace. The GAI traffic police pursued their duties with their typical zeal, dispensing twenty-ruble fines for both real and imagined offenses. Il Pomodoro, the city's trendiest Italian eatery, was holding its annual asparagus festival, and the Azerbaijani watermelon vendors had returned from their seasonal migration to the Caspian's shores. The new Versace boutique on Tverskaya continued its spring clearance sale, as though the season of prosperity would last forever.

By the end of May the market had shed a third of its value, and Roberta finally admitted that she was getting worried. Until then VSO had been taking advantage of the downturn to bargain-hunt. But now it too had lost its nerve, and orders had come from New York to stop buying Russian stocks. So far the market mayhem had not spilled over into Roberta's private-equity department—that is, fixed assets—but gloom in the investment community had a way of spreading.

Her spirits were particularly low that evening in the opening days of June when our friend Askold invited us out for dinner at the Rossiya Hotel. He insisted on the downtrodden Rossiya because he said he was fed up with the new expense-account joints and wanted a taste of the old Moscow. We agreed to his choice of venue out of prurient interest; the Rossiya's director had just been shot. By Chechen gangsters, the police speculated; but they were fresh out of leads.

The Rossiya was still State-owned and had changed little since the Soviet central planners had decided to build the world's largest hotel. In constructing the Rossiya they had succeeded only in blighting two whole blocks next to St. Basil's Cathedral and Red Square. It had been closed off and on since 1991, as fumigators fought a losing battle against roaches and rodents. Donald Trump had made noises about buying and fixing up the place, but in the end decided it was too big and too far gone to repair.

We had foolishly agreed to meet Askold in "the Rossiya lobby," forgetting that the hotel had perhaps eight of them, and we had spent the better part of an hour wandering from one dark wing to the next, looking for one another in the gloom of endless corridors. By the time we found him, it was after nine o'clock and most of the Rossiya's two dozen retrograde restaurants were closed. Just one place reluctantly agreed to serve us, after a twenty-dollar bill changed hands, and as luck would have it, the establishment overlooked a banquet hall that Vladimir Zhirinovsky had rented for his birthday party.

Zhirinovsky stood on the podium, wearing his trademark sailor's cap and a buffoon's grin. The leader of Russia's second-largest political party, and possibly the least sane individual in the Russian parliament, he waved a bottle of champagne in one hand and steadied himself against the microphone stand with the other. He was drunk. But then so were most of the other two-hundred-odd lunatics celebrating the occasion of his birthday. The ballroom at the Rossiya Hotel was festooned with balloons and Russia's worst crazies: fascists and skinheads in storm-trooper boots; brownshirts and Jew-baiters with wild blue eyes; nationalists and ultranationalists in black caps; communists and Stalinists with so many Soviet medals stuck to their breast that they listed.

This motley crew was having a grand old time, singing patriotic songs, swilling Baltika beer, and applauding their mercurial messiah. Zhirinovsky looked in fine form, his paunch tucked under a bulging red cummerbund. Though his political stock had fallen considerably since the last legislative elections, when startlingly strong public support for his inaptly named Liberal Democratic Party had terrified the West, he still attracted Russia's disaffected in alarming numbers. His constituents were invariably the losers of the capitalist transition, the humbled and humiliated who clung to old symbols of Russian glory and sought convenient scapegoats on which to blame their troubles. Some were newly pauperized, others outright nuts, and they came in all shapes and sizes, from young toughs with shaved skulls to old dinosaurs with bald pates.

There was a band that played mostly Soviet cover tunes, a type of militarized folk-pop. And there were a few young girls, pretty and reedy but unfashionable in their spiky Soviet-era white boots and rayon blouses, and many older, stouter matrons with bouffant hairdos and the purple dye jobs that were still fashionable in Russia's provinces.

The birthday boy was making a speech. We could see his lips moving but from our perch could not hear what he was saying. He stabbed the air with a maniacal finger, and his face grew flushed. Every now and then a great, approving roar from the crowd rose through the glass divider.

We took a table by the restaurant's picture window and watched the skinheads slam-dance below while the waitress brought us a beaded carafe of chilled vodka. We ordered what was available, just like in the old days, when there was so little choice that you gratefully paid eighteen dollars for a salad of canned peas, canned corn, and canned hearts of palm, doused with globs of mayonnaise whose expiration predated the fall of the Berlin Wall. Salad, or more particularly lettuce, was an unofficial barometer of economic reform in the former Soviet Union, just like that trusted barometer of inflation, the price of an imported Snickers bar. "When iceberg lettuce started appearing in stores in Moscow in late 1995, I knew Russia was on the map," reminisced Roberta. You still couldn't buy iceberg lettuce in Ukraine—except maybe, if you were really lucky, at the Nika Swiss hard-currency store.

Black bread and pickles arrived with our vodka, and some time later, green pickled tomatoes, cheese, and cold meats. The simple fare conjured further waves of nostalgia, and Roberta recounted how a friend who had helped set up the American Embassy in Ukraine in 1992 had won the hearts of the tiny expat community by distributing canned goods as party favors at her diplomatic soirées. "She had boxes full of Cheerios, and spaghetti sauce, and peanut butter, and Campbell's soup, and we used to salivate over her hoard. You couldn't buy breakfast cereal in Kiev in 1992 for all the money in the world."

We drank to old times. Everything in those hopeful early days had seemed simpler, purer. We expats were swept up in what we were doing back then, willing to suffer deprivations to be part of a great and noble effort. We saw ourselves as poverty-stricken, itinerant apostles of democracy and the free market. But the stock-market boom had changed everything, as it would a few years later in America for the "techies" of the information age. Money had entered into the equation, and now it was hard to tell if we were still playing for the good guys, or just out for ourselves.

A scuffle at Zhirinovsky's party interrupted our reminiscing. A shoving match had erupted between a skinhead and one of the black-capped boys. The black caps, like Zhirinovsky, were ultranationalists and wanted to take back Ukraine and all the other lost tsarist domains. The skinheads were at once neo-Nazis and Slavic supremacists, blissfully unaware of the contradiction. A dozen of them had recently hospitalized the daughter of a Pakistani diplomat to celebrate the anniversary of Hitler's death. In other valiant tributes to the Führer, a lone off-duty African-American Marine from the U.S. embassy was set upon, and a bomb was set off at a Moscow synagogue to which Roberta's boss was a large contributor.

"You know who's going to be blamed if there's a full-fledged financial crisis," Roberta said ominously, watching the fracas below. "If the shit hits the fan, those nuts down there are going to start screaming about the Jews robbing poor Mother Russia blind."

"Don't worry," joked Askold. "I'll hide you in my attic."

While it was true that anti-Semitism needed little encouragement to gain ground in the East, it didn't help that six out of the seven oligarchs were Jewish. Even Zhirinovsky's dimwits would be able to do the math, if the time ever came to apportion blame. Jews had traditionally played the role of scapegoats in Russian society, whether as impoverished inhabitants of *shtetls* during tsarist pogroms, or intellectual victims like my gentle friend Genady during the Soviet era. Bu it must be noted that capitalist Russia's Jewish community had its fair share of Bugsy Siegels and Meyer Lanskys. An astonishing number of the criminals on the fringes of the free-market revolution were in fact Jewish. This was partly a consequence of communist discrimination, when many Jews were forced to work outside the system. Since they couldn't rise in the Party or the bureaucracy and generally weren't admitted to the best universities, they had little stake in the old order and were among the quickest to figure out how to operate in the shadows of the new anarchy. And because hundreds of thousands of Jews, former refuseniks, had been allowed to emigrate during the 1970s and 1980s, the Jews were just about the only Soviet citizens who had international connections and long-established foreign networks when the Iron Curtain collapsed with a crash.

Nor did it help the image of Russian Jewry that countless Slavic mobsters masqueraded as Jews in order to exploit the Israeli immigration laws. Written after the Holocaust, these guarantees of safe haven granted automatic Israeli citizenship to virtually all persons declaring themselves Jewish and, most important, did not permit extradition to other countries. For criminals in the wild East, being—or pretending to be—Jewish was even better than running for parliament, since they didn't have to go through the trouble and expense of buying an election to get immunity from prosecution.

Not surprisingly, every time a gangster narrowly escaped on his new Israeli passport, the cause of anti-Semitism won new converts in Eastern Europe. I remember the public outrage in Warsaw when a pair of shifty entrepreneurs bilked State banks out of over two hundred million dollars and flew off in their Challenger jet just as prosecutors were about to descend on them. Poles woke up to blaring newspaper headlines the next day, trumpeting that taxpayers would have to foot the bill while the pair of crooks claiming to be "of Jewish origin" sunned themselves on the beach in Haifa.

Of all the oligarchs Vladimir Gusinsky was the most openly Jewish. He headed the Russian Jewish Congress, which was a sparsely populated organization despite the fact that there were still over a million and a half Jews left in Russia. Gusinsky had successfully sued the *Wall Street Journal* for libel, so we at the bureau steered well clear of him. But Roberta, just before the crash, had approached his property division to build a Hilton hotel on a site he owned on New Arbat Street. Though Gusinsky was best known for his television network, he had made his fortune as a privatization broker and banker for Luzhkov, when the City of Moscow owned virtually every building and lot in the capital and could arbitrarily decide what would be sold to whom for how much. Gusinsky's people had initially not even wanted to see Roberta, until she brought up her boss' generous contributions to synagogues. "Well, why didn't you say so?" the president of Gusinsky's bank had gushed.

"Let's crash Zhirinovsky's party," Askold suggested, as we surveyed the scene downstairs. I had had just enough vodka to agree, despite Roberta's protestations. Zhirinovsky's bully boys, she said, were a pogrom waiting to happen. She'd wait for us upstairs. "Don't stay long," she made us promise. "And don't do anything stupid."

As it was, the party was winding down. We caught Zhirinovsky on his way out, his burly bodyguards clearing a path to the door through the throng of simple-minded well-wishers. I'd seen him on television many times, but this was my first actual brush with the eccentric who gave press conferences in the shower and punched female members of parliament during live Duma debates. He floated by us in a haze of cigarette smoke and outstretched arms, reached out like an apparition and touched the delirious woman next to me, and then was gone.

We hung around for a few minutes, helping ourselves to some cognac that had been left on one of the tables, and were about to leave when a young tough in one of the black caps sauntered up and asked with marked suspicion where we were from.

"Canada," I answered quickly before Askold said something snide.

The tough mulled this over for a moment, probably plumbing the depths of his memory for any recalled slights the Russian people had suffered at the hands of the Canadians. I hoped hockey didn't count.

Apparently Canada was judged sufficiently distant and inoffensive, for the youth did not call over his buddies and instead inquired how we liked Russia.

This was trickier. We had to be quick on our feet.

"Such an exciting country," I responded enthusiastically, which at least wasn't a lie, and added: "Have you ever been to Canada?" The youth shook his head no. Berlin once, he volunteered sullenly, as if that was the same uniformly distasteful thing, the West. And what were we doing at this event, he asked, his eyes narrowing once again.

"Balloons," I explained, very pleased with the lie. "For my fiancée," I said pointing up to the restaurant windows. "She saw them and asked if I could get her one as a souvenir."

The youth squinted for what seemed like a minute but was probably an instant. "Okay," he said finally, in English, smiling for the first time as though we had passed a test. He held up a hand for us to wait and dashed off to a nearby table where half a dozen blue party balloons imprinted with Zhirinovsky's mug dangled from strings attached to a chair.

"*Shchastlivo*," he beamed, handing them to us. "Good luck to you."

Roberta hung up the balloons in our kitchen, next to a cage where we kept the pair of green lovebirds we'd picked up at the bird market. It took a week for the helium to slowly leak out of Zhirinovsky's jowls, by which time the stock exchange had lost over 40 percent of its value and the crisis had deepened considerably.

Fear, like greed, is contagious, and the capital flight from Russian stocks had spread to the GKO bond market, where now Russian banks were all selling their GKOs. The Kremlin tried everything to stop the exodus. In mid-June it nearly doubled interest rates to 150 percent, a staggering hike given that an increase of half a percentage point by the Federal Reserve in Washington typically sent investors on Wall Street flooding out of equities and into government bonds.

But no one wanted Russian paper any more. The seven hundred forty million dollars' worth of agro-bonds for collective farms that Boris Jordan's Renaissance Capital had peddled when I first arrived in Moscow had just come due, and the surprised and penniless Russian farm regions were proposing to redeem them with birdcages and barber chairs. Not surprisingly, the big monthly federal-bond auctions that the Kremlin had grown to rely on to plug tax-collection shortfalls failed to find any bidders. Yields on the ninety-day benchmark bonds spiked from 30 to 50 percent, then climbed to 80 percent and finally crossed the 110 percent mark. Still there were no takers. The Kremlin gave up and canceled its debt auctions indefinitely. The Russian government had just lost its main source of borrowing.

The crisis was beginning to take on an ominous momentum of its own. To complicate matters, Yeltsin was becoming downright volatile. Like a grumpy old bear he had emerged from hibernation in late March, and abruptly sacked his entire cabinet. Throughout April, he had fought with parliament over his choice of a complete unknown to replace the trusted time-server Chernomyrdin. The squabbling over Yeltsin's appointment of the political neophyte Sergei Kiriyenko had been so fierce that the Duma had come within a hair's breadth of being disbanded, and early parliamentary elections had very nearly been called. The dispute had done little to calm investors and had sent the entire press corps scrambling for their tea leaves. Who was this new guy? What was Yeltsin thinking? *Was* Yeltsin thinking?

The political upheavals in the Kremlin did not augur well for Gretchen's beleaguered husband. Boris Brevnov and Sergei Kiriyenko apparently had their differences stemming from their days in Nizhny Novgorod, where Kiriyenko had headed the Komsomol (Young Communist League), and those animosities carried over to Moscow.

A campaign to discredit Boris was now in full swing. His underlings at UES were intriguing away like vengeful courtiers, and the old-guard managers at the regional power stations were fomenting open rebellion against him. The mutiny was keeping him out almost every night until the early hours of the morning, and his absence was beginning to wear on Gretchen, who already refused to talk over the phone for fear of wiretaps, and who slept very little. Or so said my source, our driver Yura's wife, who was the night nanny at the Brevnov residence—but who was thinking of quitting because it didn't pay to be too closely associated with the losing faction in a Kremlin war.

When Roberta and I dropped in on Boris and Gretchen, it was clear that they had met with a series of severe disappointments in recent weeks. Boris and Gretchen had been working on a billion-dollar Eurobond issue for UES, Gretchen unofficially handling most of the negotiations with her old investment-banking contacts while Boris fended off his thieving power-plant managers. But the deal had been scrapped at the last moment, when investors balked at the prospect of being paid in lumber or sugar beets. That setback had all but sealed Boris's fate. When it had become clear that his wife's Western connections were not going to come through, the other UES bosses tried to lock him out of his office and he, in turn, tried to barricade himself in. The similarities between his spat and Umar's fight with Tatum were not lost on Gretchen, who confided to Roberta, "I've got a very bad feeling."

The intrigues were visibly taking their toll on Gretchen. As an American she was unaccustomed to the life of a Kremlin wife. Her beauty and vibrant spirit, though still considerable, had faded somewhat and she looked pale from stress. Her eyes had dark circles and her lips were thin and bloodless.

More worrisome for Boris Brevnov was the reappearance of Anatoly Chubais. The wholesale political massacre in the Kremlin had left Chubais without a job, and the wily former deputy prime minister was now openly gunning for Boris's chair. Chubais had helped create the oligarchs, and now he had apparently decided that he wanted to be one. Unfortunately for Boris, he was no match for a seasoned schemer like Chubais. Sure enough, *kompromat*, the so-called "compromising material" that was collected on every important person and locked away until someone more powerful decided to use it, was starting to surface about Boris's past as a banker. It seemed his bank, in the mid-1990s, had unwittingly accepted large deposits of embezzled funds from a shady businessman who had just been elected mayor of Nizhny Novgorod. Yeltsin had overturned the results of that election and thrown the former businessman in jail. The arrest had sent shock waves throughout Russia, for, regardless of the truth of the allegations, the move clearly subverted the democratic process. There were no charges against Boris, nor anything that I was aware of that might have substantiated any; he had a reputation, by Russian standards, for being quite honest. But in the changing climate, when everything was rapidly unwinding and scapegoats might soon be needed, that didn't mean he was safe. After all, Boris was an American collaborator, both by marriage and by conviction. Gretchen told Roberta as much that evening in the kitchen. "If there's a reckoning and they draw up a list, Boris's name will be on it."

A fresh ugliness now hung in the air over Moscow, a sense that something unpleasant was in the offing. Russia's market revolution had simply been too unjust for there to be no fallout if it failed.

As the markets continued to plummet, and the ruble, in late June, started to teeter, the cries for an international bailout rose like a great, urgent tide. They washed over the *Journal*'s sixteenth-floor office and inundated our phone lines. Why was the International Monetary Fund not stepping in, demanded the bankers? Where the hell was the World Bank, the brokers wanted to know? Why were we business reporters not writing articles condemning the foot-dragging? Didn't we know what was at stake? Surely we understood that Russia was too big, too nuclear, too dangerous to be allowed to fail.

Do something! shrieked indignant fund managers, as if we could shame the IMF into action with our copy—and just maybe salvage what was left of their battered portfolios. The phones rang incessantly. Nonna patched them through to Betsy or me with the tested patience of an air traffic controller, leaving some in a holding pattern while directing others to try again later. So many came in that Betsy started referring to them as the "bail-me-out" calls, as in "Matt, you've got another 'bail-me-out' call on line two."

The importuner in this case was the president of ABN-Amro Corporate Finance for Eastern Europe, a snappy dresser who had seemed very self-satisfied only a few months before when we had met for breakfast at the new Marriott on Tverskaya. "It's appalling," he moaned now, "how the IMF is taking its time. This is Russia, for God's sakes, not Thailand."

"If Russia doesn't get support soon, it won't be able to hold on to the situation much longer," warned a DLJ London analyst who called minutes later. Trouble was brewing in the Russian Far East. Unpaid miners near Vladivostok had just blockaded the Trans-

Siberian Railroad and were threatening to march on Moscow unless the government settled wage arrears that in some cases dated back a full year. The Kremlin had promised to pay off the back wages with domestic bond issues, but no bonds had been sold, and now money earmarked for wages was going to have to be diverted to honor T-bills that were maturing later in the summer. And billions of dollars of debt were coming due. Russia's insatiable appetite for borrowing was catching up to it. The country was running out of time.

Bill Browder, Mr. Dollar Cufflinks, was calling almost daily now that the market had shed just under half its value and his fund was fast careering from its position as the "world's best performing" towards the worst-performing slot. "This silence from the IMF is outrageous, irresponsible!" he cried. To be sure, the IMF was taking its time. After being misled by Russia so many times, after having its patience tested by the Kremlin's countless broken fiscal promises, it may have now viewed Moscow as crying wolf. Besides, it was busy putting out fires in Asia. "Why aren't you writing about the IMF dropping the ball?" Browder persisted, like a salesman who wouldn't take no for an answer.

"That's for the editorial page to decide," I snapped back. It wasn't my job to save gamblers who'd lost their chips and then cried foul.

"But think of the orphanages that will go without funds, think of the poor Russian children!"

I suspect he sensed that I was getting ready to hang up, for he quickly ditched the humanitarian approach and tried a Cold-War tack: "Think of Belarus."

That did get my attention. Belarus was the post-Soviet bogey-man, the specter that haunted every negotiation between Russia and Western donors. Whenever talks broke down over some little detail, like IMF money that had mysteriously disappeared, lost in transit over Switzerland, the image of Belarus was evoked to loosen the West's purse-strings.

On its own, Belarus was an inconsequential little pimple of a nation on Russia's western rump, a poor and isolated country of ten million hapless collective farmers and factory workers led by a neo-Stalinist lunatic bent on recreating the Soviet Union. But seen from a geopolitical perspective, it served as the ultimate nightmare scenario—a place where the capitalist and democratic experiment had failed, a blueprint, if you will, for rolling back the political clock.

Belarus happened to be part of my beat, and I had been there on November 25, 1996, the day democracy died.

A harsh, wet snow was falling over Minsk. Several hundred demonstrators remained in Lenin Square, downcast under their sodden pro-democracy banners. But their numbers dwindled as hope for the Belarusian legislators barricaded inside the besieged parliament faded.

It was over, and everyone knew it.

I looked out the window of the embattled parliament building, and through the fog and sleet made out the heavy black tracks left in the snow by the retreating armored personnel carrier. No longer needed, the carrier was being moved to a grimy side street, where President Alexander Lukashenko's elite guards had been redeployed and were passing the time playing cards and cleaning their weapons inside steamy army buses and jeeps.

Lenin Square seemed eerily empty now that all the troops were being pulled back. The Stalinist parade ground exuded a desolation and despair that could only be measured in shades of gray. Like the rest of Minsk, it was bleak, oversized and soulless, and it covered an asphalt expanse of perhaps twenty concrete football fields. On every side of this Orwellian plaza rose oppressive ministries and uniformly ugly government offices crowned with hammers and sickles. Lenin himself stood four stories high and smiled down from his granite dais on this triumph of Socialist Realist architecture.

A military helicopter clattered overhead, rattling the parliament's beaded windowpanes, but the chopper too would soon head back to the barracks.

It was just a mop-up operation from here on. Belarus, the smallest Slavic spinoff of the ex-Soviet empire, was now formally a police state. Lukashenko had won, defeated the last holdouts against his bid for authoritarian rule, and the stone-faced militia troops posted outside the legislature had given the elected officials until the end of the day to clear out.

"Only God can help us now," said Deputy Vasily Shlyndzikau,

raising bleary eyes that only the week before had flashed with indignation. The lawmaker sat slumped at his desk, his suit wrinkled, his hair disheveled, his hands unsteady from lack of sleep. The vestiges of the standoff lay cluttered on his desk: overflowing ashtrays, countless coffee mugs, a declaration calling Lukashenko's actions unconstitutional, a motion to impeach the maverick president. There was a small pistol in the drawer too, in the event that the presidential guards stormed the legislature as Yeltsin's forces had in Moscow three years before—only this time the good guys were in the parliament, not outside it.

For a while it looked very much like a replay of Yeltsin's brutal suppression of the 1993 Duma rebellion, with tanks shelling the legislature and small-arms fire being exchanged along the barricades. For weeks the tension in Minsk had mounted. The press corps had flown in en masse from Moscow, and the networks had all booked satellite time in anticipation of a bloodbath. Russia's offers to mediate had been spurned. The barricaded lawmakers had refused to budge and instead called on the people to rise against Lukashenko. The Belarusian army, in turn, had been called out and had thrown a tight cordon around Minsk. Thousands of soldiers and militiamen had taken to the capital's sullen streets. Snipers had been posted on the flat, mass-produced rooftops. Convoys of troop carriers had lined entire blocks, and military choppers had filled the gray, overcast sky.

Minsk had been a city under siege—on the brink, some said (and the reporters hoped), of civil war. Whole sections of town had been sealed off by the militia, and we journalists had run the blockades by climbing over fences and scurrying through back alleys and the rear exits of apartment buildings. It had been, I must confess, very exciting, the sort of thing I had always imagined dashing foreign correspondents did—as opposed to, say, tabulating the coupon value of bonds.

The root of the standoff had been Lukashenko's decision to hold a sham referendum that would ram through a new constitution granting him absolute power. The sweeping privileges included the right to appoint all judges, mayors, and members of parliament; extensions to his term in office; presidential immunity from prosecution for life; and the right to arrest anyone for "defamation or insult to the president." The new constitution banned unauthorized public assembly.

The Belarusian Supreme Court had dismissed the document as ridiculous, but Lukashenko had simply ignored the ruling. The country's chief elections officer had rejected the referendum as illegal, but the KGB had hauled her out of her office by the hair. Only the parliament and the people stood between Lukashenko and his naked consolidation of power.

And the people adored Lukashenko. There were no longer wage delays in Belarus as there were in Russia; no housing shortages; no layoffs at factories; no mass unemployment; no prohibitively priced goods; no hospitals without medicine. Since Lukashenko's election in 1994, there were no longer BMW-driving bankers to rub their wealth in everyone's noses or marauding mafia gangs to brazenly rob people. The trains ran on time, and Belarusians had food on their tables. And for this they were grateful. Freedom was a small price to pay.

Belarusians had tasted freedom, and found that it wasn't all that it was cracked up to be. Freedom was poverty and chaos. Freedom was suffering and uncertainty. Freedom was lawlessness and disappointment. Who needed that? Who wanted that?

What the vast majority of the people wanted was the security of the old order, to go back to the USSR. Lukashenko had been only too happy to oblige. His first order of business after being elected in 1994 had been to ban Belarus' national colors and rehoist the Soviet hammer and sickle as the State flag. The Belarusian language, a peasant tongue that, like Ukrainian, borrowed from Polish and Russian, was jettisoned in favor of Russian as the official State language. When some newspapers complained, they found that government-owned printing presses would no longer take their business. When they persisted in complaining, they found themselves the focus of vigorous KGB interrogations. Lukashenko next set his sights on a vague reunification treaty with Russia, which he signed with a reluctant Yeltsin after Chubais and Nemtsov watered down the document to offer reunification in name only. When twenty-five members of the Belarusian parliament refused to ratify the accord, Lukashenko sent in the OMON, the riot police. The vote passed— as did, eventually, the bruises on the recalcitrant legislators' foreheads.

Despite the strong-arm tactics, Belarusians applauded all these moves. The only history they knew was the reflected glory of being part of the Russian empire, and the collapse of the USSR had shattered their sense of identity.

The people cheered even louder when Lukashenko began cracking down on the tiny private sector that had managed to sprout before he came to office, "the criminals and the thieves" as he called all entrepreneurs. All businesses had to be reregistered with a newly created economic arm of the KGB, which henceforth imposed price controls on products and limited if not banned expensive imported foodstuffs. Lukashenko personally paid surprise visits to stores, accompanied by State TV, and could be seen on the evening news sternly upbraiding shopkeepers who sold eggs or milk above the government-sanctioned rates.

A campaign of nationalization was launched in the spring of 1996, and the banks that had been privatized during the early 1990s in a murky Russian fashion were targeted. Lukashenko reserved his particular contempt for bankers, whom he labeled "leeches" and accused of undermining his monetary policies, which essentially fixed the Belarusian ruble's value at whatever inflated exchange rate he dictated. The banks were eventually all taken over by Lukashenko, whose claim that he was simply "returning stolen State property to the State" played very well with the populace. Production quotas were reintroduced, and factories were soon working at full steam. GDP was up 10 percent, according to Lukashenko's creative number crunchers, making the country's Soviet-style economy one of the world's fastest growing. Of course it was all a scam, a house of cards held together by force. But the people were sold.

Small wonder so few showed up to defend the parliament. Of Belarus' ten million citizens, barely ten thousand came to democracy's aid. Even among those few who stood vigil outside parliament, a good many were rooting for the bad guys.

"President Lukashenko is increasing production. Only he can save us," exhorted Nina Kovaliova, a fifty-year-old military-factory worker who had come to Lenin Square to jeer at the deputies. "They are the traitors," she shouted, thrusting an angry finger at the 'lature. "They should all be immediately arrested."

Inside the embattled legislature, the lawmakers were conceding defeat.

"I can't blame the people for not rising in our support," said Shlyndzikau sadly, lighting a foul-smelling, filterless cigarette from the butt of another. Indeed, this had been a coup, but a popularly sanctioned coup. Lukashenko, in fact, had not needed to resort to strong-arm tactics to ram his constitutional amendments through. Belarusians would have happily given him the additional powers that he wanted.

"The president is restoring law and order," a sixty-one-year-old pensioner, Ana Dubiaga, had told me earlier in the day. "Thanks to him, I am no longer frightened to go out at night."

Like millions of other Belarusians, Dubiaga had slogged through the sleet and snow to endorse the president at the polls. She knew how to cast her ballot because State television had been telling Belarusians for weeks how to vote. And she was grateful that just in case there was any confusion, "some kind officials" were on hand at her polling station to help her answer the referendum questions "in a way that would help the president."

What little dissent there was in Belarus had been cowed into submission by the overwhelming show of force put on by Lukashenko's Interior Ministry. To discourage protesters from taking to the streets, State television devoted copious coverage to the military preparations, showing snipers at target practice and file footage of the OMON beating the daylights out of demonstrators. Government newspapers printed front-page announcements that listed detailed troop deployments, including one notable mention of "eighty-three attack dogs and other animals." The intimidation tactics worked. "What mother would allow her child to protest in the face of snipers?" sighed Stanislav Bogdankievich, one of the leading opposition figures in the legislature.

In the end, Belarusians proved too browbeaten by decades of communism to even dent the iron will of one man. The thing that struck me, as I watched the frightened deputies pack their belongings, was how easy it was, in a part of the world that had no democratic traditions, to turn back the political clock.

Sitting on the windowsill of the nearly empty parliament, I felt terribly sorry for this small, sad country. The experiment with democracy had been so short-lived here, less than five years.

Already some lawmakers had defected to the rump parliament Lukashenko had established across town, but the legislators that remained did not bear them ill will. "They have families," said Shlyndzikau simply.

Now was no longer the time to take a stand, not when Lukashenko held all the cards. "He has prepared a list of enemies," Bogdankievich declared. "There will be arrests. It is just a question of time."

The halls of the parliament building were now strangely silent, so that the echo of my boots reverberated off the marble floor. On the way out I ran into an old contact, Peter Byrne. Byrne headed the Soros Foundation for Democracy in Minsk, and had lent me his cellular phone in the past to call in stories. At times of crisis in Belarus the international connections mysteriously jammed, as did television signals from Russia, which offered Belarusians the only alternative to domestic State channels and which experienced frequent "technical difficulties."

"Welcome to Europe's North Korea." Byrne managed a weak smile.

Byrne's days in the new Belarus were numbered, and he knew it. Already a team of "fire marshals" had raided the offices of the Soros Foundation, apparently looking for flammable materials in its computer banks and files. In fact, Byrne was thrown out of the country several weeks later, accused of being in league with the CIA.

A gaggle of journalists had congregated at the end of the hall. I recognized Pavel Sheremet, a young and outspoken local reporter whom I'd visited in the past. Sheremet had tried to run an independent newspaper, but Lukashenko's goons had trashed the office, beat up its staff, and closed down its printing presses. Refusing to quit, he had hired on as the ORT (Russian TV) correspondent in Minsk and used his bully pulpit to infuriate Lukashenko.

We foreign correspondents thought ourselves brave for parachuting into places like Belarus. But just about the worst thing that could happen to us—if we really offended the government—was to get frog-marched onto the next available flight out of the country.

The local journalists were the ones with real convictions and courage, as I was reminded whenever I met someone like Sheremet. "Well," he said in English as we shook hands. "We have lost." "I'm sorry," I said. "Yes," he said. "So am I."

The Belarusian KGB arrested Sheremet and his cameraman a few months later. He spent half a year in jail, and emigrated to Moscow when he was released. His cameraman remained in Minsk. He disappeared, and is presumed by U.S. officials to have been murdered.

Boris Brevnov was fired around the time the IMF mission arrived in Moscow to start emergency talks on the bailout. To no one's surprise, Chubais had succeeded in dethroning him and had crowned himself Russia's new electricity tsar.

Roberta and I met Gretchen and her now-unemployed husband for lunch at the Eldorado, a trendy eatery near the British Embassy recommended primarily by all the Mercedes and black Hummers in its guarded parking lot. Gretchen seemed relieved, happier than I'd seen her in months. She still looked tired, but no longer frightened. Some of the color had returned to her sculpted cheeks. And she had regained her famous, disarming Southern smile. With unusually good cheer, she announced that the Brevnov clan was going on vacation. Two weeks. Somewhere nice. Maybe the South of France.

Boris and Gretchen left Moscow the following week. They never returned.

CHAPTER FOURTEEN

The End of the Experiment

I knew the economic trouble was grave when in July our cleaning lady Larisa informed me that she would no longer accept payment in rubles. When it came to the value of a ruble, Russians had an uncanny sense, an instinct honed by the painful devaluations of the early 1990s.

The financial community was also losing confidence in the government. The GKO bond market was revealed to be a giant pyramid scheme when Russia's equivalent of the Federal Reserve, the Central Bank, made it known that without new bond issues to replenish its coffers, it might not be able to repay treasury bills coming due. The word *default* was now being uttered with mounting dread. On the street, nervous Muscovites were buying dollars. And the Central Bank was running out of hard currency.

Against this backdrop of impending doom, President Boris Yeltsin made a rare television appearance. Looking frail and grim, he warned the world that Russia was careering into turmoil. "There are extremist forces," he said vaguely and ominously, "trying to destabilize the country." Whether these "forces" were striking miners, Chechen terrorists, scheming oligarchs, or panicked Western lenders, the president did not say. But preventive measures, Yeltsin assured viewers, were being taken.

With that, the camera panned back to reveal a dozen military men standing rigidly behind the president. They wore different colored uniforms—olive green for the Army, morning blue for the Interior Ministry—and each man bore the gold stars of a general on his broad epaulettes. The generals were all receiving promotions, an extra star, or increased powers, to ensure their loyalty and vigilance in the troubled times ahead, Yeltsin made it known. Among those promoted stood the new head of the Federal Security Service (as the KGB's domestic branch now called itself), a thin, sinister-looking civilian whom I did not recognize—but should have spotted as the former deputy mayor of St. Petersburg whom I had narrowly missed meeting: Vladimir Putin.

The message to any observer, but particularly to the IMF and its paymasters in Washington, was clear. Bail Russia out or suffer the consequences.

The tax police started kicking in doors a few days later. Conscripted to convince the West that Russia would make good on its oft-broken promise to increase tax collection, Yeltsin's security forces set about the task with zeal.

State television aired footage of elite troops in black ski masks and full body armor storming the hideouts of tax deadbeats, and the culprits were pictured cowering beneath the muzzles of AK-47s. Unfortunately, most of the deadbeats featured were the terror-stricken wives of American executives who had the misfortune to be home when the tax squads started randomly raiding buildings where foreigners lived.

The Kremlin had decided to make an example of just about the only people who were actually paying taxes in Russia: Westerners. Never mind that mega-outfits like Gazprom openly flaunted their multibillion-dollar overdue tax bills. Never mind that most of Russia's business elite were brazenly stashing billions abroad. Never mind that the Moscow Tax Inspectorate listed foreign-registered firms as contributing thirty-five times greater levies on average than Russian concerns. The government would squeeze the stupid foreigners some more. The Westerners would be just foolish enough or frightened enough to pony up.

At the airport, an English-language leaflet was now tucked into the passport of every new arrival. Welcome to the Russian Federation, read the warnings; if you spend more than six months in the country you are liable for Russian taxes, regardless of whether you file in your home country. Failure to comply can result in fines, jail, etc. Have a nice stay.

"The West has asked us all along to improve tax collection," Russia's top tax collector, Boris Fyodorov, shrugged innocently when we interviewed him. "So tax dodgers may be stopped at the airport and asked to stay in Russia for a few years—maybe a sojourn of three to seven years in Siberia."

While I was fairly certain that this wasn't what the IMF had in mind, the masked tax thugs had succeeded in putting the entire foreign community on notice. Everyone was nervously flipping through their passports, counting their days "in country." The tax police raided the Moscow office of Johnson & Johnson, the giant shampoo and floor-wax maker, and diligent auditors discovered a few-thousand-dollar discrepancy on a seven-figure tax bill that had *already been paid*. An arrest warrant was issued for the American executive in charge. The poor guy promptly had a heart attack.

But the IMF got the message.

As negotiations with the International Monetary Fund reached their frenzied peak, I went to the Russian White House with our foreign editor and my new bureau chief, who had just returned to Moscow after a lengthy stint in Hong Kong. The White House was a large postmodernist structure fronted by broad, pearly Romanesque steps that dipped invitingly down toward the Moskva River, giving the edifice the open, accessible air of a big beach house or a fashionable resort. Inside, however, the atmosphere was more stifling; the ceilings were low and the unmistakable whiff of bureaucracy permeated the building. You could almost feel the unbending will of authority.

"The last time I was here tanks were shelling the top floor, and plaster was falling from the ceiling," Andy, the new bureau chief, reminisced as we walked through the spare lobby. The signs of the bloody 1993 power struggle between Yeltsin and the legislature had literally been whitewashed over, and the seat of Russian government bore no visible scars from that brush with rebellion. The décor was spartan and Soviet; as in every bureaucratic outpost in the former

USSR, red, green-bordered carpet runners covered the parquet floors. Along the corridors, double doors bulged with burgundy leather soundproofing, a testament to Soviet paranoia. Some of the light fixtures had burned out, which served only to deepen the gloom.

We ran into a CBS camera crew in the hall. "Who are you seeing?" we inquired competitively.

"Kiriyenko," beamed the correspondent. "You?"

"Chubais," we said nonchalantly, and watched her face fall.

Anatoly Chubais was a far bigger catch than the new prime minister, particularly now that Russia was angling for billions in international aid. No one knew how to charm Western lenders like Chubais, and Yeltsin had shrewdly rehabilitated him to negotiate the terms of the bailout. One day you were out, one day you were in. That was Russia.

It was astonishing how many political lives Chubais had already used up. I'd lost track of how many times he had been discredited and brought back, only to be discredited again. In the name of deregulation and liberalization, Chubais had created a kleptocracy the sheer scope of whose larceny was probably unrivaled in modern times. Under the banner of fair play and open competition, he had championed conflicts of interest. Carrying the torch of progress, he had protected the entrenched. And despite all those contradictions, he was still the only man in Russia the West wanted to deal with.

The United States and Russia's other Western backers felt they had no choice but to blindly trust Chubais and his so-called reformers. The alternative was to embrace either assorted communist cabbageheads or nationalist firebrands like Zhirinovsky. Being a land of extremes, Russia offered precious little middle ground. Washington had put all its chips on Yeltsin's government and had to play those chips regardless of how they fell. And so, if necessary, the Clinton administration was willing to turn a blind eye to the shenanigans of Boris's boys. It was too late in the game to change bets.

The policy did Russia a great disservice. One reason the country was in such a mess was because Kremlin officials had grown too confident; they believed that regardless of how much they looted or mismanaged, they still could count on Washington's unwavering support. If a five-hundred-million-dollar loan from the World Bank went missing, the West would cut them another check. If two billion dollars of IMF funds was diverted, there was more where that came from. If the promised new tax codes or budget cuts were not carried out, Washington would look the other way.

Russia had been offered the same Western advice and financial assistance as Poland, or Hungary, and the Baltic States. Those countries had taken the advice, were now among Europe's fastest growing economies, and no longer needed Western aid. Russia, on the other hand, had only paid lip service to the advice in order to get money. After going through a hundred billion dollars, Moscow now needed its next fix. I couldn't help thinking that Russia was like a recovering alcoholic who kept falling off the wagon and demanding another bottle just to consider going into the twelve-step program. Call it vodka diplomacy.

We were told Chubais was running late, and were ushered into a sunny conference room on one of the upper floors, which looked out on the bridge to Kutuzovsky Prospect and the Gothic hulk of the Ukraina Hotel. Toward the shrouded American Embassy compound (where construction crews, in an atmosphere of embarrassed secrecy, were still removing all the bugs that the Soviet builders had embedded in the concrete), below and to our left squatted the miners. They had finally made good their threat to march on Moscow, and were now camped out in front of the White House by the thousands, sleeping in tents and banging their hard hats on the cement steps in a litany of woe.

For seven years Russia's miners had suffered in silence. Suddenly, when the Kremlin had to convince the West that it was in its hour of need, they conveniently chose to rise up and "spontaneously" pitch camp in the one spot in all of Russia where the IMF and the Americans couldn't miss them. When it came to extracting money from the West, Russia didn't miss a beat.

Not that I wasn't sympathetic to the miners. On the contrary. I'd been to a mine and seen the conditions they worked in. It had been in 1993, in Donetsk, "the city of a million roses," not that I saw any— only slag heaps and black, choking dust everywhere. The shafts at the bottom of the October Revolution Mine were especially perilous because there was a shortage of lumber to prop up the caverns and tunnels. Mine bosses were cannibalizing beams, so dire were their finances, and had spread out the remaining load-bearing columns way beyond safety norms.

Stepping into that mine had felt like stepping into a Dickens novel: sweaty and smeared men working without pay, crouching all day in the permanent dusk; water dripping from rusted, mineralized pipes; dim yellow lights flickering through creaky fans that beat the hot, grainy air. And at the deepest end of the nightmare, the black glinting coal face, kicking up dust as thick and noxious as the smoke from a burning tire. There is probably no closer approximation of Hell on earth than a post-Soviet coal mine. Certainly few places on the planet are as dangerous.

Fifty-three men died at the October Revolution mining complex the year after I visited, when the poorly supported tunnels collapsed, just one reason why the life expectancy of a miner in the former Soviet Union was an Industrial Age fifty-seven.

Our *Journal* delegation didn't have time to speak to the miners outside the White House, though; we had been too busy making the rounds of very important people. Just before our appointment with Chubais, we'd gone to see the finance minister. A slight, bespectacled man with a caterpillar mustache, Mikhail Zadornov sat beneath a framed oversize facsimile of a check for five hundred million dollars made out to the Russian Federation from the bond-packaging department of Morgan Stanley. On another wall hung a museum-quality portrait of Tsar Nicholas's II's last finance minister, the official who had presided over Russia's last ill-fated attempt to borrow on international capital markets, when the Bolsheviks had cheerfully defaulted on repayment of Imperial Russia's loans.

Zadornov seemed intent on not perpetuating the tradition. He would not countenance the word *default* (no finance minister ever can) when we put the question of Russia's tarnished credibility to him. This time, he vowed, it would be different. "Russia has its back to the wall," he said. "We have the greatest incentives to carry out painful reforms." Russia was going to honor its obligations, he insisted. It simply needed "some breathing room" to shore up its finances.

While we waited for Chubais, I could not help but think that if the Russians had not stolen most of their country's wealth, there would have been no need for "breathing room" or an international bailout. How many billions of dollars had been spirited out of Russia during the 1990s? No one knew for sure. But estimates ranged from one hundred fifty to three hundred *billion* dollars—the equivalent of nearly four times Russia's entire annual federal budget.

To be sure, some of the funds stashed away in Swiss numbered accounts or offshore tax havens such as Cyprus were ill-gotten gains from criminal activity. Yet the vast majority of the funds had a legitimate provenance in oil, natural gas, steel, aluminum, diamonds, gold, and timber exports. This raised a fundamental question: why did Russians not keep money in their own country, as Americans or Germans or even Poles did? The most perceptive answer I heard came from one of the country's more honest and respected industrialists, Kakha Bendzukidze. It was a matter of trust, Bendzukidze explained. "Tell me," he said when I interviewed him in the fall of 1997. "Do you feel richer owning a million-dollar factory that yields a thirty percent annual return, or having a million in cash locked away in a Swiss safe-deposit box that earns no interest?"

"The factory," I had responded, without much enthusiasm; I thought the question rhetorical. "Well," Bendzukidze went on, "I pose the same question to my Russian colleagues. They are, mind you, for the most part very wealthy men, and so have some understanding of economics. And ninety percent of them say they feel richer with money earning no interest in Switzerland. When I ask them why, they all say it is because the government can take away their factory at any time, but it can't touch that million abroad. That is what is wrong with this country. The people do not trust the government and the government does nothing to earn the trust of the people. It is a self-perpetuating problem that will stifle the development of Russia for decades to come, if we do not address it soon."

That conversation stayed with me, partly because it was the mirror opposite of what a successful Polish businessman had told me in Warsaw some years back. His story is worth recounting for the differences it highlights between the Polish and Russian capitalist experience.

During the communist era, Zbigniew Grycan had run a small ice cream parlor called the Green Shack, or Zielona Butka in Polish. The parlor had taken its name after the hard times in World War II, when Grycan's father could find only green paint and a few sodden planks with which to build his ice cream stand. The Grycans sold only one flavor, vanilla. But it was good, and long, noisy lines soon formed outside their kiosk. The Stalinist authorities, however, would not let the father-and-son team expand, instead confiscating the family's furniture and throwing the senior Grycan in jail for "undesirable economic activity." So Grycan Junior found another outlet for his entrepreneurial ambitions: he became a black-market profiteer.

He was, by all accounts, very good at it, winding his way through communism's maddening bureaucratic maze to procure sugar for sweet-toothed customers during the direst of shortages. His biggest problem was what to do with all the money he made. As he explained it to me, if he displayed too many signs of wealth the government would nab him. If he hid his ill-gotten zlotys, he ran the risk of having his savings eroded by inflation. One day, he hit upon the solution to his dilemma while passing a dusty antique store. Among old crests and standards and silverware pawned by destitute aristocrats, an ancient gold coin gleamed in the window display. Gold did not lose its value and could easily be hidden from the State's prying eyes. Grycan began discreetly buying coins and burying them.

In 1990, shortly after Lech Walesa's election and the introduction of the Shock Therapy reform program, which would eventually spawn the two million small businesses that were to be the driving engine of Poland's booming economy, Grycan dug up his treasure trove. He sold the antique currency in Germany for one and a half million dollars and used the proceeds to buy a modern line of Italian ice-cream-making equipment.

When I visited Grycan in 1995, his Green Shack Corporation was competing against the Anglo-Dutch giant Unilever, the world's second-largest food conglomerate, for first place in Poland's fast-growing ice cream market. Seventy-five brand-new Mercedes refrigerated trucks sat in the parking lot of his state-of-the-art factory on the outskirts of Warsaw. Inside the factory hundreds of workers in crisp white frocks and hygienic hairnets busied themselves over stainless steel vats while twenty-seven automated Italian-made assembly lines hummed, churning out over thirty tons of ice cream products every twenty-four hours.

"It's all about trust," he had explained, sweeping an expansive arm over the spotless and bustling hub of his ice cream empire. "I didn't trust the communists, and they didn't trust me, so I hid my money. But I trusted Walesa and the Solidarity government not to take this away from me. I believed they wanted to create the conditions for people to prosper through honest, hard work. Look around," he had added, over the clatter of expensive machinery. "I generate a lot of money for the economy. Taxes, jobs, spin-off industries. The system works."

Which brings us to Anatoly Chubais, the man who created Russian capitalism and was charged with saving it.

I had never met Chubais, other than seeing him at press conferences, and was curious to see what all the fuss was about. After some delay, he finally swept into the paneled conference room. Russia's chief beggar and "reformer" extended a firm, generous hand and slid into a high-backed chair. An aide fluttered at his shoulder, like a twitchy hen supporting her champion rooster.

It was quickly apparent why the West was so smitten with Chubais. His manner was youthful, casual, and confident, almost American, and his English was polished, right down to the idioms peppering his conversation. Purposeful and dignified in manner, he bore little resemblance to the jowly and buttoned-up bureaucrats bred by the Soviet system. He was handsome in a bookish way, with a thick, carroty mop of hair and cool, penetrating eyes, and he revealed no trace of the confrontational demeanor some Russian officials used to mask their inferiority complexes when dealing with Westerners. When you dealt with Chubais, you immediately sensed that you were dealing with an equal, even if he was groveling for billion-dollar handouts. He epitomized the new generation of Russian leaders, the bright young men with laptop computers who, it was said, would gently and skillfully nudge the country into the Western orbit.

We had been summoned to help the Pasha of Privatization push his bailout agenda. Chubais wasted no time on pleasantries, immediately launching into an impassioned plea for funds to defend the ruble. The ruble's relative stability and low inflation were Russia's greatest postcommunist achievements, Chubais argued. Jeopardizing these twin pillars of market reforms would bring the whole edifice crashing down and "set Russia back by years."

Because of the exodus from her capital markets Russia was spending two billion dollars a week, he pressed on, to prop up its shaky currency, and at this rate would run out of money by August. If international help did not arrive by then, the ruble would go into free fall, inflation would skyrocket, and panic would break out among ordinary Russians. Such a scenario, he grimaced, would be politically devastating, would wipe out seven years of hard-won market gains, and would open the way for extremists to exploit the collapse for their own unsavory political ends. The bottom line was that if the ruble fell, Russia could find itself reverting to its bad old ways.

It would also, he did not need to add, do irreparable damage to America's reputation with the Russian people. The United States, after all, was the principal backer of the capitalist reform programs that had gotten the country into such a pickle. To be sure, what passed for capitalism in Russia was a grotesque perversion of the American variety—but ordinary Russians, most of whom had never left the country, had no way of knowing this. To them it was all just one great big injustice, a foreign import they could do without.

"We are playing," concluded Chubais, "for very high stakes."

Two days later, on July 14, the IMF announced a $22.6 billion emergency aid package. The clouds over Moscow immediately lifted. The stock market, after having lost nearly two-thirds of its value, shot up 15 percent. The ruble firmed. Yeltsin beamed triumphantly. Potanin and the other oligarchs cracked open the champagne. And we reporters got to go home before midnight for a change.

Throughout expatriate Moscow you could almost hear the collective sigh of relief. Russia's crisis was over—or so everyone thought.

Roberta's and mine, however, was just about to begin.

———

Moscow was eerily quiet after the frenetic bailout. It was late July, the height of *dacha* season, and the city was dusty and deserted. Only the roads leading out of the capital were congested with Zhigulis filled with families in swimwear retreating to their crude little country homes, to tend their tiny vegetable gardens and get away from the traffic fumes for a few weeks.

This was an annual pilgrimage for the Muscovites, this exodus to dachaland, a rite as sacred as every Parisian's determination to abandon Paris before Bastille Day. The Kremlin too was all but shuttered. Now that the bailout was securely in place, most government officials had gone off on holiday as well, the lesser ones to State sanitariums in Sochi, the big shots like Chubais to the South of France to enjoy a well-earned twenty-two-billion-dollar rest.

That left us exhausted reporters virtually alone in Moscow. And with the government effectively shut down, we quickly hightailed it off to Canada to sneak a few days of badly needed R&R. It was then that I had my first inkling that my days in Russia were numbered.

Roberta and I had been driving through a suburb of Montreal when suddenly I jammed on the brakes. "Hear that?" I demanded of a startled Roberta.

"What?" she asked, fixing me with one those have-you-gone-crazy stares.

"Can't you hear it?" I pursued. "Listen."

She looked at me blankly.

"The sprinkler!" I shouted, excited, almost delirious. "It's a lawn sprinkler!" The thing was going *thack, thack, thack,* sending revolving jets of spray around the rolling front lawn of some cookie-cutter tract mansion with a minivan in its American-pastoral driveway.

Now Roberta was staring at me as if I definitely *had* gone mad.

"You know," I said, suddenly morose, "I can't remember the last time I heard that sound." In fact, it had been seven years since I had heard one of the most mundane sounds of suburban summer. In Eastern Europe and the former Soviet Union there were no front lawns to water, or to mow. Hardly a blade of grass grew in all of Moscow.

Roberta was silent for a moment. "You know," she said finally, "I think you're homesick."

She was right. That staccato rhythm triggered something in me. I couldn't quite put my finger on it at first, but later I would realize it was a yearning for normality. When we returned to Moscow, my strange behavior intensified. My idea of a good time was to drag Roberta to a picnic lunch at the new British Petroleum car wash that had opened next to a McDonald's in northwest Moscow. I'd order a Big Mac and buy a bag of jellybeans from the BP convenience store (the only place in Moscow where you could get them), and sit in our car while it went through the automated car wash. For those few minutes, while the mechanical sponges and brushes twirled over the windshield, I was not in Russia, but transported to someplace deliciously boring and civilized. The moment, alas, was invariably ruined by the beggar conscripts—scrawny young AWOL soldiers who sniffed glue and wandered the streets—who panhandled by the drying station. *Welcome back to Russia,* their unwashed military presence announced.

It had become abundantly clear that Roberta and I had a problem. I was bitterly unhappy and badly wanted to leave Russia. She wanted to stay. Neither of us was keen on compromising. Our dilemma festered, unresolved, until early August when, just as the IMF was preparing to wire Russia the first five-billion-dollar installment of the bailout loan, the gods intervened in my favor.

The unlikely instrument of my delivery turned out to be the dreaded tax police. Having terrorized various other expats, the financial fuzz were finally about to come knocking at my door. They had called the *Journal* asking for the home addresses of all the accredited correspondents. A visit from the masked men was thus imminent—not to mention highly worrisome, since my tax situation was, well, about as messy as Russia's finances.

For one thing, I was late filing my tax return. For another, I was facing a whopping fine. I think I had procrastinated because deep down I couldn't bear the thought of giving money to Russian officials, and had counted on the tax department's disorganization to try to get away with not paying at all.

Now I had the necessary ammunition to further my argument for flight. Somewhat gleefully, I broke the bad/good news to Roberta. "I'll pay your taxes," she offered. I shook my head. "No, I just want out of here."

"At least come to the accountants with me," Roberta implored. "They can clear this up." I relented, after some debate, and this proved to be a stroke of genius.

The offices of Coopers & Lybrand occupied the entire floor of a new building owned by the City of Moscow. We sat in the conference room while one of the Coopers number-crunchers glumly pecked at a large calculator. A little spool of paper in the machine unwound endlessly like the itemized tally of a supermarket bill. When the final figure was read, Roberta's face dropped. Now we were talking about *her* tax situation, and an unexpected mine had exploded: her potential tax liability if she stayed in Russia for more than 180 days in 1998 would climb into six figures. Russia, you see, had just amended its tax code, rescinded many of its international tax treaties, and—in a typically byzantine maneuver—applied all the changes retroactively.

Roberta was in shock. She was considerably more organized than I was when it came to taxes and had thought she was well covered. Like most senior executives of investment funds, she was paid offshore, and had incorporated in the United States so as to reduce her tax burden stateside. It was all completely legal, and prepared by a very sharp tax attorney in Washington—who just happened to be her mother.

But not only did Russia no longer recognize the taxes she paid in the United States, they would now want a piece of her salary from her days at the World Bank—when, like diplomats worldwide, she had been exempt from taxes. Roberta had own her own calculator out now, and was flipping through her passport tabulating her entry and exit dates to see how many days she had spent in the Russian Federation so far that year. She was just shy of the six-month mark because she had spent a good deal of time working on her big sugar-mill deal in Ukraine—which thankfully, now counted as "abroad."

I sensed victory and plunged in the knife. "Do you want to stay and give the Russians a house? That's what this is, you know, a down payment on a house—a nice one. Trust me." I was pleading now. "We have to get out of here before it's too late."

Roberta sat quietly for what seemed to be the longest time. She had, after all, devoted her entire academic and professional career to the former Soviet Union. Now it had become a zero-sum game. She could stay and risk losing her life savings—and maybe me as well—or leave her dreams behind.

"You win," she finally said. "But we have to move quickly."

I tendered my resignation the next day, and we bought our plane tickets to New York. Our departure date was August 19, just enough time for us to wrap up our affairs and be safely out of the country before the magical six-month mark lapsed.

By then, however, it would already be too late for Russia.

No one took the news of our departure harder than Larisa and Lev. For days, as we packed, our cleaning lady was a fountain of tears. Larisa sobbed uncontrollably with every moving box that was filled, sniffled at every painting that came off the wall, blew her nose remonstratingly at every book that was crated.

"I love you like a sister," she wailed to Roberta. "You are like family to me. I can't bear the thought of losing you. By the way, are you taking that camera?" The Minolta—my Minolta—went into a box labeled Larisa. That carton would fill with every outburst.

"Please don't go. Why do you have to go?" Larisa moaned as the living room emptied, and her moist eyes hungrily scanned the remains. "And what are you going to do with the television?" Even Lev choked back a few crocodile tears at the prospect of a free Panasonic, which, despite his infirmities, he managed to cart away with remarkable speed and dexterity. Thanks to Larisa's paroxysms of grief, we were increasingly shipping a lighter and lighter load.

The Russian government was also doing its best to reduce our freight costs. Our car, we were informed, would have to be donated to a Russian charity, unless we ponied up twenty-two thousand dollars in import taxes to send it back to the States. This, of course, made absolutely no sense. But Russia was not very accommodating about allowing anything of value out of the country once it was brought in—as Western investors were all about to discover.

"But we're re-exporting the car to where we bought it," Roberta had argued to the customs authorities. Tough, they said. Fine, she countered, we'll sell it here then. You'll have to ship it out first—and then ship it back in under a new registration—to sell it, and you'll *still* owe us twenty-two thousand dollars, came the response. Then we'll just abandon it in front of our building. They were unmoved. That'll be $22,000. Oh, and we only accept cash.

"Who writes these regulations, anyway?" Roberta snapped. "Kafka?"

As with many dealings with Russian officialdom, an arrangement was eventually reached, and our SUV obtained the necessary stamps to go home legally.

Our apartment was now nearly empty. Our landlord, upon hearing of the tax police's exciting new initiatives, had ripped up our lease and even offered to help us move out. Apparently he had not reported his own rental income—and was as anxious to have us gone as I was to leave. My beloved aquarium went to Betsy's husband; he had just been forced out of his business by his Russian junior partners and had wisely chosen to withdraw without a fight, apparently deciding that caring for fish was better than swimming with them.

Larisa saved her most mournful sobbing for last, as she packed up Roberta's coat closet. "You've become a daughter to me over these past two years," she lamented, mascara streaming. "I will miss you so much. I'm sorry to be so emotional. Are you leaving the mink?"

Sheremetyevo had the frantic feel of an airport on the eve of revolution or civil war. The lines at customs stretched hundreds deep, past shuttered souvenir stands and all the way to the overcrowded concourse, which was thick with passengers sitting anxiously on their suitcases. Unruly scrums formed around the check-in counters, where harried airline representatives turned people away, and there was a good deal of pushing and shouting. Above the din, I heard a baby shrieking.

The expatriate stampede to get out of Moscow had begun. Two days before, on August 17, 1998, the bottom had fallen out of Russian capitalism. It seemed that the Kremlin had taken all five billion dollars of the IMF bailout money, and traded it to the oligarchs so that they could get rid of their remaining rubles at a favorable exchange rate before the government abandoned its defense of the currency. Once the oligarchs had the bailout funds, the Kremlin declared a massive default and devaluation.

As a result, the ruble was in free fall, plunging hourly—as in the worst of the hyperinflation years. The prices of basic foodstuffs were soaring and there was panic; Muscovites emptied the shelves of their neighborhood shops as they tried to unload Russia's currency before it devalued into irrelevance or merchants stopped accepting it. There were runs on all the major banks. Outside of some branches riots broke out when it became clear that hundreds of thousands of people would never see their deposits again. On the trading floors of the brokerage houses, stock prices were falling so fast that the brokers just gave up and went home.

The Kremlin, having perpetuated one last con on its unwitting Western supporters, announced a forty-billion-dollar default on its government bonds, suspended trading of all T-bills, and placed a moratorium on the repayment of another forty billion dollars' worth of private corporate and bank debt to foreign creditors. Western commentators were calling the crash the biggest disaster in international financial history.

The International Monetary Fund was stunned. Stock markets around the world were reeling. In Russia's parliament, both the communists and the nationalists were howling for purges, prison terms, and Jewish heads. And in the Kremlin, Kiriyenko and his fellow "reformers" were already packing their bags. "Russia's worst nightmare," to quote my colleagues in the August 18 edition of the *Wall Street Journal*, had just come to pass. But it was Moscow Mayor Yuri Luzhkov who best summed up how millions of Russians now felt about their country's ill-fated attempt to adopt a Western-style society. His angry face filled the big screen television at Sheremetyevo's crowded airport bar, and was one of the last things I saw as we prepared to make our final exit from Russia. "Ladies and gentlemen," he declared, "the experiment is over."

Epilogue

Russia's experiment with democracy effectively ended on the last day of the old millennium, when Boris Yeltsin abruptly abdicated and anointed Vladimir Putin acting president.

In a late-night resignation speech that doubtless had a sobering effect on Russian New Year's revelers, Tsar Boris the Failed apologized to his subjects for the injustices committed in the name of freedom and the free market. Russia, he declared, needed a young, strong hand to crush corruption and chaos—one, in this case, attached to a KGB veteran with a black belt in judo. That same evening, Putin launched his "dictatorship of the law" by granting Yeltsin and his family immunity from prosecution. That bloodless palace coup brought to a close the *bankirshchina*, the rule of the bankers.

Putin's reign was inaugurated, in traditional fashion, with a search for scapegoats. Fortunately for Russia's Jews, the Chechens proved a more convenient target. A rash of mysterious apartment bombings in Moscow in late 1999 was blamed on Chechen terrorists, and a second war against Chechnya was unleashed. The campaign rallied the Russian populace around its obscure new leader, who flew to the front in a MiG fighter jet, and who rode the wave of rekindled nationalism to stand virtually unopposed in the March 2000 presidential election. (Would-be presidential contenders like Luzhkov, faced with a mountain of *kompromat* unearthed by Putin's friends in the secret police, prudently decided to sit this one out.)

Chubais, Nemtsov, Kiriyenko, and many of the other "young reformers" quickly pledged allegiance to Russia's new master. So did Potanin and most of the other oligarchs, who, thanks to shady stratagems learned from their Western hirelings, weathered the financial crash with a series of spectacular but apparently profitable bankruptcies. Putin allowed the tycoons to keep their fortunes so long as they kept out of politics, and his prosecutors ensured their continuing cooperation with the threat of corruption investigations.

Only Vladimir Gusinsky refused the Faustian bargain; he used his media properties to expose the ethnic cleansing in Chechnya and to criticize Putin's revival of such Soviet symbols as the playing of the USSR national anthem, the display of the Red Army flag, and the use of secret-police informers. He was thrown in jail and eventually fled to his villa in Spain—where, at this writing, he sits under house arrest, fighting extradition to Moscow while the Russian government tries to seize his television network.

Russia's other media mogul, financier Boris Berezovsky, also fled the country with Moscow prosecutors close on his heels. There was much that investigators might have had cause to question him about, but it was his stake in ORT-TV that the government was after. In trying to resurrect State control over the press, Putin declared that he was simply rectifying a "destructive mistake" of the Yeltsin years—allowing the media to be independently owned.

Another Yeltsin legacy that Putin rolled back in his first year in office was the hard-won autonomy of Russia's eighty-nine regions, which during the 1990s had obtained the right to elect their own leaders and to manage (or mismanage) their own affairs. Although the regional governors were all too often incompetent or crooked or more than likely both, they did provide the provinces with more self-determination than they had enjoyed at any other time in Russia's history. With the connivance of the communist-dominated parliament, Putin reinstated a Soviet-style system of vertical authority; regional leaders now serve at the president's pleasure; he can fire them any time he wants.

Unsurprisingly, relations between Russia and the West have cooled considerably over the last several years. In Washington, where Roberta and I now live, the ascension of Putin and his KGB cohorts sparked furious debate over "Who lost Russia?" Republicans blamed the Clinton administration, accusing Vice President Al Gore and the Democrats of promoting Russian corruption by turning a blind eye to it. Congress held hearings on the matter, and recriminations flew in the editorial pages of the *Washington Post* and the *New York Times*.

The truth of the matter is that no one lost Russia but the Russians themselves. Russia during the 1990s was offered the identical assistance package received by Poland, Hungary, and the Czech Republic. But unlike those prospering countries, which have been rewarded with NATO membership, or the thriving Baltic states, which seek to join the European Union, Russia's postcommunist leaders never truly wanted to be part of the Western family of nations. They wanted the West's money and admired its gadgetry, its luxury cars and cellular phones, but were never sold on its ideals; they particularly rejected the notion that government is for the people and not the other way around.

The same held true for corporate Russia; the *biznesmeni* had also been only too happy to take the West's money, but were not interested in adopting the transparency that is essential to join the global business community in earnest. That Wall Street fell for the hundred-billion-dollar con is a testament to the blinding power of greed.

But if we in the West need to blame someone specific for losing both Russia and our billions, Boris Yeltsin is as good a candidate as we will find. Yeltsin's heroic stand atop a tank in 1991 started the democratic experiment. His charisma and courage helped dismember the totalitarian system. He was, for a brief period, a man of the people. But then both his health and his vision failed, and his ambition undermined everything he had achieved. He sold out his country for a second term in office, then withdrew into sickly isolation while Russia was pillaged from within. Then, when everything fell apart, he sold Putin what was left of Russia in exchange for his own personal safety. For that historians should treat him harshly.

For now, Putin seems to have a popular mandate to use a "strong hand" to restore order and dignity to Russia. The Russian people were never too enthusiastic about their distorted versions of democracy and capitalism anyway. Whether Putin will offer Russians stability and economic development through a Latin American–style dictatorship, or continue along the African-style path of kleptocracy, remains to be seen. But what is fairly certain is that those heady days of the roaring nineties, when more foreigners called Moscow home than at any previous time in Russia's thousand-year history, are over.

The financial crash decimated Moscow's expatriate community with remarkable speed. Within days of the default, the investment bankers, lawyers, and chartered accountants were hightailing it for New York. (There, another boom just getting under way, the dot-com frenzy, urgently required their services.) The stockbrokers and bond salesmen were not far behind, followed by the corporate types. By the end of 1998, every member of our party from that drunken evening at the White Sun of the Sands had left Russia. Moscow, in expatriate terms, was now a ghost town.

A great deal of soul-searching and more than a few career changes accompanied the crash. VSO lost two billion dollars and most of its staff. Boris Jordan laid off hundreds of workers and was nearly wiped out. George Soros groused that investing in Russia had been the biggest mistake of his forty-year career, while a bond buyer I knew abandoned his ten-thousand-dollar-a-month apartment for an ashram in India. Another acquaintance traded in his Land Rover for a room at his mother-in-law's house. Then there's the uplifting story of how one enterprising colleague managed to get around the freeze on all wire transfers out of Russia by using his ATM card. By going to virtually every ATM machine in his home state and withdrawing the maximum permitted amount each time, he managed to empty his Moscow bank account of nearly two hundred thousand dollars. When he deposited the resulting garbage bag full of bills at his home-town bank branch, the manager thought he was a drug dealer.

Betsy McKay stayed in Russia for a full year, and she and her new colleagues at the *Journal*'s Moscow bureau were rewarded in 1999 with journalism's highest honor for their coverage of the aftermath of the crash—the Pulitzer Prize for international reporting.

Roberta and I bought that old house in Georgetown with the money we might have otherwise given the Russian tax authorities, and the only time I have ever regretted leaving Moscow was the morning that the winners of the Pulitzer were announced. Roberta is more nostalgic; she often reminisces about the early days of the postcommunist transition, when we were all part of something we thought was big. She now invests in Asia, but her heart is still in the former Soviet Union. As for me, my passion for sprinkler systems and normalcy has ebbed now that I water my own lawn, paint my own shutters, and walk my own dog three times a day. Soon I will be a father, and Roberta and I already look back on our days in the Wild East as a distant and dimming adventure.

We see Boris and Gretchen Brevnov from time to time. They live on a multimillion-dollar horse farm in Virginia's most exclusive hunt country, and their poolside patio overlooks rolling paddocks where Thoroughbred racehorses graze. Boris is now a vice president of a major publicly-listed American energy conglomerate. He can be seen on weekends in his tennis whites leaving his country club in his Suburban SUV, perhaps the ultimate survivor.

Acknowledgments

There are a great many people without whom this book would not have been written, most of all my family, who lent their support in Montreal, Warsaw, and Washington; my wife, who served as both character and muse; and my editors, who gave shape to the incredible things I witnessed.

I want to thank Jane Perlez and Ray Bonner for eight years of patience and good will, and Fred Kempe for his leadership and confidence. They are all accomplished and inspiring journalists, and I'm proud to call them my mentors. At the *Journal* I had occasion to work with some of the world's best reporters and editors, and a few deserve special mention. Dan Michaels, for exhibiting that rare quality in our competitive field, generosity of spirit; Betsy McKay, for starting as a colleague and becoming a friend; Matthew Kaminski for many a hangover; and John Bussey, Jeff Burke, and Jim Pressley for their often sobering comments.

Many of those who shared my Eastern adventure remain in my thoughts: Askold Krushelnycki, Chrystia Freeland, Ghena Mishuris, Natalia Feduschak, Tom Kearney, Alans Cullison and Bigman, my cousins Mark and Ian, Jamie Hamilton (even though we didn't overlap), and my Polish friend Darek who put me up in his Kiev apartment after my unfortunate run-in with Buzz, not to mention a few ex-girlfriends from my Warsaw days that it is no longer appropriate for a married man to name. I wish them all success and happiness.

Last, but not least, I am indebted to my agent Scott Waxman and everyone at the Free Press and Simon & Schuster: Paul Golob for buying the book, my editor Rachel Klayman and her assistant Brian Selfon, Camilla Hewitt, and many others. Any libel suits or other legal unpleasantries resulting from the publication of this book should be referred to them.

About the Author

MATTHEW BRZEZINSKI was a staff writer for *The Wall Street Journal* in Kiev and in Moscow from 1996 through 1998, having previously reported from Poland and other Eastern European countries for *The New York Times, The Economist, The Guardian* (London), and *The Toronto Globe and Mail.* He is currently a freelance writer and his work has most recently appeared in *The New York Times Magazine.* He lives in Washington, D.C.

Printed in the United States
By Bookmasters